anglistik & englischunterricht

Youth Identities

Hans-Jürgen Diller · Erwin Otto
Gerd Stratmann (Hrsg.)

anglistik & englischunterricht

Band 63

Youth Identities

UNIVERSITÄTSVERLAG C. WINTER
HEIDELBERG

Youth Identities

Teens and Twens in British Culture

Verantwortliche Herausgeber
für den thematischen Teil des Bandes:
Gerd Stratmann, Merle Tönnies und Claus-Ulrich Viol

UNIVERSITÄTSVERLAG C. WINTER
HEIDELBERG

Die Deutsche Bibliothek – CIP-Einheitsaufnahme

Youth identities: teens and twens in British culture /
verantw. Hrsg. des Bd.: Gerd Stratmann … –
Heidelberg: Winter, 2000.
(Anglistik & Englischunterricht; Bd. 63)
ISBN 3-8253-1134-1

Herausgeber:
Prof. Dr. Hans-Jürgen Diller
Dr. Erwin Otto · Prof. Dr. Gerd Stratmann

ISBN 3-8253-1134-1
ISSN 0344-8266

Anschrift der Redaktion:
Ruhr-Universität Bochum, Englisches Seminar
Universitätsstraße 150 · 44801 Bochum

Imprimé en Allemagne. Printed in Germany
Satz: OLD-Satz digital, Neckarsteinach
Druck: Strauss Offsetdruck, Mörlenbach

Contents

Bill Osgerby, Southampton

'The Young Ones'. Youth, Consumption and Representations of the 'Teenager' in Post-War Britain

The young ones
Darling, we're the young ones
And the young ones
Shouldn't be afraid
To give love
While the flame is strong
'Cos we may not be the young ones very long.

Cliff Richard, *The Young Ones* (Columbia Records, 1962)

1. Images of Youth and Social Change in Post-War Britain

The 1961 British pop musical *The Young Ones* is a study in zestful sparkle. A light-hearted romp, the film elaborates a sprightly tale of swinging adolescent life in west London. Facing the demolition of their favourite youth club by a money-grabbing property tycoon, chirpy youngsters resolve to raise funds to save the building by organizing an all-singing, all-dancing musical extravaganza. Needless to say, a happy ending sees all concerned joining together in a spirited and up-lifting grand finale. While it hardly boasts the most original plot, *The Young Ones* nevertheless possesses historical significance in a number of respects. Firstly, the release of the film points towards some important elements of economic and cultural change taking place in the lives of young people in Britain during the late 1950s and early 1960s. Secondly, the themes and tone of the film are indicative of some of the ways in which youth was socially, economically and politically represented and responded to during this period.

Essentially a vehicle for rising pop star Cliff Richard, the release of *The Young Ones* testifies to the augmented economic importance of the youth market in post-war Britain. During the late 1950s and early 1960s film-makers and popular music promoters joined a literally boundless range of commercial entrepreneurs in an attempt to woo the spending power of British youngsters. Pop-oriented films like *The Young Ones* were just one example of a multitude of products geared to the post-war youth market, consumer industries interacting with and mutually re-enforcing one another in their scramble to cash-in on youth spending. Indeed, during this period young people's earning power and levels of disposable income seemed to have grown to unprecedented heights as shifts in the British employment market saw an intensified demand for young people's labour – and the release of *The Young Ones* stands as an illustrative example of the commercial and entertainment industries' response to the perceived growth in young people's economic muscle.

More than this, however, *The Young Ones* is also significant for the way that it constructed particular notions of youth and youth culture. The "young ones" of the film's title come from a wide variety of social and economic backgrounds, yet all share the same culture of vibrant and vivacious fun. Nowhere is this clearer than in the film's opening sequence and the way in which it draws together a range of working youngsters in a celebration of adolescent good times. *The Young Ones* opens as a Friday afternoon draws to its weary end. Across London a legion of youngsters from all walks of life – a construction worker, a shop girl, a ballet dancer, a delivery boy and a young, bowler-hatted accountant – race home, all buoyant with anticipation for an evening of dancing, music, fun and excitement. *The Young Ones*, therefore, evokes a sense of a classless and homogenous 'culture of youth' in which social divisions and conflicts are effaced by youngsters' common involvement in, and commitment to, a shared culture of enjoyment and hedonistic leisure. In this respect the film testifies to the broader ideological construction of 'youth' in Britain during the late 1950s and early 1960s.

During the 1950s and 1960s the popular iconography of youth came to function as an ideological vehicle that encapsulated sentiments about the more general contours of social, economic and cultural change. This period saw the 'youth question' mobilized as a medium through which fundamental shifts in Britain's social boundaries and cultural relationships were explored, made sense of and interpreted by the media, politicians and a wide array of social commentators. In particular, the media constructed and deployed the themes and images of 'youth' as a shorthand signifier for progress, modernity and conspicuous consumption in what seemed to be a dawning age of political consensus and economic growth. *The Young Ones* exemplifies this ideological construction of youth. The film, of course, does not mirror wider social beliefs and attitudes in any simple, linear fashion, but is nevertheless significant for the way it frames a specific account and interpretation of the nature of post-war youth culture. Moreover, the representations and connotations of 'dynamic youth' that lie at the heart of *The Young Ones* were constituent in a much wider set of ideological strategies that sought to actively explain and interpret the trajectories of social development in post-war Britain. In these terms, therefore, the representations of young people in the film *The Young Ones* can be seen as part of an ideological discourse in which 'the teenager' was promoted as the symbolic figurehead of Britain's march into what appeared to be a new era of social harmony and economic prosperity.

2. The 'Institutionalization' and 'Formalization' of Youth

'Youth' was not a social category unique to post-war Britain. Many features of young people's lives after 1945 had been anticipated by earlier social, economic and cultural trends. Since at least the nineteenth century spectacular subcultural groups had existed among sections of working class youth,[1] while the degree of disposable income possessed by many working youngsters laid the basis for a commercial youth market which steadily blossomed between the wars.[2] Nevertheless, while dimensions of continuity can certainly be identified, there remain strong grounds for understanding the post-war period as marking a crucial turning-point in the development of British youth culture. In the two decades that followed 1945 a concatenation of factors served to accentuate young people's social and cultural profile – to the degree that many contemporary commentators became convinced that post-war youngsters were palpably different, and culturally distinct, from earlier generations of British youth.

Demographic changes undoubtedly played a role in emphasizing the identifiability of post-war youth. A 'baby-boom' in the wake of the Second World War was temporary but significant, ensuring that the British youth population during the 1950s and 1960s grew both in absolute numbers and as a percentage of national totals.[3] Additionally, scientific evidence suggested that with higher standards of living children were beginning to reach puberty at an earlier age, this further contributing to ideas of a qualitatively distinct younger generation.[4] These factors may, in themselves, have been sufficient to enhance the social profile of youth in post-war Britain, though they were further reinforced and augmented by additional developments which worked to 'formalize' and 'institutionalize' notions of young people as an identifiable social group.

As part of a wider package of social reforms the British school-leaving age had been due to be raised to fifteen in 1939, but with the outbreak of war this had been postponed. During wartime, however, the conviction grew that the expansion of Britain's education system should be a fundamental priority in any programme of post-war reconstruction, with youth seen as a national resource whose potential had too often been squandered through educational inadequacy. As a consequence the 1944 Education Act established free secondary education for all children, while in 1947 the school-leaving age was finally raised to fifteen. The formalization of age categories within the sphere of education was complemented by the simultaneous expansion of the youth service. During the war a scarcity of 'respectable' leisure provision came to be regarded as a significant gap in the socialization of young people, with the consequence that a National Youth Committee was established to administer grants to youth organizations that, it was felt, could be trusted to marshal young people's leisure in a reliable and responsible fashion. Under the 1944 Education Act, furthermore, it became the statutory responsibility of Local Education Authorities to provide adequate recreational facilities for young people in their area. Taken together, therefore, the post-war reorganization of the education system and expansion of the youth service worked to formalize and institutionalize concepts of 'youth' as a discrete social entity associated with specific needs and problems.

This institutionalization of youth as a distinct age category was further augmented by the introduction of National Service in 1948. Deferment was available to youngsters completing apprenticeships or courses of education (and about 16 % were exempted on medical grounds), but on average 160,000 young men were annually conscripted for two years of military training. Conscription further fostered a sense of 'generational consciousness' in Britain – National Service detaching young men from the ties of their domestic environment and gathering them together with thousands of others undergoing the same experience.[5] Moreover, the practice of posting young National Servicemen to military bases in the heart of the British countryside brought the styles of urban youth to rural communities which might otherwise have been relatively untouched by rock 'n' roll, winkle-picker shoes and the whole gamut of post-war youth culture.

Demographic shifts, the expansion of secondary education and other institutions of youth provision, together with the introduction of conscription, undoubtedly all contributed to the greater social profile of British youth during the 1950s and early 1960s. More important than these factors, however, was the intensification of long-term trends in the British economy – the decline of heavy industries, the movement of capital into lighter forms of production (especially the manufacture of consumer goods), the expansion of production line technologies, trends towards 'de-skilling' and the movement of labour out of direct production and into distribution and service. The impact of these trends registered on the workforce as a whole but held their greatest consequences for young workers.[6] De-skilling and production-line technologies created a demand for a flexible, though not especially skilled, workforce. Cheaper to employ than adults, young people were an ideal source for this labour. Indeed, rather than undertaking a period of relatively poorly paid training or apprenticeship, many youngsters much preferred the relatively high immediate rewards offered by unskilled and semi-skilled work.

The consequent rise of youth as an economic force made a profound impression on contemporary commentators. As early as 1947 a Ministry of Education report drew attention to the financial power accruing to young workers, observing that

> when juvenile workers are scarce, as they are now, and are likely to continue to be, he [*sic*] quickly realises that he may not be so unimportant as he seemed at first; and after two or three years his income may be larger compared with his needs and with his contribution to his maintenance than at any other period of his life.[7]

This equation of 'youth' with 'affluence' became a powerful and recurring theme during the post-war decades.

Especially important in sedimenting images of a generation of young workers possessing unprecedented wealth was the research of Mark Abrams. Conducted for the London Press Exchange during the late 1950s, Abrams' research purported to show that youth, more than any other social group, had materially prospered in the post-war years. Abrams calculated that since 1945 young people's real earnings had risen by 50 % (roughly double that of adults), while youth's 'discretionary' spending had risen by as much as 100 % – representing an annual expenditure of around £830 million.[8] Furthermore, Abrams maintained that this spending power was concentrated in particular consumer markets (for instance representing 44 % of total spending on records and record players and 39 % of spending on bicycles and motorcycles), which, he postulated, represented the rise of "distinctive teenage spending for distinctive teenage ends in a distinctive teenage world".[9]

Routinely cited in an array of official reports, books, newspapers and magazines, Abrams' statistics played a key role in crystallizing the idea of a newly affluent body of youngsters patronizing a commercial youth market of remarkable scale. Many of his observations, however, demand qualification. Firstly, Abrams' somewhat idiosyncratic definition of teenagers as "those young people who have reached the age of fifteen but are not yet twenty-five years of age and are unmarried"[10] would have encompassed a large number of older, higher-earning subjects – and therefore would have undoubtedly concealed significant differences of earnings and expenditure within the whole group. Secondly, his discussion of *total* expenditure and *average* earnings would, again, have disguised major disparities. Lastly, Abrams took no account of the degree of regional variation. Indeed, though less widely publicized, locally-based studies conducted in the same period suggest levels of youth consumption much lower than those estimated by Abrams.[11] Nevertheless, while Abrams' findings may have exaggerated the scale of young people's economic power, the broad sweep of his arguments was accurate. During the 1950s and 1960s the earning power of young British workers was certainly not huge, yet compared to earlier generations their levels of disposable income were tangibly enhanced. Post-war notions of 'affluent youth', therefore, may well have been distorted and exaggerated by some commentators, yet were not pure myth. The 1950s and 1960s saw many young people enjoy a degree of relative prosperity on entering the world of work – an affluence which underpinned an exponential expansion of Britain's commercial youth market.

3. The Growth of the Commercial Youth Market

The 1950s and 1960s saw growing levels of consumer spending within the British working class as a whole, but it was young workers – unencumbered by family obligations – who were most able to enjoy the benefits of a higher disposable income. Indeed, the sheer enormity and diversity of the range of consumer products geared to the youth market was often a topic for awed wonderment among commentators. Surveying the commercial youth scene in 1965, for example, Peter Leslie was breathless at the scale of the phenomenon:

> Today, the teenagers pay the piper – largely because they are the most numerous group with money to spare *on this kind of thing* – and the tunes they call have their elders in a whirl. With astonishment, dismay, curiosity or even fear, the adults find themselves on the outside, looking in at a vast industry with an annual turnover of many millions which is entirely devoted to the satisfaction of caprices and whims expressed by those who, only a few years ago, were expected to be seen and not heard.[12]

The growing importance of the youth market had an especially notable impact in the realm of popular music. Indicative of youth's growing importance to the music industry was the rise of the 7 inch, 45 r.p.m single (launched in 1952 and accounting for 80% of British record sales by 1963), as well as the introduction of sales-based singles' charts (the first British singles' chart appearing in *New Musical Express* in 1952, followed by *Record Mirror*'s "Top Fifty" in 1954) and the emergence of the pop star as a cultural phenomenon – most strikingly manifested in 1956 with the arrival from America of rock 'n' roll. The initial wave of American stars such as Bill Haley, Little Richard, Chuck Berry and Elvis Presley was soon joined by home-grown talent such as Cliff Richard, Tommy Steele, Adam Faith and Marty Wilde and, with the rise of British beat and rhythm and blues in the early sixties, bands such as the Beatles and the Rolling Stones were soon dominating the world of popular music.

As adult audiences declined, the film industry also began to focus more concertedly on the youth market. In America producers such as Roger Corman and Sam Katzman pioneered the 'teenpic' – low-budget, quickly produced movies geared to a young audience, especially the drive-in market.[13] The British film industry also attempted to gear itself more explicitly to youth demand. Britain could never match the scale and prolificity of the American 'teenpic' industry, yet the fifties and sixties saw the release of numerous British films that courted a young audience through featuring pop idols such as Cliff Richard, Tommy Steele and, later, the Beatles.[14]

In contrast to the cinema, British radio came to grips much more slowly with the changing universe of popular music and youth culture. During the late fifties rock 'n' roll could only be heard by tuning in to the American Forces Network or Radio Luxembourg since it was largely ignored by the BBC as a consequence of restrictions on 'needle time'[15] and a mandarin disdain for forms of music that officialdom deemed inferior and crassly commercial. It was not, therefore, until the appearance of unlicensed (so-called 'pirate') stations such as Radio Caroline and Radio London in the early sixties, and the subsequent launch of the BBC's Radio One in 1967, that Britain saw radio programmes specifically geared to the 'youth' audience.[16] On the other hand, the younger medium of television responded relatively swiftly to the developing 'youth scene' and the fifties and sixties saw both the BBC and ITV (Britain's first commercial TV channel, launched in 1955) make numerous forays into the field. Initially programmes such as *Hit Parade* (1952), *Music Shop* (1955) and *Off the Record* (1956) were rather muted in the explicitness of their appeal to youth. By the later fifties, however, a more fully formed youth-oriented genre had begun to emerge with shows such as *Six-Five Special* (1957), *Oh Boy!* (1958) and *Juke Box Jury* (1959).[17]

The explosion of British pop music in the mid-fifties was also a boon to many traditional entertainment venues whose adult clientele had begun to drift away. In their place a younger generation of patrons packed into variety theatres, dance halls and clubs – young audiences flocking to see concert tour 'packages' of pop stars organized by impresarios such as Larry Parnes and, later, appearances by headline bands such as the Beatles and the Rolling Stones. Other business interests also thrived on the growing youth market. The brewing industry did not seriously attempt to appeal to younger consumers until the late sixties and as a consequence pubs retained a dull, colourless (even rather boring) image. Coffee bars, on the other hand, thrived. The leading focal point to British teenage life, during the fifties and early sixties the coffee bar was a place where youngsters could gather and freely chat amongst themselves or dance to their favourite records on the juke box (itself appearing in much greater numbers from the mid-fifties) – all for the price of a cup of foamy espresso or a bottle of Coca-Cola. The most famous coffee bars were in London – the Gyre and Gymble in Charing Cross, the Breadbasket near Middlesex Hospital and the Two I's (where, legend has it, Tommy Steele was discovered by his agent) in Old Compton Street – though most provincial towns also developed their own network of espresso bars and local 'dives'. Often furnished in a vaguely exotic style (with bull-fight posters, bamboo fixtures, tropical plants and an occasional shell or Mexican mask) coffee bars generated an excitingly cosmopolitan allure and stand as one of the most enduring images of not only fifties' youth style but of British cultural life more generally during the period.

The two decades that followed the Second World War, therefore, witnessed a proliferation of the commercial youth market in Britain. Increases in many young workers' disposable income laid the foundation for this burgeoning commercial sector, its scale serving from reinforce notions of the post-war youth experience as qualitatively different from that of preceding generations. Beyond this, however, the period also saw the youth market take on symbolic significance. Perceived changes in the lifestyles of young people were increasingly treated as a benchmark of wider and more fundamental changes in patterns of culture and social relations, with 'the affluent teenager' promoted as the figurehead of Britain's march into what had the appearance of a new era of prosperous consumerism.

4. The 'Metaphorical' Dimension to Youth in Post-War Britain

Conceptions of 'youth' and chronological age almost inevitably figure in attempts to make sense of social change. At moments of particularly profound transformation, however, youth's symbolic capacity becomes powerfully extended. In Britain the 1950s and early 1960s represented just such a period – the 'youth question' coming to operate as a forum for debate about the wider social, economic and cultural state of the nation.[18]

It is impossible to understand the post-war saliency of youth as a cultural category in Britain without considering the wider societal context. During the war German bombing, lack of investment and the sheer weight of wartime demand had taken a heavy toll on the British economy. By the beginning of the fifties, however, recovery was underway. Over the next decade full employment underpinned rises in real earnings and laid the basis for a steady growth in consumer spending. Moreover, between 1951 and 1964 three consecutive terms of Conservative government saw reductions in interest rates and taxes and the relaxation of hire purchase controls – promoting high street sales and prompting, in 1957, Prime Minister Harold Macmillan's famous remark that the British people had 'never had it so good'. It is difficult to measure precisely the extent to which this new spending lay in the hands of the working class, though they clearly benefited, with a growing number of working-class households boasting televisions, motor cars, washing machines and a growing range of domestic appliances and consumer durables.

During the late 1950s and early 1960s the imagery of youth was deployed as a shorthand signifier for these wider shifts – young people seeming to embody all that the consumer dream stood for. Throughout the late fifties and early sixties, for example, there appeared a wealth of official research, both nationally and locally based, which presented youth as a category integral to wider social changes. The tone of much of this work was optimistic and reassuring. Certainly, studies such as that produced by the Labour Party's Youth Commission (1959) and the British Medical Association (1961) voiced a number of reservations about trends in the lifestyles of young people, yet overall their conclusions were favourable, indeed almost celebratory, presenting young people as a group whose lively energy was kept in check by their mature sense of responsibility.

The media, too, often presented young people in glowing terms. Newspapers and magazines, especially, helped popularize notions of 'youth' as an excitingly positive social force – a vibrant and uplifting contrast to the tired and out-moded conventions of the traditional social order. Leading this field was the *Daily Mirror*, where the theme of 'youth' (along with an explicit appeal to a young readership) became a recurring feature as the paper sought to maintain its share of market sales as well as offering a meaningful response to the rapid pace of social change. The 1950s saw the *Mirror* increasingly jump on the youth 'bandwagon', the paper publishing several books on the quickly developing universe of pop music and, in 1957, sponsoring a 'Rock 'n' Roll Express' to take American rock 'n' rollers Bill Haley and the Comets to London after they had arrived at the port of Southampton for their first British tour. An enthusiastic interest in youth culture was also demonstrated by the magazine *Picture Post*. Despite its share of histrionic articles on "Boy Gangsters",[19] the tone of *Picture Post*'s coverage was generally positive, culminating in 1957 with an optimistic four-part series entitled "The Truth About Teenagers", which revealed "what teenagers are, what they hate and what they hope for".[20]

This positive stereotyping of British youth reached its apex in the milieu of 'Swinging London' during the early sixties. Here, the throbbing dance-floors of the capital's night-clubs and the fashionable clothes boutiques of Carnaby Street came to embody notions of a Britain that was moving boldly into a new age of growth and modernity. In the world of fashion, especially, designers such as Mary Quant pioneered an image of youthful chic, their impact underlined in 1962 when the first edition of the

Sunday Times Magazine featured on its cover a teenage Jean Shrimpton modelling a sleeveless Quant dress – the same newspaper later awarding Quant for "jolting England out of its conventional attitude towards clothes".[21]

This equation of the imagery of youth with notions of general economic growth and increasing consumer consumption was exemplified, above all, by the addition of the term 'teenager' to everyday vocabulary. First coined by American market researchers during the mid-1940s, the term was formalized in the early 1950s through the research endeavours of bodies such as the Student Marketing Institute, Teenage Survey Incorporated and Eugene Gilbert and Company which, in conjunction with an avalanche of books, magazine and newspaper articles, revealed to the American public what appeared to be a new social caste with its own culture and lifestyle.[22] By the late forties the word 'teenager' had been imported into Britain and was swiftly integrated into popular discourse, the media making liberal use of the term by the early fifties.

In the image of the 'teenager' post-war notions of affluent prosperity found their purest manifestation. Taken as the quintessence of social transformation, 'teenagers' were perceived as being in the vanguard of the new consumer culture, distinguished not simply by their youth but by a particular style of conspicuous and leisure-oriented consumption. As Peter Laurie contended in his taxonomy of *The Teenage Revolution*, published in 1965, "[t]he distinctive fact about teenagers' behaviour is economic: they spend a lot of money on clothes, records, concerts, make-up, magazines: all things that give immediate pleasure and little lasting use".[23] The 'teenager', therefore, was much more than a simple descriptive term. Rather, the 'teenager' was an ideological terrain upon which a particular definition of post-war change was constructed. Central to notions of the 'teenager' was the idea that traditional class boundaries were being eroded by the fashions and lifestyles of newly affluent "gilded youth".[24] 'Teenagers' were presented as a class in themselves, or what Laurie termed a "solidly integrated social bloc",[25] a group whose vibrant, hedonistic culture seemed to be a symbolic foretaste of good times that would soon be available to everyone. Teenage consumption, therefore, became the defining emblem for the economic changes which, many commentators argued, were steadily ameliorating social divisions, neutralizing traditional class conflicts and ushering in a new epoch of prosperous 'postcapitalism'.

5. Negative Stereotyping and the 'Demonology' of British Youth Subcultures

Social responses to youth, however, were never unanimously positive. Throughout the post-war period a recurring duality saw young people both celebrated as the exciting precursor to a prosperous future and, almost simultaneously, vilified as the most deplorable evidence of cultural bankruptcy. Alongside the positive and optimistic representations of youth there always co-existed important elements of apprehension and uncertainty.

While economic prosperity and rising living standards were warmly greeted, commentators from across the political spectrum also viewed the cultural implications of these changes with a degree of anxiety. Antipathy toward the forms and institutions of what was seen as a 'commercialized', 'mass' culture was nothing new. Identical fears had existed in the late nineteenth century, while the 1930s saw notions of a cultural 'levelling-down' increasingly centre on the idea of 'Americanization' – America, the home of monopoly capitalism and commercial culture, coming to epitomize the processes of debasement and decline that many commentators saw as increasingly characteristic of popular cultural forms and practices in Britain. As Dick Hebdige shows, this use of America as a paradigm "for the future threatening every advanced industrial democracy in the western world"[26] intensified after 1945, the growth of working-class affluence prompting heightened anxieties that British culture was set to become a degraded and desocialized mass.

Developments in British youth culture were treated as symbolic of this trajectory of cultural decline. The work of writer and academic Richard Hoggart was exemplary of these concerns. In *The Uses of Literacy* (1958) Hoggart decried the emergence of a "candy-floss world" with its "canned entertainment and packeted provision" which, he contended, offered a culture that was shallow and banal compared with that which had existed before the war. Moreover, it was typical of the period that Hoggart should single out the younger generation as symptomatic of the growing paucity of contemporary cultural life. Contemporary youth was, for Hoggart, a "hedonistic but passive barbarian", the writer lamenting "the juke box boys" with their "drape suits, picture ties and American slouch" who spent their evenings in "harshly lighted milk bars" putting "copper after copper into the mechanical record player".[27]

A perceived rise in rates of juvenile crime was also taken as evidence of cultural decline. Within both popular opinion and academic enquiry there arose the widely held belief that wartime destruction, the absence of fathers and the long working hours of mothers had all contributed to a steady break-down in processes of socialization and an ensuing rise in levels of delinquency. One of the leading exponents of this perspective was the journalist T.R. Fyvel who, through a number of articles and his study *The Insecure Offenders*, helped popularize the notion that post-war increases in juvenile crime were, at least partly, "the expression of a particularly disturbed generation, a delayed effect of the war".[28] Fyvel's opinions found empirical support from research conducted for the Home Office by Leslie Wilkins and subsequently published as *Delinquent Generations* in 1960. Juggling with a host of statistics, Wilkins claimed that children born between 1935 and 1942 were more prone to delinquency than those born in any other seven year period with, he claimed, the highest delinquency rates existing among youngsters who had been aged between four and five years during the war.[29] Wilkins, however, judged that wartime conditions were not solely to blame for subsequent rises in levels of juvenile crime. In addition to the destabilizing effects of the war Wilkins also cited the recent stylistic preferences of the young as an important contributory factor, postulating that

> [o]ne of the most disturbing features of the pattern of post-war criminal statistics is the recent crime-wave among young adult males between seventeen and twenty-one years of age. The crime wave among young males has been associated with certain forms of dress and other social phenomena.[30]

Nor was Wilkins alone in his speculation. Throughout the post-war period the new fashions of the young were a recurring theme in attempts to understand the apparent upsurge of juvenile crime. In the early 1950s the association of particular styles of dress with what was perceived to be a 'new wave' of vicious delinquency crystallized around two dramatic murder cases. The first, in 1952, saw the controversial conviction and subsequent execution of nineteen-year-old Derek Bentley for the shooting of a police officer in Croydon. The second, in 1953, saw twenty-year-old Michael Davies convicted and sentenced to death (later commuted to life imprisonment) for the stabbing of a youth on London's Clapham Common.[31] In both cases the dress of the young defendants became symbolically charged. The press drew attention to their 'flashy', 'American-style' clothes and demeanour, the two accused being presented as the embodiment of a dissipation of traditional culture and values which was judged to be a growing feature of life in post-war Britain.

Throughout the post-war decades it became commonplace to draw an association between young people's sartorial styles, growing levels of crime and a general decline in cultural standards. During the early fifties, for example, these anxieties cohered around the figure of the Teddy boy. First identified by the media in the working-class neighbourhoods of south London in 1954, the Ted was soon presented as a shockingly new spectre haunting street corners and dance halls all over the country. The Teddy boys' negative image was further compounded as they were cited by the press as central protagonists in both a spate of cinema 'riots' that followed screenings of the film *Rock Around the Clock* in August 1956 and a wave of racist attacks in Nottingham and Notting Hill in 1958.

By the end of the fifties the Ted's drape-suit had been superseded by the 'Italian' look of short, 'bum-freezer' jackets and 'slim Jim' ties, though dominant reactions to the mods of the early sixties replicated many of the anxieties that had earlier attended the arrival of the Teds. Like the Teddy boys before them, the mods' style was often judged by the media and other social commentators to represent not simply a mode of dress, but a symbol of national decline and cultural degradation. Negative responses to the mods were exemplified, above all, in the outrage that surrounded the 'invasion' of several seaside towns in 1964. Working-class youngsters had traditionally visited seaside resorts at holiday times, but Easter 1964 was cold and wet and facilities for young people were poor – with the result that a few scuffles broke out between local youths and visiting Londoners. In reality the violence was sporadic and small-scale, yet the media response was melodramatic and overwrought, newspaper reporters regaling their readers with stories of a 'day of terror' in which whole towns had been overrun by marauding mobs 'hell-bent on destruction'.[32]

Yet dominant responses to the mods were always ambiguous. At the same time as they were reviled as the *bête noire* of the affluent society, the mods were also hailed as stylish consumers *par excellence*. Superficially clean-cut and well-dressed, the mod's appearance was amenable to co-option within notions of post-war dynamism and modernity. The mods, therefore, were treated as the trend-setters of sixties' stylishness and élan and the press eagerly charted changes in the minutiae of their dress and music. Even in 1964, at the height of concerns about mod violence, the *Sunday Times Magazine* featured a sumptuous nine-page photo-spread chronicling the intricacies and finesse of mod style.[33]

6. Social Change and Shifting Representations of British Youth

The contrasting representations of youth in Britain during the fifties and sixties were obviously stereotypes which often bore only a tenuous relation to social reality. Nevertheless, these images of youth possessed potent symbolic power and served as a key motif around which dominant interpretations of social change were constructed. While social responses to youth were always marked out by a degree of ambiguity, however, the late fifties and early sixties saw a set of generally positive images come to the fore – with 'the young ones' taken as the epitome of a Britain in which the sheer pace of economic growth seemed set to engender a newly prosperous age of fun, freedom and social accord.

This 'teenage mythology', however, was generated from an unstable set of social and economic conditions. In retrospect the prosperity of the post-war decades can be seen as insecure and transient, the ephemeral trappings of a precarious "age of illusion".[34] The consumer 'boom' was, for example, to a large part based on the vulnerable economic foundation of short-term credit, Britain's hire purchase debt rising faster between 1956 and 1959 than at any other time either before or since. Moreover, post-war 'affluence' depended on a level of growth that Britain's weakened economic infrastructure was simply unable to maintain. By the late 1960s, therefore, the scale of these problems was becoming apparent, as the period was punctuated by a series of deepening economic crises. By the end of the sixties an atmosphere of social discord and political conflict had come to characterize British society. As a consequence, the ideologies of affluence, prosperity and consent which had articulated social relations during the fifties and early sixties became untenable and gave way to political programmes more visibly coercive and confrontational.[35]

Against this background representations of young people also began to change. Responses to youth were never exclusively negative, yet the late 1960s and early 1970s saw a more marked degree of hostility within political comment and media coverage. For example, the skinhead style, which first began to make its presence felt in British youth culture in the mid-sixties,[36] was unequivocally presented as a violent and menacing presence stalking British streets. Whereas the mods' style of slick and conspicuous consumption allowed them to be integrated relatively easily within a discourse of classless affluence, no such co-option was possible with the skinheads, whose self-conscious invocation of a 'traditional' working-class heritage (through their distinctive 'uniform' of steel toe-capped work boots, rolled-up jeans, braces and convict-style cropped hair) was incompatible with notions of disappearing social divisions in a prosperous Britain. However, whereas working-class subcultures such as the skinheads were understood as socially delinquent *symptoms* of deterioration, the emergence of a more middle-class counter-culture (especially its more overtly political elements) was cast as an active cause of cultural degeneration and social instability.[37] Amid the revolutionary ferment of 1968, therefore, media and political responses stigmatized and vilified the counter-culture, and a coercive backlash saw increasingly repressive measures directed against social elements deemed either 'permissive' or 'subversive'.[38]

Notions and representations of 'youth', therefore, have the capacity to play a metaphorical role in the ways sense is made of more general social developments, especially at times of dramatic change. This was especially true of Britain in the two decades that followed the Second World War, young people becoming an important (possibly the *most* important) ideological vehicle for the discussion of wider shifts in social relations and changes in cultural life. During the late fifties and early sixties 'the affluent teenager' was exalted as the figurehead of Britain's march into a new era of prosperous consumerism. By the end of the sixties, however, the confident rhetoric of growth and social cohesion had begun to crumble in the face of industrial decline and economic crisis – a shift which found its corollary in the rise of an increasingly negative set of social responses to 'the young ones'.

Notes

1 The most authoritative account of working-class youth subcultures in Victorian and Edwardian Britain is provided in Pearson (1983).
2 The work of David Fowler (1992, 1995) offers a meticulous survey of British youngsters' life and culture between the wars.
3 According to Department of Employment statistics (1971: 206-207), numbers of young people in Britain grew from just over three million in 1951 (representing 8% of the national population) to just over four million in 1966 (10% of the national population).
4 This perspective was exemplified in "Growing Up Faster", an article written by Alex Comfort and published in *The Listener* in 1960. See also "The Beanstalk Generation", a series of articles featured in the *Daily Mirror* between 15 and 19 September 1958.
5 Strangely, the experience of National Service has been subject to relatively little scrutiny by British historians. The best existing accounts of National Service, its history and the experiences of National Servicemen are provided in Chambers & Landreth (1955), Johnson (1973) and Royale (1988).
6 A concise overview of the impact of economic change on employment patterns among British youth is provided in Roberts (1995).
7 Ministry of Education (1947: 47).
8 Abrams (1959: 9).
9 *Ibid.*, 10.
10 Abrams (1961: 3).
11 Research such as Smith's (1966) study of youth in the town of Bury and Jephcott's (1967) survey of Scottish youth produced figures for earnings and consumption much less than those arrived at by Abrams. "The popular picture of affluent teenagers", Smith concluded, "grossly simplifies the very real differences in income among them." (1966: 17)
12 Leslie (1965: 15).
13 The history of the American 'teenpic' industry is documented in Doherty (1988).
14 The rise and fall of the British pop film is meticulously charted in Medhurst (1995).
15 Since the 1930s an agreement between the BBC and representatives of the record industry and the Musicians' Union had placed time limits on the radio

broadcast of commercially produced records. This had originally been intended as a measure to protect both the profits of British record companies (who blamed falling record sales on the broadcast of recorded music) and the interests of musicians (who were anxious that records should not be used as a cheap alternative to live performance).

16 Accounts of the development of pop radio during this period are provided in Hind & Mosco (1985: 7-18) and Barnard (1989: 32-49).

17 A history of British television's early forays into the field of pop music can be found in Hill (1991).

18 For further exploration of this 'metaphorical' facet to youth debates see Smith, Immirizi & Blackwell (1975: 242), Clarke *et al.* (1976: 9-74) and Davis (1990).

19 Marchant (1953: 16-18).

20 Philpott (1957: 11).

21 Quant (1967: 139).

22 For overviews of the growth of the commercial youth industries in America during this period see Gilbert (1986: 196-211), Doherty (1988: 17-41) and Palladino (1996: 96-174).

23 Laurie (1965: 9).

24 *The Economist*, 11 January 1958.

25 Laurie (1965: 11).

26 Hebdige (1988: 52-53).

27 Hoggart (1958: 248-250).

28 Fyvel (1963: 51).

29 Wilkins' calculations and conclusions were, in fact, seriously flawed. Not only were his statistical inferences invalid but he failed to consider variations of delinquency rate between different types of offence and ignored non-indictable offences altogether. Moreover, by the 1960s the generation of youngsters born in the years following the war had begun to register rates of delinquency even higher than their immediate predecessors.

30 Wilkins (1960: 9).

31 In both cases serious doubt exists as to the guilt of the accused. It is possible that the authorities sought to make salutary examples of both Bentley and Davies, demonstrating to the public that the juvenile 'crime-wave' was being firmly dealt with. For details of the Bentley and Davies cases see, respectively, Yallop (1990) and Parker (1965).

32 In his now classic study Cohen (1973) shows how the melodramatic press coverage of these events actually served to engender and amplify subsequent disturbances.

33 Halton (1964: 12-19).

34 Bogdanor & Skidelsky (1970: 7).

35 According to authors associated with the Birmingham Centre for Contemporary Cultural Studies, Britain during the late sixties and early seventies saw the rise of a political order which was increasingly willing to rule through force and compulsion rather than consensus and consent. See Hall *et al.* (1978).

36 Informed and well documented histories of the development of skinhead style are provided in Knight (1982) and Marshall (1991).

37 These arguments were originally developed in Clarke *et al.* (1976: 72).

38 This more coercive shift was marked by a more determined enforcement of drug laws, followed by police raids on the offices of underground publications

such as *It* and the closure of clubs like Middle Earth and UFO after police raids had prompted landlords to withdraw leases. In 1970 the authoritarian offensive against the underground press continued, with *Oz* editors Richard Neville, Jim Anderson and Felix Dennis prosecuted, and subsequently imprisoned, for obscenity. A more coercive set of official responses also made itself felt in the sphere of public order. In 1968 demonstrations against the Vietnam war were subject to aggressive and often brutal policing, with the intimidatory use of mounted officers and police 'snatch squads', while in February 1970 punitive prison sentences were passed on six defendants after police had battled with protesters objecting to the presence of representatives of the Greek military junta at the Garden House Hotel in Cambridge.

Bibliography

Abrams, Mark: *The Teenage Consumer*, London, 1959.

---: *Teenage Consumer Spending in 1959*, London, 1961.

Barnard, Stephen: *On the Radio. Music Radio in Britain*, Milton Keynes, 1989.

Bogdanor, Vernon & Robert Skidelsky (Eds.): *The Age of Affluence, 1951-64*, London, 1970.

British Medical Association: *The Adolescent. Observations Arising from Discussion Among Members of the British Medical Association*, London, 1961.

Chambers, P. & A. Landreth: *Called Up. The Personal Experiences of Sixteen National Servicemen*, London, 1955.

Clarke, John *et al.*: "Subcultures, Cultures and Class. A Theoretical Overview". – In Stuart Hall & Tony Jefferson (Eds.): *Resistance Through Rituals. Youth Subcultures in Post-War Britain*, London, 1976, pp. 9-74.

Cohen, Stanley: *Folk Devils and Moral Panics. The Creation of the Mods and Rockers*, St Albans, 1973.

Comfort, Alex: "Growing Up Faster", *The Listener* 64, no. 1632, 7 July 1960, 15-16.

Davis, John: *Youth and the Condition of Britain. Images of Adolescent Conflict*, London, 1990.

Department of Employment: *British Labour Statistics Historical Abstract 1886-1968*, London, 1971.

Doherty, Thomas: *Teenagers and Teenpics. The Juvenilization of American Movies in the 1950s*, London, 1988.

The Economist, 11 January 1958.

Fowler, David: "Teenage Consumers? Young Wage-Earners and Leisure in Manchester, 1919-39". – In Andrew Davies & Steven Fielding (Eds.): *Workers' Worlds. Cultures and Communities in Manchester and Salford, 1880-1939*, Manchester, 1992, pp. 133-155.

---: *The First Teenager. The Lifestyle of Young Wage-Earners in Interwar Britain*, London, 1995.

Fyvel, T.R.: *The Insecure Offenders. Rebellious Youth in the Welfare State*, Harmondsworth, 1963.

Gilbert, James: *A Cycle of Outrage. America's Reaction to the Juvenile Delinquent in the 1950s*, Oxford, 1986.

Hall, Stuart *et al.*: *Policing the Crisis. Mugging, the State, and Law and Order*, London, 1978.
Halton, Kathleen: "Changing Faces", *Sunday Times Magazine*, 2 August 1964, 12-19.
Hebdige, Dick: "Towards a Cartography of Taste, 1935-1962". – In D.H.: *Hiding in the Light. On Images and Things*, London, 1988, pp. 45-76.
Hill, John: "Television and Pop. The Case of the 1950s". – In John Corner (Ed.): *Popular Television in Britain. Studies in Cultural History*, London, 1991, pp. 90-107.
Hind, John & Stephen Mosco: *Rebel Radio. The Full Story of British Pirate Radio*, London, 1985.
Hoggart, Richard: *The Uses of Literacy*, Harmondsworth, 1958.
Jephcott, Pearl: *A Time of One's Own*, Edinburgh, 1967.
Johnson, B.S. (Ed.): *All Bull. The National Servicemen*, London, 1973.
Knight, Nick: *Skinhead*, London, 1982.
Labour Party Youth Commission: *The Younger Generation*, London, 1959.
Laurie, Peter: *The Teenage Revolution*, London, 1965.
Leslie, Peter: *Fab. The Anatomy of a Phenomenon*, London, 1965.
Marchant, Hilde: "The Making of Boy Gangsters", *Picture Post* 61, no. 2, 10 October 1953, 16-18.
Marshall, George: *Spirit of '69. A Skinhead Bible*, Dunoon, 1991.
Medhurst, Andy: "It Sort of Happened Here. The Strange, Brief Life of the British Pop Film". – In Jonathan Romney & Adrian Wootton (Eds.): *Celluloid Jukebox. Popular Music and the Movies Since the 1950s*, London, 1995, pp. 60-71.
Ministry of Education: *School Life. A First Enquiry into the Transition from School to Independent Life* (Clarke Report), London, 1947.
Palladino, Grace: *Teenagers. An American History*, New York, 1996.
Parker, Tony: *The Ploughboy*, London, 1965.
Pearson, Geoffrey: *Hooligan. A History of Respectable Fears*, London, 1983.
Philpott, Trevor: "The Truth about Teenagers", *Picture Post* 74, no. 11, 18 March 1957, 11.
Quant, Mary: *Quant by Quant*, London, 1967.
Roberts, Kenneth: *Youth and Employment in Modern Britain*, Oxford, 1995.
Royale, Trevor: *The Best Years of Their Lives. The National Service Experience 1943-63*, London, 1988.
Smith, A.C.H., Elizabeth Immirizi & Trevor Blackwell: *Paper Voices. The Popular Press and Social Change, 1935-65*, London, 1975.
Smith, Cyril: *Young People. A Report on Bury*, Manchester, 1966.
Wilkins, Leslie: *Delinquent Generations*, London, 1960.
Yallop, David: *To Encourage the Others*, London, 1990.

Rachel Thomson / Janet Holland, London

Sexual Relationships, Negotiation and Decision Making[1]

Over the course of a generation there have been many changes in the attitudes and practices of adolescents, and this is nowhere so true as in the area of sexuality. Young people have become increasingly liberal and tolerant in the area of personal morality,[2] they are sexually active at an earlier age and there is growing evidence of convergence in the patterns of female and male sexual behaviour.[3] Yet there is also evidence of a 'gender lag' in these changes – the attitudes, expectations and aspirations of young women are changing more quickly than those of young men, and a significant proportion of young men continue to hold traditional expectations of gender roles.[4]

The religious and ethnic diversity of many developed societies means that there continues to be variation in attitudes towards sexual relationships and levels of sexual experience, but sexual activity is both statistically and culturally a 'normal' part of late adolescence. While it may be 'normal' for young people to have sex, evidence of regret and the inability of realising intentions to practise safer sex, suggest that many young people are uncertain about the pleasure, perils and precautions that are involved in sexual relationships.[5]

In this paper we explore the social context of young people's sexual relationships, how expectations of conventional femininity and masculinity shape communication and decision making in their intimate encounters, and suggest practical ways in which those working with young people might address these issues. We draw on material from two studies undertaken by the authors[6] but the points that we raise in the paper have been confirmed by many studies in Britain and other developed countries.[7]

1. Expectations and Reality: First Sex

The processes through which young people learn about sex are those through which they learn about being feminine and masculine, and young men and young women arrive at their first sexual experience with very different expectations.

1.1. How was it for him?

Becoming sexually active appears to be a crucial part of the process of moving from the status of a boy to that of a man:

> I mean it's the old saying, 'you enter the bed a boy and you leave it a man' or words to that effect. I felt the same, I didn't alter physically, but I felt different after that first time. I did definitely feel different.
> [*young man, aged 19, ESW,*[8] *working class*]

Studies with young men have found that sexual experience is highly prized within the male peer group and is generally understood as being inherently positive, even if it fails to meet with prior expectations. Young men experience pressure from their peers to be sexually active and knowledgeable, and sexual experience can provide them with a passport to status and affirmation. The opinions of male friends seemed to be paramount in the first sexual experiences of some of the young men in our study:

> At the time I was thinking, if only my mates could see me now, and stuff like that, and I must admit I didn't really think of the girl at the time.
> [*young man, aged 16, African Caribbean, working class*]

The dynamics of the adolescent male peer group mean that it can be difficult for young men to demonstrate ignorance or innocence about sex to their peers or to their sexual partners. They feel under pressure to 'do sex well' and often suffer anxiety about their 'performance'.

> Q. Did you feel confident?
> A. No, I felt bloody nervous. I thought, what if I don't get a hard-on? It all goes to pot.
> [*young man, aged 19, ESW, working class*]

This anxiety can eclipse concern for their partner and in our study was often associated with a preference for having first sexual encounters with partners whose judgements would not get back to their friends (for example holiday romances, older more experienced partners).

> Q. Is there a sort of feeling do you think amongst men to think they have to be good at sex?
> A. I think so yes, especially if you have seen the girl about and stuff like that, and like you know she is going to open her mouth to everyone else if you are not good, so yes, you have to perform quite well, if you know the girl like, and you have seen her about.
> [*young man, aged 16, African Caribbean, working class*]

There were exceptions to this pattern, some young men had their first sexual experience in the context of longer-term relationships and friendships, and in these cases there tended to be greater equality and communication:

> Q. How was it [with] both of you being virgins? Was it all right the first time? I mean sometimes it's a bit problematic.
>
> A. No, it was funny. I mean you've got to get rid of your embarrassment and you're both in the same boat. You both know, and it's just a laugh isn't it? It's not a … I didn't find it like a nerve-racking experience like lot of people do. I just sort of took it as it comes. If it doesn't work the first time you have another go. You laugh about it.
> [*young man, aged 18, white/Asian ethnicity, middle class*]

1.2. How was it for her?

Although sexual practice has undergone enormous changes over a generation, sexual attitudes have not always kept pace. The convergence in the patterns of male and female sexual activity has not been entirely paralleled by a convergence in the social meanings associated with sexual behaviour. In many cultures conventional femininity continues to require that young women should not be seen to be sexually desiring or assertive, and while young men are expected to seek sexual access, young women are expected to resist their sexual advances. This can be illustrated by the words of the following young man interviewed in our study who questioned his partner's claims to virginity on basis of her unseemly lack of resistance to his advances.

> Q. Was it her first time?
>
> A. She said it was but I – I don't know whether it was or not. Because like it was too quick like for her like, for a girl to say it was, like in a couple of hours. It would have been more if like she was a virgin, so I reckon she wasn't.
> [*young man, aged 18, ESW, working class*]

It appears that young men approach sex from the position of the sexual actor (the person who does sex) whereas young women are generally positioned as the objects of sex (the person who has sex done to them). The lack of power involved in the latter position (other than the negative power to 'say no') was apparent to many young women.

> And I suppose he must been on a right high, you know, just, you know, broke someone's virginity – a sixteen-year-old girl.
> [*young woman, aged 19, ESW, working class*]

Many of the young women we interviewed found it difficult to articulate their own agency in such sexual encounters and frequently described sex as something that 'happened to them'. Faced only with the choice of saying no or yes to sex effectively silences any voice that a young woman may have in negotiating the context and meaning of the sexual encounter:

> [...] normally when you just know a boy's going to try it on or something, you know like, – and, you know, that's when you say 'No' or something, but I didn't. I wanted – I did want to do it. It wasn't like I was – like I say – I wasn't forced or anything. I knew what was going to happen and, you know, I wasn't worried.
> [*young woman, aged 19, ESW, working class*]

Young women in our study dealt with this lack of agency in different ways. Some sought to escape it by rushing into their first sexual experience and 'getting it over and done with'. Unfortunately this was frequently associated with frustration and regret:

> Q. Do you think you made the right decision the first time?
> A. No. I suppose I wanted to just get it over and done with – I didn't want to rush into it, just because he was there, and I'd been going out with him anyway. I didn't like him. I just finished with him. I hated it. It's not great the first time. Never.
> [*young woman, aged 18, ESW, working class*]

A number of studies have documented the way in which being positioned as the objects of male sexual desire can render young women passive in heterosexual sexual relationships, irrespective of the existence of force or pressure on the part of male partners.[9] These studies have observed that being the object of male desire can effectively silence female desire and lead to self-surveillance on the part of women both young and old. Self-surveillance can be manifested as 'nurturance' (fulfilling the needs of their male partner) and/or pragmatism (accepting that consent to sexual experience may be easier than offering resistance). Many of the young women's accounts of their first sexual experiences reflect this ambivalence, and a frequent response to such confusion was self-blame:

> Q. Why did you do it?
> A. I don't know. I liked him, but I don't know why – I wish I didn't do it.
> [*young woman, aged 16, ESW, middle class*]

The lack of emphasis on female sexual pleasure in formal and informal sex education and in the wider society means that many young women enter sexual relationships aware of the sexual needs of men but without a clear sense of their own sexual self-interest. As the following woman explains:

A. [...] if I could go back then and change my mind I would, not because I lost my virginity, but because he was so horrible [*laughs*]. But I can't. And it wasn't very nice, like it was –
Q. You didn't enjoy it?
A. Oh. Well, not like – you know, like you were saying do I like my job. But – because I've got nothing to compare it against, then you don't know. ... In one sense I think you might enjoy it because, you know, like you're having sex and, you know, you don't really know what to enjoy it is like.
[*young woman, aged 19, ESW, working class*]

The contrasting accounts given by young men and young women of their first sexual experiences illustrate the differently gendered worlds within which adolescents become sexually active. Not all the young women in our study gave negative accounts of their first sexual experiences, but they reported significantly less satisfaction than did the young men.

The most positive accounts of first sexual experience tended to come from young people who were able to communicate openly with their partner and express their individual needs and desires within the privacy of a relationship or sexual encounter. It is important to remember that while adolescent sexual relationships may technically take place in private, they are located within complicated social networks of peers where information is exchanged and reputations are constructed. Conventional heterosexual identities are frequently enforced through the mechanism of sexual reputation, where a young woman is in danger of being labelled a 'slag' if she is seen to be sexually assertive and a young man is in danger of being labelled a 'wimp' or 'gay' if he is not.[10] The extent to which young people conform to or transgress conventional masculinity and femininity in their intimate relationships depends in part on the climate of the peer culture within which they are located.

Young people may also have a vested interest in not communicating about sex in early sexual encounters. One study found that silence can enable ambiguity to be maintained by both partners as to whether sex will actually happen. To mention condoms presumes that sex is on the cards, thereby opening the possibility of rejection. In the absence of communication the meanings and associations of conventional masculinity and femininity tend to fill the silence, overshadowing the needs and desires of the individuals involved and concerns for sexual safety. Commentators have observed that 'hegemonic masculinity' (a socially shared understanding of successful masculinity, constituted in opposition to femininity and other subordinate forms of masculinity including homosexuality) dominates the sexual cultures of both young and adult men and women.[11] Challenging hegemonic masculinity takes individual courage and may be punished by peers and partners. In the following section we explore the ways in which hegemonic masculinity and associated expectations frame the conditions within which sexual encounters are negotiated and which structure the possibilities of safer sex for young people.

2. Trusting to Love: The Logic of Sexual Risk Taking

A number of studies have confirmed that unsafe sex, in terms of pregnancy and protection against sexually transmitted diseases, is a 'normal' part of adolescent sexual experience. Unsafe sex is particularly associated with first sexual encounters, with those who begin their sexual career at a relatively early age and with those who have higher numbers of sexual partners.[12] In our studies we found that the practice of safer sex (particularly for protection against STDs) was uneven and inconsistent, and we have argued that this inconsistency is the outcome of the contradictory pressures of conventional masculinity and femininity on sexual encounters. The demands of conventional femininity militated directly against the demands of sexual health, and in many cases the former proved more compelling.

The belief that sexual decision making is a rational, individual process predicated on free choice has received sustained criticism, and it has been recognized that the arena of intimate sexual relations is subject to deeply rooted symbolic and social meanings and is structured by unequal power relationships.[13] If achieving safer sex was merely a process of rational decision making, the ability to negotiate would develop with growing experience and awareness. In contrast, we found that young people's ability to negotiate safer sex was conditional on the circumstances and contingencies of individual sexual encounters and relationships. Safer sex might be negotiated in one relationship but this did not necessarily imply that it could be successfully negotiated in the next. In some cases this negotiation was easier in early and 'casual' sexual encounters than in more established relationships, a finding that appears to hold for both heterosexual and gay relationships.[14]

The symbolic meanings of safer sex for heterosexuals also involves the meanings and practices associated with contraception. Developments in contraceptive technology have affected the meanings that we associate with heterosexual sex and the kind of sex that is practised. The move from the condom and withdrawal as the most common forms of contraception in the 1960s to the pill in the 1980s and 1990s has been paralleled by a shift from men to women for the responsibility for sexual safety. The use of a particular contraceptive can profoundly construct both the expectation and practice of sex. The pill, unlike barrier methods, does not intrude on the act of sexual intercourse. Condoms are visible, require negotiation, disrupt the act of intercourse and bring attention to the potential for both pregnancy and disease. Within a culture where contraception has become an invisible female responsibility the negotiation of condom use can be highly disruptive.

Many of the young women to whom we spoke considered the 'spontaneity' enabled by the pill to be a central defining factor of sexual interaction and expressed opposition to condom use for reasons related to the disruption of this ideal. One young woman said:

> The climax to intercourse is all passion and kissing and I think to actually just stop and he puts a condom on, or me to turn around and say I want you to put this on, it just ruins the whole thing then.
> [*young woman, aged 20, ESW, middle class*]

A young man specifically referred to the way in which condoms and the pill enable different kinds of sexual practice:

> Well condoms are a bit mechanical – not in themselves – it's just that you put one on, then you have sex under cover, then you take it off again. You can't sort of roll around with somebody for hours and sort of have penetrative sex, then stop that for a while, do something else, go back to that.
> [*young man, aged 20, ESW, middle class*]

The belief that sex should be spontaneous is particularly attractive to young women, removing as it does the necessity of female sexual agency and masking a lack of confidence in and knowledge of their bodies. The 'rational' safer sex messages ("you know the risks, the choice is yours") can be seen as antithetical to discourses of conventional femininity, romance and passion which construct sex as relinquishing control in the face of love. Whether it is because it offers greater potential for pleasure and exploration, or because it requires less communication and engagement in the messy realities of sex, the understanding of sex made possible by the pill acts as a disincentive to the use of condoms and the practice of safer sex.

3. Symbolic Meanings: Condoms, Romance and Trust

The dual imperative on young people to protect against both pregnancy and sexually transmitted diseases complicates the practice of safer sex. Studies have found young people to be aware of the risks of HIV and AIDS (less so about other STDs) but more concerned about the possibility of pregnancy. Decision making about the use of contraception and/or prophylactic protection in different sexual encounters ultimately owes as much to the symbolic meanings attached to these methods as to rational assessments of risk. Condoms are not neutral objects. They are associated with certain types of sex, significantly with sporadic sexual encounters, whether these are one-night stands, early sexual experiences or sexual encounters outside an established relationship. Not using a condom is associated with the expression and demonstration of trust. The demonstration of trust is a significant factor in decision making about condom use, and can in itself become a euphemism for monogamy or love.

In our studies we found that while condom use characterizes the early stages of a sexual relationship, when a relationship was felt to be established, young people would often cease condom use and transfer to the pill as a method of contraception. Continued condom use at this point would distinguish between its function as prophylactic and contraceptive at a time when the display of trust is considered to be crucial. This transition from condoms with a new partner to the pill with a steady partner is laden with symbolic meaning and can be used to signify the seriousness of a relationship, a way of demonstrating to a partner that they are special. As one of our respondents put it, "I went on the pill for him". If condoms signify 'casual', 'illicit' or inexperienced sex, the pill is associated with grown-up status and grown-up sex. This makes the prospect of long-term condom use highly problematic, as some of our respondents clearly indicated:

> If you want to have relationships then you've got to trust them. Otherwise it's no good from the start. You have to believe what they tell you. You just hope they tell the truth. You can't find out if it's lies or not.
> [*young woman, aged 20, ESW, working class*]

> You've got to trust somebody at some time, you can't meet somebody and start, first time say, 'I know, let's use condoms I'm not on the pill' (even if you are) and then a week later still be saying 'Let's use condoms' and a week after that still be saying 'Let's use condoms'.
> [*young woman, aged 21, ESW, working class*]

But what is a 'serious', 'steady' or 'long-term' relationship? We found that there was a good deal of pressure on young women to define any relationship they were in as 'serious' (and therefore steady) in order to justify sex within a model of conventional femininity. Most young women are reluctant to describe themselves as having casual sex when the culturally approved objective is to be in a steady, preferably monogamous relationship. They are likely to expect or to express the hope that relationships of short duration, including one-night stands, will in fact last – relationships are 'steady' until proved otherwise.

> If I sleep with anyone I intend it to be a long terms relationship – so I don't know, because you don't like to think of the end of a relationship when you start it.
> [*young woman, aged 16, ESW, working class*]

In contrast, young men seemed much more able to see sexual relationships as 'casual' and as potentially risky. The young men in our study tended to distinguish sexual relationships with 'girlfriends', which were considered to be safe, and sexual relationships with 'slags', 'dodgy' and 'slack' girls, which were considered to be sexually risky.

> Safe sex is for a one-off. For one-night stands it's alright, but for long-term relationships, I don't think – I think people who have long-term relationships don't use condoms.
> [*young man, aged 18, white/Asian, middle class*]

4. Power, Pleasure and Control in Sexual Situations

Perhaps the most important constraint experienced by young people wishing to practise safer heterosexual sex is the degree of control which they have within sexual encounters. In general we found that young women had far less control over their sexual encounters than did young men. One obvious way in which power is manifest in sexual relationships is the presence of violence or its threat. Pressure, ranging from rape to persuasion, was reported by a quarter of the young women in our study. Interviews with young men confirmed that 'persuasion' is a legitimate (even requisite) component of the masculine sexual role.

Yet power is present within sexual relationships in some far less explicit but still crucial ways. Research by ourselves and others has identified the privileging of male sexual pleasure as an important expression of power in sexual relationships that places young women at a significant disadvantage in negotiating safer sex.[15] One expression of the privileging of male sexual pleasure is the definition of what counts as 'sex'. The majority of young men and women in our study understood sex to mean vaginal penetration (beginning with an erection and ending with ejaculation). Other sexual practices such as touching, mutual masturbation and oral sex were seen as either a prelude or afterthought to sexual intercourse. A significant proportion of the young women in the study reported that they experienced relatively little pleasure from sexual intercourse and relatively more from other forms of sexual practice but it was clear that vaginal intercourse was equated with 'real' and 'normal' sex.

Many of the young men's objections to condom use were centred on the way in which they disrupted their performance and pleasure.

I think they're horrible, I never come with one.
[*young man, aged 17, ESW, working class*]

They make your penis look pathetic.
[*young man, aged 19, ESW, working class*]

It's like everything's ok, and then its, 'Oh God, I've got to put a condom on' and then, you know, I kind of – I just lose my erection completely.
[*young man, aged 17, ESW, working class*]

Many of the objections to condom use, reported by young women in our study, were also related to ideas about male sexual pleasure and fears of its disruption. Both sexes used similar terms to describe the problems of condom use: 'having a bath with your boots on', 'eating a toffee with a wrapper on', but few cited criticisms which focussed on the ways in which condoms affect female pleasure. One young man reflected sensitively on this:

Q. Did she feel the same about it being sort of uncomfortable?
A. It – well, yeah. I don't know. She said she didn't really like them. I don't know if it made an awful lot of difference to her really... But maybe she was also saying it because she knew I was uncomfortable about it.
[*young man, aged 17, ESW, working class*]

The privileging of male sexual pleasure within our culture is experienced particularly strongly by young women who are unsure of their own sexual potential and agency. The absence of sexual self-interest on the part of young women involved in sexual relationships can place them at a disadvantage in the negotiation of sexual encounters. It is interesting that young women's reports of male opposition to condom use were not entirely confirmed by the reports of male respondents. This may be a characteristic of the sample (these were not the same young men with whom the young women were having sex) or may reflect the difficulties of communication between the sexes. It is possible that young women are policing their own behaviour, assuming male opposition to condoms, having internalized beliefs about the priority of male sexual pleasure. It was clear from our study that young women found consistent condom use very difficult. In our interview sample, 67 % of the sexually active young women had asked for condom use at some point in their sexual career. Of these 21 % had asked and had been refused for varying reasons. Others had not even been able to ask, finding themselves muted by the contradictions of their situation, and despite their intentions were unable to initiate condom use. In very few cases did young women report young men as taking responsibility in this area, and these were perceived to be exceptional.

> I know I have been in situations where I haven't [used a condom]. I have simply thought to myself, well look, well. When I got pregnant, I thought to myself, 'I'm not using a condom here, I'm not using anything', but I just couldn't say, just couldn't force myself to say, 'look you know' – and then the consequences were disastrous. But at the time I knew what I was doing, and I knew that I just couldn't say it and I knew that it was wrong.
> [*young woman, aged 21, ESW, working class*]

> About two weeks ago I ended up not asking him [to use a condom] and had to go and get the morning-after pill. I wouldn't say anything, and kept thinking I'll say something in a minute, it's just so difficult. I thought I'd say something in a minute and then it was too late, and I thought 'Oh no!' I didn't even know this person anyway.
> [*young woman, aged 18, ESW, middle class*]

5. Strategies for Safer Sex

In this paper we have shown that young women hold much of the responsibility for negotiating sexual safety; however, the demands of conventional masculinity and femininity mean that they rarely have the power or the skills necessary to realize this responsibility. Yet young women are not simply passive victims and we found that many of the young women in our study were resourceful in their responses to this situation.

A small number of the young women we interviewed reported adopting a strategy of 'subterfuge', which entailed being on the pill but using its invisibility as a cover to request condom use on the basis of fear of pregnancy.

> Rather than saying, 'Will you wear something, because I don't want to get AIDS?', which sounds really bad, doesn't it, we would say, 'you'll have to wear something because I'm not on the pill'.
> [*young woman, aged 18, ESW, working class*]

In this way, problems associated with trust, with appearances of sexual innocence and the taboo associated with the prophylactic function of the condom could effectively be avoided in the short term. The young women who used this strategy preferred it since it did not place them in the position of having to challenge the sexual politics of the sexual encounter. But it is also a strategy which demands the acknowledgement of the transient nature of a sexual encounter, thereby challenging the romantic expectations of potential relationships. Not all young women are able to do this and the strategy became problematic if the relationship did in fact last.

A second strategy adopted by young women was the avoidance of vulnerability by establishing relationships with men who were younger and/or significantly less experienced or mature than themselves. This was usually not specifically in order to practise safer sex, but related to more general fears of vulnerability around sexuality and relationships. These young women seemed able to ensure that their own sexual needs were given status within their relationships. In most cases this included shared responsibility for sexual safety and contraception. A number of young men in our study also reported equivalent sexual relationships, characterized by openness, equality and mutual learning. Many of the young women involved in such relationships expressed concern that they might not be able to negotiate the same relationship with future partners, particularly if that partner was sexually experienced.

Another group of young women who perceived themselves to be effectively 'safe' were those in monogamous relationships which they felt confident to actually be so. In a few cases the young women had negotiated an HIV-test before the relationship became sexual. In others partners' sexual histories were known due to small and static social networks. The ability of young people to communicate openly and effectively about sexual histories has been shown to be problematic; while they may be able to communicate about numbers and names of sexual partners, it is more difficult to discuss details of sexual practice and condom use.[16] In effect it may be difficult to openly explore questions of 'risk' in the face of the imperatives of trust and commitment involved in negotiating a relationship, and partners remain vulnerable to the possibility of infidelity. The safety of such relationships was often based on informal judgements as to the moral categories into which partners were seen to fall. For many young men, these categories divided into 'girlfriends' and 'slags', while contraception would be used with the former, prophylactic protection might be used with the latter. For young women such distinctions were harder to make.

A small number of the young women to whom we spoke had considered safer sex to be a more significant project going far beyond condom use and part of a wider reconsideration of their own sexual practice, pleasure and desire. They were young women who had reflected upon their sexual experiences and found them wanting in terms of their own agency and access to sexual pleasure. The safer sex repertoire of these young heterosexual women was considerably wider than with those who perceived it simply to mean using a condom, and they were prepared to have to educate their partners about the validity and worth of a range of non-penetrative sexual practices. These young women experienced few if any problems negotiating condom use within this context. Such a strategy was effective precisely because it entailed challenging a definition of sex structured by expectations of men's needs and desires and in doing so challenged the implicit constraints to safer sex as mentioned above, spontaneity, loss of control, trusting to love and lack of self-esteem. Unlike the others described above, this particular strategy was not dependent on the context of the sexual encounter or relationship but could travel with the person from relationship to relationship.

One young woman described her understanding of safer sex and the means by which she employed these practices as follows:

> A. Safe sex is as pleasurable an experience as actual penetration. Oral sex, just things like touching somebody else's body in a very gentle way. Kissing. Appreciating one another's bodies. I think it's just as [much] fun, if not more. You concentrate on each other's needs a lot more, you're a lot more aware of them. You're aware of each other's bodies a lot more ... Instead of 20 minutes of bang, bang, bang, you've got a whole night; you watch the dawn come up and you're still there.
>
> Q. Have you had to convert your partners? Have you come across men who understand sex as being more than penetration?
>
> A. Yes ... I've said, 'I don't want to do that', or 'Why don't you try this?' Before they know it they're converted, and they suddenly realize – 'Well we haven't actually done it!' – 'Well I'm tired now, haven't you had a good time?' You can change a lot of people's ideas. [*young woman, aged 18, ESW, working class*]

It takes a special combination of circumstance and communication for young women to gain sufficient control in sexual encounters to ensure sexual safety, a secure feminine identity and their own sexual pleasure. Maintaining a sense of personal empowerment which is independent of context and relationship can be difficult and lonely. It requires young women to negotiate a new model of sexuality which treats female sexual pleasure as a priority. While the accounts that we received from young men in our study suggest that some felt threatened by sexually knowing and confident young women, there also existed a minority who welcome this change.

Masculinity and femininity are mutually dependent. Effecting change in one leads to changes in the other. The development of a positive sexual agency for young women will mean that young men must also be prepared to re-evaluate their own beliefs about masculine sexuality. The evidence from studies with young people suggests that the individual needs and desires of young men and young women, both heterosexual and gay, are constrained by conventional masculinity and femininity and that they all share a vested interest in such changes.

6. Conclusions

Many would argue that women's increasing participation and success in education and employment, and concomitant economic independence, are leading to changes in the ways in which masculinity and femininity are lived and experienced. In relation to sexuality, for example, attention can be drawn to the changes in the public representations in the mass media in recent years. Since the late 1980s, strategies to control the spread of HIV and AIDS have necessitated a considerable flow of information about sex. The need to publicize what people actually do when they have sex, and to promote non-penetrative sexual practices has produced a plethora of surveys, studies, leaflets, campaigns and debates that have brought knowledge of intimate practices into the public realm.

New public spaces have emerged for talking about sex which may enable young people to renegotiate the rules of desire and heterosexuality. There has been a growing acknowledgement of the 'female pleasure principle' in popular culture, particularly in young women's magazines. There is also a growing body of research on the impact of sexual politics on the institutions of heterosexuality which has rendered its structures increasingly visible.[17] If the first step in the loss of authority is the ability to name and describe that which was previously unquestioned, then this can be taken as evidence that these structures are under some threat, or at least that they are opening for negotiation.

But these changes are characterized by contradiction. There has also been, for example, a blossoming of pornographic imagery in the media mainstream, and it is often difficult to distinguish between a new, ironic, post-feminist stance and an old familiar sexism in some public representations of women. The extent to which shifts in public talk about sex constitute a new discourse of sexuality, in the sense of establishing new 'truths' about masculinity and femininity is far from clear. Even in a context of increasing openness and increasing tolerance, social transformation is neither obvious nor inevitable. In practice unprotected sex continues to be a heterosexual norm in the UK.[18] The rising incidence of sexually transmitted infections and the extent of unwanted teenage pregnancies among some groups of young women suggest that public examination of sexual activity, changing values and expectations and female empowerment do not necessarily go hand in hand. The pattern of sexual health that characterizes the UK (and the US) is increasing distinct from the trends in other northern European countries where the sexuality of the young is less taboo and access to educational and health services less controversial.

Despite the recent increase in openness about sexuality and sexual pleasure, our own study indicates some of the enduring power of heterosexuality to reproduce itself through interlocking gender identities. At the level of individual agency and action we found that active resistance to masculinity and femininity on the part of both young men and young women could be contained within their private relationships, leaving the broad terms of the heterosexual contract intact. While individuals can sometimes create their own personal solutions and can certainly find happiness in heterosexual relationships, they cannot always manage safety, nor claim legitimacy for these solutions in a wider social context.

As women raise their expectations of sex and relationships, and as men seek shelter from the pressures of manhood, they may experience growing contradiction. The unbalanced interdependence of masculinity and femininity that characterizes heterosexuality is increasingly out of step with other aspects of young people's lives, leaving them to work through these contradictions and confusions. While young people are under great pressure to reproduce the hidden power relations of heterosexuality as they form relationships, reproduce, live together or get married, it is through changes in these intimate relationships that such power relations will be challenged.

Notes

1 This paper is an amended version of a paper originally published in Coleman & Roker (1998: 59-81).
2 Halpern (1995).
3 Wellings *et al.* (1994).
4 Oakley (1996); Wilkinson (1994).
5 Wellings *et al.* (1994).
6 The Women, Risk and AIDS Project (1988-1990) staffed by the authors, Caroline Ramazanoglu, Sue Sharpe and Sue Scott; The Men, Risk and AIDS Project (1991-1992) staffed by the authors, Caroline Ramazanoglu, Sue Sharpe and Tim Rhodes.
7 See Wight (1992); Kippax *et al.* (1990); Moore & Rosenthal (1992); Reinders & Vermeer (1995).
8 "ESW" indicates 'English/Scottish/Welsh', which was used in our purposive sample as a category of ethnic origin.
9 See Gavey (1992); Kippax *et al.* (1990); Donovan (1996); Fine (1988).
10 See Lees (1993); Holland *et al.* (1996).
11 Connell (1995).
12 Wellings *et al.* (1994).
13 Wight (1992).
14 Weatherburn *et al.* (1992); Frankham (1996).
15 Holland *et al.* (1990); Holland, Ramazanoglu & Sharpe (1993); Gavey (1992); Kippax *et al.* (1990); Richardson (1996a).
16 Ingham, Woodcock & Stenner (1991).
17 Maynard & Purvis (1995); Richardson (1996b).
18 Adler (1997).

Bibliography

Adler, Michael: "Sexual Health – A Health of the Nation Failure", *British Medical Journal* 314, 1997, 1743-1747.
Coleman, John & Debbie Roker (Eds.): *Teenage Sexuality. Health, Risk and Education*, Reading, 1998.
Connell, Robert W.: *Masculinities*, Cambridge, 1995.
Donovan, Catherine: "Young People, Alcohol and Sex. Taking Advantage", *Youth and Policy* 52, 1996, 30-37.
Fine, Michelle: "Sexuality, Schooling and Adolescent Females. The Missing Discourse of Desire", *Harvard Educational Review* 58, no. 1, 1988, 29-53.
Frankham, Jo: *Young Gay Men and HIV Infection*, London, 1996.
Gavey, Nicola: "Technologies and Effects of Heterosexual Coercion", *Feminism and Psychology* 2, no. 3, 1992, 774-775.
Halpern, David: "Values, Morals and Modernity. The Values, Constraints and Norms of European Youth". – In Michael Rutter & David Smith (Eds.): *Psychosocial Disorders in Young People. Time Trends and their Causes*, Chichester, 1995, pp. 324-387.
Holland, Janet *et al.*: *"Don't Die of Ignorance – I Nearly Died of Embarrassment". Condoms in Context*, London, 1990.
---, Caroline Ramazanoglu & Sue Sharpe: *Wimp or Gladiator. Contradictions in Acquiring Masculine Sexuality*, London, 1993.
--- *et al.*: "Reputations. Journeying into Gendered Power Relations". – In Jeffrey Weeks & Janet Holland (Eds.): *Sexual Cultures. Communities, Values and Intimacy*, London, 1996, pp. 239-260.
Ingham, Roger, Alison Woodcock & Karen Stenner: "Getting to Know You ... Young People's Knowledge of their Partners at First Intercourse", *Journal of Community and Applied Psychology* 1, 1991, 117-132.
Kippax, Susan *et al.*: "Women Negotiating Heterosex. Implications for AIDS Prevention", *Women's Studies International Forum* 13, 1990, 533-542.
Lees, Sue: *Sugar and Spice. Sexuality and Adolescent Girls*, London, 1993.
Maynard, Mary & June Purvis (Eds.): *(Hetero)Sexual Politics*, London, 1995.
Moore, Susan M. & Diane A. Rosenthal: "The Social Context of Adolescent Sexuality. Safe Sex Implications", *Journal of Adolescence* 6, 1992, 164-180.
Oakley, Ann: "Gender Matters. Man the Hunter". – In Helen Roberts & Darshan Sachdev (Eds.): *Young People's Social Attitudes – Having Their Say. The Views of 12-19 Year Olds*, London, pp. 23-43.
Reinders, Jo & Veroon Vermeer (Eds.): *Gender Specific AIDS Prevention for Youth. A Working Document*, Utrecht, 1995.
Richardson, Diane: "Contradictions in Discourse. Gender, Sexuality and HIV/AIDS". – In Janet Holland & Lisa Adkins (Eds.): *Sex, Sensibility and the Gendered Body*, London, 1996a, pp. 161-177.
--- (Ed.): *Telling it Straight. Theorising Heterosexuality*, Buckingham, 1996b.
Weatherburn, Peter *et al.*: *The Sexual Lifestyles of Gay and Bisexual Men in England and Wales*, London, 1992.
Wellings, Kay *et al.*: *Sexual Behaviour in Britain*, London, 1994.
Wight, Daniel: "Impediments to Safer Heterosexual Sex. A Review of Research with Young People", *AIDS Care* 4, no. 1, 1992, 11-12.
Wilkinson, Helen: *No Turning Back. Generations and the Genderquake*, London, 1994.

Mike Storry, Liverpool

Teenagers and Advertising

This essay aims to give an account of the relationship between teenagers and advertising in Britain in 1999. It seeks to show how the ads are designed to work and how they are targeted. It will deal with four areas of advertising: 'General' (street hoardings, bus shelters, railway stations etc.), 'Cinema', 'Magazines' and 'Television'. It will examine debates centring on whether teenagers are exploited by adverts or are genuinely savvy consumers who can distinguish between the lures laid down for them and the pleasures to be got from simply enjoying the ads themselves.

Most of the essay will be concerned with popular culture. The latter enjoys a totally different status in Britain and the US. Nominally it is more welcomed in American than in British academic circles – for example the Popular Culture Association of America was set up in 1974 while to date there is no UK equivalent. In practice, however, American academia seems to be more suspicious of popular culture, especially where culture integrates with commercial and consumerist practices. Thus, many US commentators complain about the destruction of childhood and the inroads made on youth by commercialism. Despite this difference in outlook, there are similarities between American and British culture and much of what is said about US teenagers can be applied to those in Britain. Also, in many respects Britain follows American trends. Hence one can benefit from reading the American experience while being aware also of the differences.

Broadly speaking, commentators on teenage culture regard recent changes in society, in particular the development of consumerism and changes in family structures, as either malign or benign. So for example Shirley Steinberg and Joe Kincheloe in the US argue that there has been a paradigm shift since about 1950 in the patterns and condition of childhood. They are fearful that the upbringing and education of children has been taken away from both parents and educators by various corporate forces. They say that corporate America has revolutionized childhood through its use of the medium of television: "The world views produced by corporate advertisers [...] always let children know that the most exciting things life can provide are produced by your friends in corporate America. The economics lesson is powerful when it is repeated hundreds of thousands of times [...]."[1] They call the environment that this has produced "Kinderculture" and say that it is "primarily a pedagogy of pleasure and, as such, cannot be countered merely by ostracizing ourselves and our children from it".[2]

Advertisers do have designs on children which include situating them as consumers needing to be force-fed products made by corporate America, and critics do thus see children as hapless individuals at the mercy of a society which is much more sophisticated than they are. As they are preyed on by advertisers, businessmen and TV moguls, they are in need of protection.

Under "Kinderculture" children are exposed, inside and outside of school, to a barrage of influences. The whole world has become their learning arena: "Pedagogical sites are those places where power is organized and deployed, including libraries, TV, movies, newspapers, magazines, toys, advertisements, video games, books, sports, and so on."[3] Steinberg and Kincheloe see this shift from learning in the classroom to learning in the world as one which requires extra vigilance on the part of educators. For them, advertising is going to play a major part in the corporate takeover of children and this trend must therefore be flagged as dangerous and be resisted.

From a mainstream British perspective, these anxieties do have a distinctly American flavour. Parental responsibility in the US is seen as a more formal and literal duty in a more rigidly religious, even puritanical society than in Britain. But one shouldn't discount this position entirely. Many families from Britain's ethnic minorities hold similar values to Americans, and emphasize duties and responsibilities rather than rights within the family. And even in mainstream Britain, the death of the family has been exaggerated. The nuclear family may no longer be the only norm, but single-parent families are still cohesive units which struggle for the same stable growing-up environment that parents have always sought for their children and expect to regulate them. Undeniably, recent changes in family structures have made it more difficult for parents to police their teenage children, should they wish to do so, but in Britain parents do not yet see the principal threats to their children as coming from corporate entities whose weapon is advertising. Instead many British commentators, including Paul Willis and others, see positive aspects to advertising.

1. Advertising

Overall expenditure on advertising in Europe is currently only at 60 % of US levels. The 1994 per capita figures are $320 for the US versus $200 for Britain/Germany. Europe's culture appears to be more 'literate' in that the proportion of the spending on TV ads versus print media is lower in Europe than the US at 70 % versus 91 %. However with the globalization of culture and the increasing dominance of the US it seems likely that TV will assume relatively more importance for all advertising including that to teens.

Most teen-related advertising money is spent, in descending order, on TV, magazines (*Just Seventeen*, *Smash Hits*), style magazines (*The Face*, *GQ*), cinema advertising and street hoardings. Though some ads for e.g. jeans and trainers are now unisex, the majority are still aimed discretely at males and females. More are targeted at teenage girls than boys and for them they cover a more diverse range of products – fashion, cosmetics, records, concerts. Most of the ads beamed at males are to do with technology, computers, video games and sport.

2. Hoardings

Adverts on billboards in the street have traditionally not been directed so much to specific age groups as to social classes and to males and females. Dick Hebdige in his *Subculture. The Meaning of Style* (1979) distinguished separate subcultures among teenagers, but until recently advertisers have tended to treat consumers as a group differentiated principally by gender.

One of the few types of adverts in public places directed at teenagers is ads for gigs and night clubs, fly-posted on derelict city-centre buildings. Otherwise the public is seen in public space as a mass, differentiated only as above, in which it is hard to discern specifically targeted groups. However, a number of advertisers are beginning to specifically target teenagers.

The series of Tango ads is particularly clever. In one, commonly placed in bus shelters where young people have time on their hands, they are invited to lean on the ad. In another they are asked to imagine that the person nearest them is naked. In a third, a youth with a large love bite on his neck looks skywards above a caption saying: "You've been Tango'd." The name of the drink product is 'Cherry Love Bites'. These ads appeal to teenage knowingness. You are mature, self-possessed and street-smart if you drink Tango. Likewise certain sweets, particularly Twix and Smarties, are seen as desirable and sophisticated because of the ads associated with them. Teens want the sophistication that goes with eating them; it's cool to buy Smarties. Smarties ads supply teenagers with a means of differentiating themselves from pre-teens. Purchasers are invited to understand and interpret the arcane language and signifiers of a privileged club. This makes them savvy consumers, who know more than their parents and other members of the fuddy-duddy society of which they find themselves a part. Curiously, the sweet wrappers themselves are not made particularly alluring. They picture the contents alone. This is odd when compared with magazine covers which are adorned with the faces of pop stars, bands and features, and thus make much more explicit promises about the imaginative buzz that the consumer will experience.

3. Cinema

Teenagers are particularly susceptible to ads through their familiarity with films. 40 % of British teenagers go to the cinema at least once every three months. There they are, to a degree, specifically addressed by advertisers. Cult teenage movies such as *Austin Powers II* are accompanied by ads for Levi Jeans, Coca Cola and other 'youth' products. Ads are commonly set in overseas locations to appeal to British teenagers; Australia and America being the commonest variants. However, the cinema is still seen as a 'family' venue and the same screening session will promote cars and other products outside the ambit of teenage purchase.

4. Print Media

In their advertising, newspapers virtually ignore teenagers, who in turn also ignore newspapers. The General Household Survey of 1983 says that 98 % of the population of Britain watches more than 25 hours of TV per month, but only 10 % of teenagers regularly read a newspaper. Hence in print media it is left to magazines to stage the major assault on teenage pockets. The most successful teen magazines in terms of circulation are: *Smash Hits* 274,000; *Just Seventeen* 242,000; *19* (monthly) 200,000; *Mizz* (weekly) 183,000. Only *Smash Hits* has a substantial male readership (31 % men, 69 % women), and more will be said about this later.

As with other areas of popular culture, opinion is divided on whether teenage magazines are 'a good thing'. Some adults suggest that magazines encourage teens to while away their time in idle fantasies, whilst selling them unnecessary fashion products. Others say they offer them much needed advice on the problems of adolescence and enable them to share culture through promotion of pop CDs etc.

In 1996 controversy erupted about the content of magazines aimed at teenage girls, after a Tory back-bench MP, Peter Luff, made an unsuccessful attempt to introduce a Periodical Protection Bill. Luff's main objection to magazines such as *Just Seventeen*, *TV Hits* and *Bliss* was that they encourage young girls to be obsessed with sex because they deal too explicitly with sexual issues. Indeed some magazines aimed at children of twelve years upwards are very sexually explicit. The advertising, however, in these magazines possibly supplies a more 'truthful' record of the concerns of the readership, in that a high proportion of it is directed towards the relief of spots or acne, and other common concerns of the age group. In a sense then, the magazines do appear to be 'ahead' of, rather than responding to the readership. What is most telling about the debates which surrounded Luff's crusade, however, is the polarization of the arguments. For some people in 1990s Britain, childhood is in danger of becoming entirely eroded, while for others, young people can never know too much.

Mary Jane Kehily conducted a study in a school in the East Midlands in 1997 of the relationship between magazine reading and sexuality. She puts a positive spin on her results by suggesting that teen magazines can be seen as cultural resources for teaching and learning about issues of sexuality. In her study of school pupils, she discovered that girls read magazines together and concludes that reading in this way "offers the group the opportunity for dialogue at the level of collective experience",[4] and thus supplies a form of social bonding which is not available to boys, in whose lives magazines are not as important. When Kehily asked boys if they wished there were boys' magazines, the response was "Nah, you'd get called a sissy wouldn't you?" She concludes from the shared laughter that follows this remark that "there is group recognition/surveillance relating to gender-appropriate behaviour for young males".[5] Much comment has been directed to the fact that there is really no equivalent for boys of the magazines available to teenage girls. *Loaded*, *Q*, *Maxim Front* and *Bizarre* have a fraction of the readerships of *Jackie*, *Just Seventeen*, *Mizz*, *Bliss* or *Sugar*. If magazine reading is valuable, boys here are missing out.

Janice Radway says that women read magazines because they "restore them to that good health needed to cope with the endless routines of housework".[6] Clearly that does not apply to teenagers. Girls read for fantasy and Angela McRobbie highlights the fact that their romantic fantasies have been replaced with consumerist ones. She points out that in *Just Seventeen* elements of youth culture and advertising have become blurred. Readers are given a sense of immediacy and empowerment by the fact that they are bombarded with 'hot off the press' information. It appears on the page in snippets, boxes, simulated faxes. Adverts are mixed with clips from stars' biographies, photos etc. A recent anti-drug ad campaign could barely be distinguished from the rest of the text.

McRobbie highlights the decline of stories in *Jackie*. *Jackie* used to be all about romance, giving teens narratives to help them make sense of their lives – though often along the narrowly prescribed routes of heterosexual love and marriage. But it and other magazines now contain few stories. They are about adverts which involve identification of the readers as teenagers and active consumers. So in some ways they are more positive but in others they are more sinister/manipulative. She catalogues the failure of *Jackie* to hold onto its audience. It tried to anchor its stories in a more down-market, recognizably working-class environment, while other titles chose to move towards the world of pop. The latter strategy proved much more successful and was adopted by *Just Seventeen*.

To exemplify the blurring of 'factual' and consumerist material in magazines, McRobbie describes how pin-up pictures of pop stars are placed alongside details of celebrities' lives and intermingled with ads. This fusion leads to a whole series of other things whose effects complement one another:

> Looking at the pictures is connected to a whole chain of events and activities. It points the reader to the record and therefore to the radio, the television set where she can see the latest video, the record shop and the concert hall. A wide range of media products have some stake in the careful placing of visual material other than (and alongside) the straightforward advertising copy. As Bros 'make it big', magazine sales rise according to their coverage of Bros. In turn Bros use the magazines to thank the fans for their loyalty and to reassure them that no matter what they read, it is the fans about whom the band care most. [7]

The job of the reader is to classify and decode the message coming from this mixture of 'information', fantasy and advertising rather than to accept the limiting role offered under a diet of romantic stories.

In many ways the move from reading stories in magazines may be seen as beneficial to teenage girls. Their interest in pop, encouraged by *Just Seventeen*, has meant they have become less 'bedroom centred', less concerned with romantic love, which for them has proved either a disappointment or a *cul de sac*. The prospect of consumption and the adverts paraded before them in their magazines offer them in many ways more choices than did romance. They are encouraged to express their femininity, not just via cosmetics ads and offers of endless 'cleansers', but are presented with an endless series of choices, in terms not only of goods but of the pop stars, music and personalities to whom the magazine introduces them. They share these choices with their friends and express their difference from each other through their individual selections. They are not fashion victims but use faction to express their awakening identities. Such expressions of desire are often likely to be more fulfilling than the old romantic possibilities that they were offered in their romantic stories – and more tangible.

Some commentators feel that watching ads is about negotiating one's inferior position through an 'empowerment' which, because mediated via ads within a dominant/subordinate relationship between seller and purchaser, is illusory. Ads fix you firmly as a consumer at the bottom of a hierarchy. But cultural differences, produced as above by expressions of choice in the market, can yield openings and possibilities rather than articulating a mere subservience to dire controlling economic and social forces. Ads for cosmetics for example are directed to girls engaged in the construction of femininity as one of the key forms of adolescent identity in transition. Hence these ads reveal not just youth aspirations and fantasies about lifestyles and money in a crucial period of their identity formation, but highlight the communal sense of lack that teenagers feel in relation to desirable products. Ads incorporate them into the process of consumption, but they meanwhile only accept ads through the medium of their own youth culture and music.

This potentially 'liberating' aspect of consumerism may be attributed to postmodernism which has increased the status of fantasy in the everyday workings of culture. Because postmodernism is concerned with surfaces and refuses to make hierarchical distinctions between popular and high culture, ads in postmodern magazines are no longer dominant and controlling. Thus pop music, which is more about pure entertainment than control, has assumed much higher significance in both youth culture and marketing. Currently many manufacturers are trying to capture individual pop songs as 'theirs' in order to promote their products.

Thus the relationship between teenagers and ads is not one in which they are simply controlled by advertisers. The fact that they are forming their identities complicates the process. The psychoanalyst Jacqueline Rose, among many others, has pointed out the fluidity of identity among adults, but especially among adolescents, whose transitions involve a repeated series of failures. This fact makes teenagers particularly more of a moving target. They cannot be controlled by advertising:

> The unconscious constantly reveals the 'failure' of identity. Because there is no continuity of psychic life, so there is no stability of sexual identity, no position […] which is ever simply achieved […]. Failure is not a moment to be regretted in a process of adaptation, or development into normality which ideally takes its course […]. Instead failure is something endlessly repeated and relived moment by moment throughout our individual histories.[8]

People are not 'socially imprisoned' by dominant cultural forms. Ads can indicate our continuous refusals of, anxieties about and disassociations from them. Advertising and consumerism lead to the formation of difference which enables people to assert their identities within power structures which view them as pawns but within which they, in reality, gain collective strength. The marketers are more anxious than teens are about their ostensible lack of power and consequently try to harness their culture rather than feeding them the dominant brand.

5. Sophistication

Any study of advertising must take account of the changes which have occurred in the knowledge concerning people's motivation and identity formation. Thus advertising is continually changing. Much of it directed towards teenagers is still straightforwardly aspirational. The subtitle of the shoe stylist Patrick Cox is significantly "wannabe". His loafers are modeled by a leggy long-haired wafer-thin model who contemplates her navel (see illustr. 1).[9] Some ads are just funny. In *The Face* Virgin Clothing Company runs an ad where the reader is invited to insert his arm into the 'sleeve' of a shirt and jacket, printed on two pages.[10] But a lot of advertising to teens has become very sophisticated.

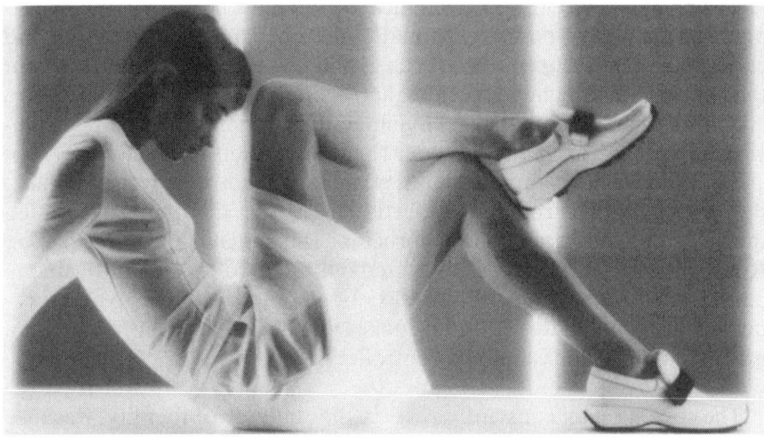

Illustr. 1
from: *The Face*, April 1999, 14-15

This is probably more true of Europe than America. Ads in the British edition of *Marie Claire* are much more sophisticated than are those in the American version. In Britain, casual readers of ads in *Just Seventeen* or certainly *The Face* are occasionally mystified as to what product is being advertised. Cigarette advertising seems to have started this trend. Only smokers could identify the cryptic signals which invited them to buy either Benson & Hedges or Silk Cut. Non-smokers had no idea of what was going on. That bewilderment has spread to other products, particularly youth ones. As adverts become even more sophisticated, it is sometimes difficult to know precisely what is being offered for sale. For example in *The Face* for April 1999, only by reading the very small print can one discover that a striking photograph of a stubble-faced young man with a voluptuous female torso, in a low-cut bra, is an advert for a music CD made by the band Windowlicker (see illustr. 2).[11]

Illustr. 2
from: *The Face*, April 1999, 85

Another trend is to disperse the single focus of an ad. Products from 'third parties' appear in the mainstream ad. For example many fashion ads show identifiable products such as an Apple computer or a Jaguar car in the background, hoping to capitalize on the fact that readers will identify with the high net earners who are reputed to own Apples and Jaguars and will make an association between the products and buy the clothes advertised.

The concept of youth culture is used in advertisements to sell to a much wider audience than to youth. Youth culture is seen as sexy. It is incorporated into ads aimed at many different types of older consumers who want to be associated with youth. Often this association is used to flatter a target audience which has become staid and unadventurous. Hence ads in the magazine *The Face* feature teenagers, but the selling is directed at twenty-somethings. So for example an ad for Diesel clothing aimed at both sexes makes use of teenagers' sense of alienation and hurt at adult disapproval (see illustr. 3). It features three trendily dressed kids, two boys who are raiding an orchard and a girl who is acting as lookout. She holds a rosy red apple in her hand, while one boy gives the other a leg up to steal from a tree. The scene conjures up Eve the temptress helping man the hunter-gatherer, and as such could be trite but in reality is wittily self-parodying. Both of the male youths are tattooed, implying perhaps the kind of prejudiced association between body adornment and criminality which ignorant adults might be inclined to make when condemning the young. The teenagers are identified as a cohesive oppressed subgroup and the audience is invited to empathize and identify with them and to be a part of their social scene by buying Diesel clothes.

Illustr. 3
from: *The Face*, April 1999, 106-107

Meanwhile text at the bottom of the ad articulates a teenage viewpoint in the kind of breathless, single-minded and intense language that adolescents might use:

STOP CRIME NOW!
Why should we jeopardize the future of our society by letting minor things like stealing an apple from a tree go? Young people doing things like this will probably turn into violent train robbers if we dont [*sic*] take drastic action today. Thank you for agreeing with us.

IF WE PUT ALL YOUNG PEOPLE IN JAIL TODAY, WE WILL HAVE NO CRIMINALS TOMORROW!

The text, in white type, is almost subliminal, but its message is clear enough. It is a parody of what teenagers are assumed to imagine is a prevalent adult attitude towards them. It situates *The Face* readers in a position from which to buy from a 'friendly' clothing company which condones teenagers' peccadilloes and 'understands' them. It sides with them against simplistic condemnations from the old and pays shameless homage to the dictum 'the customer is always right'. It describes the ad as "number 99 […] [i]n a series of Diesel 'How to …' guides to SUCCESSFUL LIVING".[12] The same legend appears on the company's web site. The advertiser really cares about you and wants to help you to conduct your life.

As mentioned above, American and Australian locations are used to appeal to British teenagers, whereas the Continent is more commonly used to sell (especially cars) to their parents. There is still little expectation of either audience to understand a foreign language although the occasional ad in *Marie Claire* contains untranslated French – to be chic rather than literally intelligible.

An advert for the hair cream fudge copies the style of Roy Lichtenstein (see illustr. 4).[13] In a surreal street scene, using the technique referred to earlier of introducing third party products, shop signs are brand names such as Licorice, pump up, HEAD and dynamite. Girls in the car in front display their buttocks. The driver of the car we are in, appears in profile in the rear-view mirror. He is the gazer, the pursuer, the predator – if presumably he buys fudge. The ad deliberately excludes older readers, who are unlikely to buy this product, and appeals to the rebel in their youthful audience. The by-line for the ad is "fudge … it's an Australian thing". Australia is 'the young country'. Older people wouldn't understand.

6. Advertising as Postmodern Playfulness

While 'the media', which is seen as including advertising, pop videos, teen magazines, etc., is continually offered as a scapegoat for inducing teenagers to do its bidding and so is indicted for example for encouraging copycat crimes, several commentators, including Paul Willis, refute suggestions

Illustr. 4
from: *The Face*, April 1999, 20-21

that teenagers are influenced negatively in this way. They welcome the role of popular media, including advertising, arguing that through their experience of watching television young people learn to distinguish between reality and artifice. According to Willis, horror films "engender simultaneously fear and appreciation of artifice". They thus turn a potentially threatening experience into a pleasurable one. "By laughing with friends at the terrifying bits one can put the feelings of terror in perspective, acknowledge artifice and affirm one's own sense of reality."[14] He points out that there is a generation gap when it comes to reading advertisements. The young are sophisticated and use ads as tokens in a system of social exchange. I have seen this in my own discussions with teenagers of the film *Titanic*. They focus on its special effects, take great pleasure in them. They hardly refer to the loss of life involved in the tragedy of the original event.

Willis presents teenagers as sophisticated consumers who can distinguish between aesthetically appealing products and the products themselves. Some teenagers undoubtedly have this capability but even those are perhaps influenced by the buying behaviour of their peers. Thus by blending 'clever' ads which flatter the teenage viewers with promotion of the product, advertisers can expect to ultimately draw in the whole of the age group.

Many commentators recognize that advertising to the young is about situating them within various hierarchies of power. McRobbie offers an interesting recantation of her position that class rather than gender is central. But she still sees the process as being about the power or powerlessness of teenagers. Some years ago she published a study of the lives of teenage girls.

> Being working class meant little or nothing to these girls – but being a girl over-determined their every moment. Unable to grapple with this uncomfortable fact, I made sure that, in my account anyway, class *did* count. If I had to go back and consider this problem now, I would go about it in a very different fashion. I would not harbour such a monolithic notion of class, and instead I would investigate how relations of power and powerlessness permeated the girls' lives – in the context of school, authority, language, job opportunities, the family, the community and sexuality. And from this I would begin once again, perhaps to think about class.[15]

7. Television

This is the television age and undoubtedly the present generation of teenagers is much more visual than literate. TV is the medium which is most likely to be effective when selling to them because it plays such a major part in forming and reflecting their values. They watch on average five hours of television a day and 'grow up' with the TV via programmes like *Blue Peter*, *Grange Hill* and *Top of the Pops*. Advertising directed at them is centred around the programmes they like. For example *The Chart Show* is sponsored by Twix. *Grange Hill*, *Neighbours* and *TFI Friday* are heavily interspersed with ads for a range of products likely to appeal to teens, from cosmetics to computer games.

TV is a much more powerful advertising medium than print. Parents will often restrict the amount of viewing for their children, though rarely discourage them from reading. Parents see TV watching as an essentially passive activity despite the numerous challenges to that notion from children themselves and from some academics. (Enrolment in university media and cultural studies courses which analyse soap operas etc. has burgeoned in recent years.) Undoubtedly parents are right to want to help children to learn self-discipline by teaching them to arbitrate the competing demands of leisure and homework, in forming their viewing habits. However, teenagers do take away something valuable from their TV watching and this becomes especially evident when they discuss their viewing with their friends. Much of their discussion centres on advertisements. "What's your favourite advertisement?", asks a teenager in Paul Willis's *Common Culture*.[16] This leads to a discussion about contemporary TV ads in which another teenager says, "some are better than the programmes", and indeed teens differ from their parents in welcoming TV ads. Where their parents see them as intrusions into, or interruptions of, the TV narratives they are trying to follow, 'MTV Generation' children welcome the lack of necessity for a prolonged attention span.

Provided discussions like this do take place, material presented to teenagers which may be seen as corrupting them – either video games like Doom, videos like *Texas Chainsaw Massacre*, magazines which offer advice 'unpalatable' to adults or ads which sexualize children in the course of their pitch – may be neutralized. Once the material is in the public domain, so to speak, and is shared and discussed by teens, its potential effects change. Teens discuss horror films and take an 'active' stance in administering them to themselves. Likewise they are not the passive consumers of adverts that their parents are, incapable of resisting them, but instead can appreciate them aesthetically and then not buy the product. In class, the occasional teenager will start off by claiming that they are totally uninfluenced by advertisements. In the course of discussion they will usually be forced to concede that they are so influenced, and in the process of making that acknowledgment have armed themselves to resist, along with their peers, some of the goods which are presented to them.

Because cinema is so popular among the young, advertisers use actors from cinema and TV in commercials to sell youth products. Lenny Henry promoted Alpen breakfast cereal. Rowan Atkinson sells Barclaycards. The footballer Gary Lineker appears in crisps ads. Advertisers flatter their audience by treating them as televisually literate and often do this by reference to and parody of other adverts.

As TV ads have become ever more sophisticated, teenagers tend not particularly to be more fooled by them but to appreciate them more. Through their exposure to ads on TV virtually from birth, young people have acquired a sophistication which arguably makes them the group of consumers most resistant to the wiles of advertisers. They take pleasure in reading the ads, and ads themselves are made purposely to give aesthetic pleasure as well as to sell the product. The Clerkenwell (East London) advertising agency Mother claims it thinks like its audience, rather than telling its audience what to think.

New ads are often self-deprecating or zany. Current ones for Levi's are humorous and use the cult character Flat Eric. Cellnet's have a lazy student, Nike's a very long-distance runner. These ads emphasize the boring ordinariness of everyday life. They have none of the aspirational gloss that typified eighties advertising, nor do they talk down to 'yoof', as they did in the early nineties. The traditional hard sell and dependence on aspirational appeal seem sometimes to have vanished altogether. As Stephen Armstrong says: "The great thing about such ads – both for advertisers wary of putting people off and consumers suspicious of being patronized – is that many don't appear to be selling anything. In many cases, the pitch is as important as the product."[17] Advertising agencies' campaigns consist of a series of narratives under a single theme. For example in an episode of Bartle Bogle Hegarty's Flat Eric campaign a young man drives around Los Angeles with an orange puppet in the back of his car. He is pulled over by a cop who inspects the Levi's Sta-Prest trousers in the boot. The product is an incidental part of the story.

AMV BBDO's ad for a mobile phone appeals to teenagers' slovenliness. A couch-potato student surrounded by cold pizza wants to drink his glass of Pepsi. He is too idle to reach for it and pulls the table towards him with his foot. The drink falls off the table and soaks the carpet. This is clearly a regular occurrence. The voice-over says: "Clean it up? Don't clean it up? It's your call", in other words, buy or don't buy the phone. Be hip and take it or leave it. Obviously the implication that the viewer is empowered by being given that choice is designed to sell the product, but it's deliberately not a *hard* sell.

The Ammirati Puris Lintas' ad for Batchelors Cup-a-Soup Extra is also directed towards male youth. The product is the UK version of the German original Heiße Tasse. The ad incorporates a laddish practical joke where anarchic building workers aim noodles from their soup at the boss's baggy trousers several floors below. Disaffected or anarchic teenagers can still become adults (and retain their irresponsibility) if they buy this product.

In Wieden and Kennedy's Nike ads based on The Cow pub in Notting Hill, an overweight athlete is impressed with the fact that all the pub's occupants are wearing top-of-the-range Nike trainers. The ad tacitly reconciles the contradictory suggestions that Nike trainers are only for elite runners *and* are fashion shoes, but acknowledges what Nike itself doesn't officially, that sales are dominated by fashion rather than sports considerations. The ad ostensibly identifies *no* target audience; there is *no* hard sell. Teenagers like this kind of anarchic pitch.

The ad for Levi's Buttonfly Cords is a cleverly staged photo of a young man evidently standing to shoot an arrow with a small Cupid style bow.[18] The inside of his arm has a heart on it to continue the Cupid theme and to connect the young man with romantic love. The trajectory of the arrow appears to peak and turn down in what, it then becomes clear, is a road sign painted on the highway. We realize we are looking down on him from a bird's-eye perspective. Thus one has to rethink the whole ad: the model is lying in the street, bracing his feet against the curb. The *trompe l'oeil* is completed by a standard [US] turning-right sign and one notices the tyre marks on the road. Clearly if you buy these trousers you will be zany, adventurous, unconventional, clever, imaginative and employ alternative perspectives. You will "Think Different" [*sic*] as Apple would say, and maybe even lie down in the road.

These are the kind of ads which appeal to Generation X (the group aged from 13-32 identified as such by Douglas Coupland in his eponymous 1992 novel). Team Saatchi, the advertising agency, in 1995 listed a number of characteristics of these young people. They included the following: Clique maintenance (they look down on the generation which follows them); centred on the self; liking technology; alienated from their parents; more than 50% 'latch-key children' (parents out working); DIY identity (they take their ideas and beliefs from a wide range of cultures); global in outlook (via the internet); loyal to ads not brands.

From this list one can see that teenagers are in control to the extent that they choose their products and administer them to themselves often without the help of advertisers. This applies particularly to the kinds of computer games which boys buy. Most of those bought depend on word of mouth. Recommendations in electronic gaming magazines and the availability of the games on the internet (Starcraft, Quake 2, Diablo) are given greater weight than advertisements in decisions to purchase the games. Computer games are advertised to a unisex audience but it is predominantly boys who play them. Their games are mostly ones involving fighting: Tekken 3, Resident Evil, Tomb Raider, Streetfighter Alpha 3. The most popular game with girls is the music-based game Parapper the Lapper.

One can, however, over-emphasize the influence of advertising on teenagers. This applies for example in the case of smoking. Thus, although it is established that in the age range 14 to 19, a substantial percentage of children periodically smoke cigarettes (an estimated 40% of girls versus 25% of boys), this hasn't been achieved by discrete advertising to them. Tobacco advertising is banned on TV, and tobacco ads do not appear in magazines such as *Smash Hits* etc. even though smoking is legal at 16 in Britain. Manufacturers rely instead on general ads and peer pressure to sell their product.

Moreover, however clever the pitch, it is well to be reminded that although a film like *Star Wars* for example has had lots of consumer products tied into it via advertising, Furbies [computerized talking dolls] and yo-yos have been given no advertising at all, and yet they are currently the two most popular teenage toys in Britain.

Notes

1 Steinberg & Kincheloe (1997: 4).
2 *Ibid.*
3 *Ibid.*

4 Kehily (1999: 70).
5 *Ibid.*, 71.
6 Radway (1984: 139).
7 McRobbie (1991: 171-172).
8 Rose (1986: 184).
9 *The Face,* April 1999, 14-15.
10 *The Face,* October 1998, 85-86.
11 *The Face,* April 1999, 85.
12 *Ibid.*, 106-107.
13 *Ibid.*, 20-21.
14 Willis (1990: 49).
15 McRobbie (1991: 64-65).
16 Willis (1990: 49).
17 Armstrong (1999).
18 *The Face,* October 1998, 106-107.

Bibliography

Armstrong, Stephen: "How to Get Ahead in Advertising", *The Face*, April 1999, 136-140.
The Face, October 1998.
The Face, April 1999.
Hebdige, Dick: *Subculture. The Meaning of Style*, London, 1979.
Kehily, Mary Jane: "More Sugar? Teenage Magazines, Gender Displays and Sexual Learning", *European Journal of Cultural Studies* 2, no. 1, 1999, 65-89.
McRobbie, Angela: *Feminism and Youth Culture. From* Jackie *to* Just Seventeen, Basingstoke, 1991.
Radway, Janice: *Reading the Romance. Women, Patriarchy and Popular Literature*, Chapel Hill, 1984.
Rose, Jacqueline: *Sexuality in the Field of Vision*, London, 1986.
Steinberg, Shirley & Joe Kincheloe (Eds.): *Kinderculture. The Corporate Construction of Childhood*, Boulder, 1997.
Williamson, Judith: *Decoding Advertisements. Ideology and Meaning in Advertising*, repr., London, 1994.
Willis, Paul: *Common Culture. Symbolic Work at Play in the Everyday Cultures of the Young*, Milton Keynes, 1990.

Peter Bennett, Hannover

Teen Pop and Teenage Identity in Britain

Teenagers listen to various types of pop music, as one might expect. In this article, however, I deal expressly with a category of music loosely defined by reference to its putative audience and usually referred to as teen pop. The term is not entirely new, but it has acquired a new currency in the late 1990s, the period on which I shall be focusing my attention. In current practice, teen pop is generally associated with an audience of people whose ages range from the pre-teens (nine or ten years and even younger) up to the mid-teens, whilst the performers are mostly aged between 17 and about 25. With regard to the music, I do not hold that there is any essential aesthetic difference between teen pop and any other pop. Teen pop is simply pop packaged for teens. I would also like to make it clear that, in referring to the pop music industry in Britain, I mean precisely that and not the industry of British pop music. The consumer culture I am looking at is British, but the marketed product is not necessarily or exclusively British. American performers such as the Backstreet Boys or Britney Spears, for example, are very much a part of the teen-pop industry in Britain. In short, then, I shall be exploring a particular segment of the pop music market in a particular place and at a particular time.

In exploring the relationship between teenage identity and the teen-pop industry in Britain I shall be concentrating my attention on the practices and workings of representation. My handling of the topic of representation is derived directly from a particular understanding of the meaning of culture which has been developed through the work of numerous people occupied within the discipline of Cultural Studies in Britain. I begin with a short explanation of this particular conceptualization of culture, of the important role that representation plays in culture, and of the relevance of all this to the question of identities within a culture. Readers who are already familiar with the conceptual framework may wish to skip over those paragraphs and come straight to the main part of the article. This consists of the discussion and analysis of representation within the cultural sphere of teen pop, in particular in teen-pop magazines and in the performance of teen pop. Some general tendencies will be observed, especially in respect of the images and idea of teen pop which the industry fosters and the relation of these to teenage identity. I conclude by drawing attention to a few contradictions which the industry either suppresses or accommodates in the process of trying to control representation.

Music fashions and labels come and go unpredictably, often quite suddenly. It is conceivable that teen pop will no longer be booming by the time this paper comes off the press. Whether or not that is the case, I still hope that readers, and especially those who teach, will feel able to make use of elements of my approach in order to explore other segments and types of popular music culture and, for that matter, other areas of cultural activity where the relations between representation and identity seem worth examining.

1. Culture, Representation and Identity[1]

Culture, in the sense I use it here, is regarded as a social process rather than a fixed entity. This process consists of the operation of what are known as signifying practices; that is, cultural practices in and through which meanings are produced and exchanged. For the exchange of meaning to be possible, it is necessary that people share not only a system of concepts and a system of signs (i.e. language) but also the codes which, by convention, more or less fix the correlation between concepts and language. There would be no socially functional meaning in the letters or phonemes of a word like 'water' or in the sound of a fire alarm if there were not also a code or convention to regularize an otherwise arbitrary relationship. The term 'representation' is used to refer to the process by which meaning is created through language. It is important to stress here that language is understood in the very broad sense of any system of representation or signification. It is therefore not restricted to verbal systems of communication but includes all practices which are capable of interpretation within a community of people. So, for people who share the same culture, meanings are produced and can be exchanged (consciously or unconsciously, intentionally or unintentionally) by body language, for example, or by the visual imagery of television, or by any of the many facets of personal lifestyle (type of car, leisure activities, clothing, domestic furnishing), or through the public rituals of sport and artistic performance. When we come to look at the cultural phenomenon of the production and consumption of teenage pop music, we shall see that it is a zone where a variety of signifying practices flourish alongside one another.

Contemporary cultural studies usually takes what is known as a constructionist approach to representation. All meaning is regarded as being produced in and through the language and other representational systems of cultures. Not only our signs but also our concepts are cultural products. The material world, which exists independently of any representational systems, does not itself contain or produce meaning. People are only able to think about, talk about, and give meaning to the material world and everything in it, including themselves as subjects, through socially developed systems of representation.

The idea that representation constructs meaning opens up the possibility for two types of approach, both of which I shall draw upon in discussing teen pop culture. One of these approaches is semiotics, derived from Saussure's structural linguistics and useful for showing how meaning is constructed in the various signifying practices of teenage pop culture. The other approach is derived from Foucault's concept of discourse and the associated idea of discursive formations. Although the semiotic approach can be very fruitful and stimulating in analysing cultural signification, as Roland Barthes's pioneering essays in *Mythologies* illustrate, one of the drawbacks is that its application is usually restricted to single signifiers, to isolated events and objects which, in the linguistic analogy, correspond to words or phrases. As Stuart Hall points out, however, meaning in a culture "often depends on larger units of analysis – narratives, statements, groups of images, whole discourses which operate across a variety of texts".[2] Foucault's concept of discourse enlarges the scale of analysis to take account of this. Discourse amounts to an accumulation of practices which produce meaning and, in the process, effectively establish the norms of knowledge and therefore also of behaviour within particular fields of cultural activity. The concept therefore entails the recognition that there is a connection between representational practices and modes of behaviour. It also brings relations of power into consideration. Foucault's historically specific inquiries were largely directed at fields of human knowledge and practice (referred to as 'discursive formations') which we can now see were especially regulatory: those which dealt with madness or social and sexual deviance, for example. The discursive practices of madness or deviance defined the terms, established and normalized a set of social responses, and fostered a deceptive sense of objectivity or truth. They also produced the human subject in so far as the discourse of the specific historical period determined who was mad or deviant and who was not.

Given the scale of Foucault's work, the profound seriousness of his purpose, and the gloomy nature of many of the practices in which he located the mechanisms of discourse and traced the inherent power relations, it might be considered rather facile to enlist the theory of discourse in a study of pop music. Nevertheless, and despite criticism that Foucault's idea of discourse is too deterministic[3] or that he makes it unacceptably all-pervasive,[4] it remains the case that it has been fruitfully, if eclectically, utilized by modern cultural studies in analysing the workings of representation. As Stuart Hall has pointed out, "since all social practices entail meaning, and meanings shape and influence what we do – our conduct – all practices have a discursive aspect".[5]

The whole cultural environment of teenage pop music readily lends itself to analysis as a discursive formation. Two aspects of discourse theory are particularly helpful. Firstly, it is possible to consider under one umbrella, as I shall be doing, the representational processes of several different but interconnected practices and media. Secondly, and of special relevance to the question of teenage identity, the theory enables us to consider how the discursive practices of teen pop construct subject positions for the consumers (and also, for that matter, for the performers and other agents and practitioners). Nobody – and not least the teenager – is obliged to accept these subject positions but, since the discourse offers positions which are in harmony with the whole cultural practice, those who adopt such a position subject themselves at least intermittently to the discourse and to the meanings and identity which are constructed in it and through it.

2. *Teen Pop and the Media of Representation*

I regret that I cannot present the following section in a live seminar or lecture but must do it here through the written word, because visual images, both still and moving, as well as the acoustic images of the music itself mediate representation in teen pop culture as much as the various verbal texts which I can at least quote here. I shall do my best to describe the visual and the acoustic in words, but I would like to stress that what I am attempting is partly intended as a demonstration or model and that the best thing would be for interested readers to get hold of some source material themselves and try some analysis of their own, preferably with students or school pupils. There are two broad types of question one may usefully ask about specific examples. Firstly, and bearing in mind that what we hear, see and read is largely the result of planned efforts to create intended effects, how do the various forms and specific instances of representation generate meaning? What sort of images and effects do the producers create, or seem to wish to create? Secondly, how do the various representations within teen pop seem to position the consumer? What sort of subject do they construct? What sort of identity do they seem to offer?

I shall be focusing most of my attention on teen-pop magazines, on selected aspects of the music and performance, and on related television and video production.[6] These elements, together with live concerts and certain internet websites, combine to form the media mix which represents and thus constitutes teen-pop culture. For reasons I have explained, it would be vain to look for an essence of teen pop, precisely because it is a construct of representation. Nevertheless, the concept and the means of referring to it can be found flourishing in the multi-media representations

I am about to illustrate and in the lives of everyone who comes into contact with them. It is therefore possible to learn to recognize the cultural codes and get an idea of what counts as teen pop and what does not. For one thing, all the discursive practices are directly or indirectly related to the personalities and performances of a particular constellation of pop stars. The characteristics of the constellation are constant enough for it to remain recognizable despite a gradual turnover in its membership. New stars appear, existing ones fade into oblivion, and others develop beyond the limits of conformity and get consigned to other constellations. By observing which stars and performances are included and which are excluded and by noticing how the former are represented, we can begin to work out what teen pop is supposed to be and how it differs from other types of pop culture.

3. Magazines

It only requires a quick glance through the host of pop music magazines on display in British newsagents and supermarkets to see that the publishers are competing for and catering to a number of distinct segments of the consumer market. Teen pop is just one such segment. It may be impossible to define the genre of teen-pop music by musical criteria, but there can be little doubt about the generic nature of the pop magazines for the pre- to mid-teens. The main rivals at the time of writing, as I have already mentioned in an endnote, are *Top of the Pops* and *Smash Hits*. It is hard in most respects to tell them apart. The optical effect of their layout is a kaleidoscopic and seemingly hyperactive mixture of colours, pictures, typefaces, font sizes and other graphical tricks. They also share the same palette of editorial content: posters and photographs of pop stars, the lyrics of the latest chart entries, interviews, numerous titbits of news and gossip, reviews, feature articles, and readers' letters, all oriented towards the same constellation of stars and their activities.

How do these magazines address their readers? How do they foster in them the feeling that they belong to the culture of teen pop? The purely formal elements of layout and content which I have just listed are part of the mode of address. They present themselves to the reader as the appropriate style of communication for teen pop. At the same time, they help to create a significant sense of difference from the discursive modes of non-teen-pop culture. This is clear if we compare the layout and editorial content of *Top of the Pops* and *Smash Hits* with other British pop magazines such as *Q* or *Mojo*, which are intended for older readers with supposedly different musical tastes. The optical effect of *Q*, for example, though undoubtedly dynamic, is restrained in comparison with the teen-pop magazines. Its page backgrounds are mostly white, whereas *Top of the Pops* and *Smash Hits* use any number of background colours. Both types of magazine insert graphical images within text but the framing in *Q* and similar magazines is typically rectangular, whereas the teen-pop magazines mix their graphical images and verbal texts in zany layouts in defiance of the rectangular. As to editorial content, both types of magazine offer a similar mix of interviews, feature articles, news, gossip, reviews, and readers' letters, but with important differences. For example, pin-up posters and song lyrics are only to be found in the teenage magazines, where they are a prominent feature; and all the items in the teenage magazines, whether they be snippets of news or longer feature articles, are proportionately much shorter than their counterparts in the likes of *Q*. They are also far more preoccupied with personal trivia than with music and performance.

Another conspicuous aspect of the way teen magazines draw readers into a distinct cultural community is the distinctive use of language. As to be expected, the style is very informal. It also has much in common with that of the British tabloid press: "Cleopatra in drag queen mix-up" runs a typical gossip page headline about the British girl band. The text below it also has a tabloid tang:

> Cleo, Zainam and Yonah, seen here modelling their clothing range from the new Index catalogue, have had to change their name in Canada. The girls have discovered a Canadian drag queen is already shaking her bootie under the name of Cleopatra and have changed their name to Cleopatra ZYC to avoid any confusion![7]

The gossip columns in particular adopt the tabloid habit of using puns in their headlines. "I don't *knee*-d that!" heads the short piece of news that Britney Spears has twisted her knee and will have to cancel a planned visit to Britain. "Nic [i.e. nice] to see you!" refers to the boy band 911's unexpected pleasure at meeting All Saints member Nicky (Nic) Appleton during a photo-shoot.[8]

The tabloid habits are not necessarily tokens of either teen or pop discourse. They are simply marks of journalistic informality. More specific to the discourse of teen pop is the practice of almost always referring to the individual members of pop bands by their familiar forename followed by the name of the band. Nicky Appleton, mentioned above, is thus typically referred to as Nic All Saint. In the same vein one reads of Kevin Backstreet, Lisa Steps, or Sinéad B*witched. Lexical blends pertaining to pop music are also common in the teen magazines: "Inside sources have told us it [i.e. the Backstreet Boys' new single] sounds fantabulous."[9] 'Poptastic' is another favourite. Or I could say 'fave', because clipped words occur everywhere, along with phonetic spellings, contractions and other orthographic deviations. An album review of *Pete Tong: Essential Selection – Spring 1999* is described as "another collection of Tongy's fave choons".[10] Other recurrent clipped words include 'goss' for 'gossip', 'pic' for 'picture', 'vid' for 'video', and 'versh' for 'version'. Alongside well-established contractions like 'cos' and 'wanna' there are contractions of colloquialisms such as 'helluva' for 'hell of a', 'loadsa' for 'loads of' and, with a friendly nod to Liverpudlian pronunciation, 'birrova' for 'bit of a'. The effect of these sorts of modification can be better appreciated in whole sentences. Here are a few examples:

> What do you think of B*witched's new hair? A total improvement or a birrova state?
>
> Look out for the brilliant vid, which shows the fellas [i.e. Westlife] performing on stage with a full orchestra and showgirls. Glam or wot?!
>
> Martine [McCutcheon]'s debut is what is known as a slow builder, i.e. BIG finish but a helluva climb. The pace picks up once Martine starts really givin' it some welly.[11]

So far I have only been describing the way the readers of teen-pop magazines are addressed. The next question to ask is how the formal and stylistic elements combine to position the notional readers. In reality, not all readers comply with the positioning. I myself do not, for example. The fact that I feel alienated, or perhaps I should say uninvited, by the teen-pop magazines suggests I have recognized that they are asking for my complicity in a particular identity group. Readers who yield to the appeal of the magazines are less likely to be conscious of the fact. Even if they are aware, however, (and I do not think one should underestimate the ability of some of the older readers in the age-group to recognize the artificiality and humour) their submission nevertheless shows a willingness to take on board the identity or subject position which the text constructs for the readers. Naturally enough, one would also expect them to be attracted by other aspects of teen-pop culture, and not least by the stars and their performances. And it is to the representation of the stars in the magazines that I now want to turn.

The photographic image and the interview are probably the two most influential modes of representing pop stars in teen magazines. I will deal with them separately. One of the factors distinguishing the teen magazines from those targeted at other groups of readers is the sheer quantity and style of the photographs. Posed and orchestrated photographs predominate almost exclusively. Candid and spontaneous shots are significantly rare. Strange though it may seem to anyone unfamiliar with teen-pop magazines, there seems to be a policy of not printing photographs of the artists in performance. They are represented simply as personalities, with nothing in the pictures to suggest that they are singers or dancers.

The posed photographs can be put into two classes, depending on how the magazine editors decide to present them. Either they are printed and arranged so that they can easily be removed and displayed on bedroom walls, or they are printed to accompany editorial text. The provision of pin-ups is one of the main selling points of the teen-pop magazines. This mainly dictates the layout and printing, however, and not the style and composition of the photographs themselves, which have many uniform characteristics. So much so, in fact, that a set of aesthetic rules seems to be in force.

I cannot say whether these rules have been expressly formulated or whether they are 'natural' to the practice. In either case, however, they are instrumental in affecting the way the pop stars are represented. The orchestration of the posed photographs can be seen as having three aspects. Firstly there are technical decisions: creating the studio background or selecting the environmental location, determining the lighting, and choosing the angles and other such elements of the shots. Then there is the arrangement of the poses and tableaux of the subjects. Finally come the contributions of the stars themselves and their stylists in matters of clothing, hairstyle and make-up. Everything is done to foreground the stars unequivocally. Hence most of the studio shots have plain colour backgrounds with the subjects sharply in focus and fully lit to eliminate shadows. Location shots for posters are often constructed with the background out of focus so that the attention does not wander from the subjects and one merely has a vague impression of forest or park or whatever. Alternatively, the background may be in focus, but it is still likely to be devoid of any details that might draw the gaze away from the subjects. I came across the Backstreet Boys standing to their knees in an unidentifiable sea and the Moffats disposed on a grassy bank before an unidentifiable lake.[12] Location shots designed to accompany feature articles tend to include just enough indexical information to signify, for example, that Martine McCutcheon is shopping in New York, or the American group Take Five are enjoying a visit to London.[13]

With regard to the orchestration of poses and tableaux, it is noteworthy that the subjects' eyes are always directed at the camera, in effect and intent at the observer, of course. In group portraits the artists are almost invariably smiling or laughing. The same is generally true of individual portraits, although the editors sometimes select a dreamy or cheeky expression, particularly for male subjects. Presumably this is thought to be of special interest to young female readers. Groups are arranged in tableaux to suggest fun, vitality and sometimes 'wackiness'. There are none of the signs of angst, disillusionment or rebellion which have been and sometimes still are the hallmarks of other waves and niches in popular music. This youthful exuberance is represented as containing a mixture of individuality and unity. Hence the heads in group portraits are contrived to be at different heights and angles, with each member adopting an individual posture. These differences are usually accentuated by the practice of the individual members each wearing their own distinctive clothing and hairstyle, even though a loose uniformity may be apparent, as is sometimes the case with a band like Steps, whose dance routines are as important as their singing and who often appear wearing the same colours. This marked diversity is then cemented into unity not merely by the smiling and laughing signs of collective happiness but very often also by a great deal of body contact between the members, a typical practice no matter whether the bands are male, female or mixed. The touching, hugging and sprawling over each other is made to suggest friendship and playfulness with never a hint of sexuality.

The theme of togetherness, unity and friendship leads me to a further observation: namely, about the industry's desire to represent the contemporary teen-pop scene more broadly as a happy family. At the 1999 annual ceremony of the British music industry, popularly known as the Brit Awards, much was made of the legacy of the Swedish band Abba and the twenty-fifth anniversary of their winning the Eurovision Song Contest in 1974 with their song "Waterloo". In particular, the teen-pop groups Cleopatra, B*witched and Steps and the female solo singers Tina Cousins and Billie came together under the *ad hoc* name of the Super Troupers to perform "Thank Abba for the Music", a tribute medley of Abba songs. *Smash Hits* conducted and printed an interview-cum-feature article with four members of this "poptastic assemblage of talent" (Billie plus one member from each of the three bands) and depicted them in a happy foursome cuddle, prominently on the front cover and twice within the article.[14]

The photographic representations of teen pop consistently project images of fun, playfulness, openness and togetherness. And (at least, as I read them) these images, whether of bands, individual band members, or solo artists, are virtually all constructed so as to engage the spectator with their eyes and their outgoing body language generally, and to invite identification with and participation in a notional community of teen pop.

Interviews are another regular feature of teen-pop magazines. They have a certain amount in common with the posed photographs in the general ways in which they represent the stars and position the reader. At the same time, though, interviews are a distinct form of representation. They make their own contribution to the discourse of teen pop in the particularities of the combined process by which they make the stars knowable, shape the idea of teen pop, and offer readers the opportunity to identify with the 'community' of teen pop. Two aspects particularly distinguish the interviews from the photographic images: their ability to introduce and in fact to determine the particular discussion topics in terms of which the performers are made known to the readers; and their function of letting the artists speak. The limited menu of discussion topics is dominated by matters of love and romance, but the other main fields of interest are clothing and fashion, lifestyle, relations with other performers, and the mixture of pleasures and tribulations of being a pop star. Music is not discussed. On the whole, the interviews try in their selective way to show what sort of people the pop stars are. This often brings out a contradictory duality in that the teen stars seem, on the one hand, to be just like the teenage readers but on the other hand, because of their fame, wealth and occupation, quite different from them.

The style of the interviews is very casual, as one might expect. The questions are usually of a trivial nature and seldom more than superficially linked to one another. Accordingly, there is no structure of development, no sense of gradually penetrating or enlightening discovery, and no expectation that the stars will be required to reflect very deeply before answering. Light digestibility is the key quality. Many interviews are printed in the form of a questionnaire: a quickfire series of questions or prompts followed by short responses. Others involve the same sort of questioning procedure but they differ in that the stars are permitted to answer at greater length and, if a group is being interviewed together, interjections are incorporated and a degree of extended dialogue is allowed to develop. Occasionally there are longer interviews written up in continuous prose with the journalist's presence chummily asserted in the teenspeak of the narrating voice.

In my opinion the particular contribution of magazine interviews to the discourse of teen pop lies in the combination of the predetermined range of discussion topics with the characteristic interview styles and language register. The following illustrations are necessarily selective and fragmentary, but I hope they will suffice to make the point. One aspect more apparent in magazine interviews than in other sources of teen-pop discourse is the impression that the consumer orientation is more to girls than to boys. For example, the implicit romantic interest for young female readers is the guiding principle of a quickfire interview with the newcomer Irish boy group Mytown, whose four members (aged between 18 and 22) respond in turn to a sequence of prompts that include my best date ("I went to an amusement arcade for the evening with this lovely girl, and then we went to a field near my house and snogged!"), my first kiss ("I was about 12, and it was round the side of my old primary school. I was really nervous, but once it started, I was like 'Waaaay, I like this!'"), my most romantic moment ("I was going out with this girl who'd had a really bad day at work, so I lit candles, brought her dinner and gave her a massage to cheer her up."), my first love, my first heartbreak, and my perfect girlfriend.[15] Mytown are represented here as relatively 'normal' boys-next-door. I have listed and quoted selectively but not unrepresentatively, for this particular interview is restricted exclusively to the sort of prompts I have exemplified and no reference is made at all to the music world or stardom or anything else. This has the effect of making the boys come across as being very knowable and notionally within the reach of aspiring teenage girl readers rather than as rising stars in an inaccessible firmament. This in turn creates a corresponding position for the female reader, if she is willing to occupy it, of a young person who could relate to one or more of these boys if she were given the opportunity.

The reverse does not seem to be true, however, when girl groups are being interviewed. The topic of romance probably comes up more often with them than with boy groups, but one does not get the impression that the female artists are generally being represented in such a way as to nourish the interest of male readers. On the contrary, they tend to come across rather as girls talking amongst themselves in a way that addresses readers as 'girls like us'. Consider the two following extracts from an interview with the Honeyz printed under the rubric of "Girls' Night In":

> What topics of conversation do you cover on a girlie night in?
> Celena: Boys! It's got to be boys!
> Naima: *(Quick to reassure us that the Honeyz aren't boy-obsessed.)* We do talk about things to do with the group too!
> Celena: Yes, but if it's not to do with the group it'll be about boys and relationships.

Boys and romance are not the only subject. The three girls talk about what food they would get in and what they would watch on television. Then comes a sub-heading "Getting Girlie":

> Do you get the beauty products out at any point?
> Heavenli: Yeah, I'm the nail person. I do my nails quite often when I'm sitting down.
> Naima: We're tweezers people!
> Celena: Naima and I are always plucking!
> Naima: I couldn't live without my tweezers!
>
> What about swapping clothes?
> Celena: We do anyway.
> Heavenli: We all wear each others' clothes.
> Celena: There's certain things that are special to us that we won't let the others borrow.
> Naima: Celena's got this Morgan dress that I'm always asking to borrow but she won't let me.

Heavenli: I got the same one for £15 in the sales!
Naima: Well, I'll borrow Heavenli's then![16]

They may talk about boys, but they are not talking *for* boys. They are simply 'doing' girl talk and it comes across as fairly natural, not just affected for the interview. The point is reinforced in the interview already referred to with the Super Troupers:

> But what do pop girls talk about when they get together? "Boys!" shouts Cleo, inevitably. "And we talk about work, emotions, the problems we've had," says Billie, "and then we talk about new makes of clothes and make-up, and guys we've seen working at different radio stations that we all agree are good-looking!" So basically, the stuff that girls everywhere talk about? "Yeah, it's just like getting together with your mates," grins Billie.[17]

The preceding examples show the female artists being encouraged to stereotype themselves as 'girlie'. Later in the same interview, however, the interviewer leads them to consider the changes that have taken place concerning women in pop and they agree that, compared to a few years ago, girl groups can now hold their own against male groups in the pop world and are even predominant, a development that was initiated by the Spice Girls. Not only that but, as Claire Steps then adds significantly, "I think the Spice Girls made it quite cool for girls to like girl bands." The four interviewees then go on to agree that, whilst female fans "just seem to go mad over the boys, and start screaming whenever they see them, [...] girls will come up and just treat you [i.e. a female artist] like a proper mate, like we've known each other for ages".[18]

The preceding discussion of interviews is intended only as a demonstration of some of the ways they work to construct the artists and, in a less conspicuous way, the readers, too. Limitation of space prevents me from illustrating the full range of variations, which I think would be well worth exploring. I hope, however, that the point has been sufficiently made for interested readers to feel able to pick up teen-pop magazines for themselves and undertake their own analysis.

4. The Songs and Performance of Teen Pop

Turning now to the songs of teen pop and their performance, I want to highlight separately and in turn certain aspects of the music, the lyrics and the dancing respectively. One might reasonably ask whether it is appropriate to discuss music in connection with representation, since music is generally considered to be a non-representational art form. That does not mean, however, that music does not carry or construct cultural meaning. It is, after all, a cultural practice. It employs (and is at liberty to subvert) codes which are culturally produced. Music does not carry inherent meaning, but there are conventions whereby most members of a culture would agree that certain pieces of music accord with or suggest certain ideas such as, for example, Spanishness or psychodelia or funerals. The causes can be traced to formal elements such as harmony, rhythm, tempo or timbre which, alone and in combination, are capable of prompting common responses, but only through recognizable codes.

I think it is fair to say that the teen pop of the late 1990s, like pop music generally over the last four decades, is characterized by danceability (except for the occasional dreamy ballad), catchy melody, harmonic simplicity, a tendency towards lush instrumentation and orchestration (real or synthetic), and lavish production textures. These features play an important role in constituting a definite signifying practice. They flourish together in a way which can be expected to produce a particular range of responses and is generally calculated to do so. A cynic might call the effect anodyne. The strong emphasis on chirpy and catchy melodies makes for light-heartedness. The effect is supported by rhythms and tempi which, except in the case of ballad numbers, are energetic but not frenetic, animated but not agitated. The tonal and harmonic structures are fundamental and safely anchored, always providing resolution and avoiding any sort of disturbance, perplexity or adventure. The vocal timbres and styles are appropriately mellifluous. They vary quite considerably, not just from artist to artist but between and even within individual songs by the same artists. This variety, however, is contained within obvious limits. The voices may be dramatic, soulful, plaintive, vulnerable, or raunchy, but they are always tuneful and perceptibly obedient to mainstream showbiz aesthetics. There is no room here for the screaming, wailing, croaking or droning that are perfectly acceptable and expressive in other strands of popular music. A similar sort of controlled aesthetics can be heard in the instrumentation. Polished production styles compensate for the musical simplicity of the songs by adding a rich variety of texture. The teen-pop sound is also apt to appropriate stylistic elements from other types of popular music. Consider the following review, taken from a teen-pop magazine, of Britney Spears's 1999 album *Baby, One More Time*:

> Blimey! Britney's debut album is a well-tasty cocktail of tunes, from sweet piano ballads to upbeat catchy numbers. The strong beat underlying her current hit [i.e. the single of the same title, which was topping the singles charts at the time of the review] is a theme that flows all through her alb and, aside from the BSB [i.e. Backstreet Boys]-style big beats, stand-out styles include the tropical calypso rhythm of *Soda Pop*,

the taste of Spanish flamenco on *Born to Make You Happy* (strongly reminiscent of the Spices' *Viva Forever*) and the reggae-tinged summer vibe of *Thinkin' About You*.[19]

That is just one album, but the stylistic range is typical of teen-pop output. Listening to albums by other performers, I was particularly struck by the frequent presence of Motown, soul and funk. At the same time, though, other sounds from the spectrum of popular music, such as guitar rock, grunge, goth, metal, hardcore, trance or drum'n'bass are patently excluded from teen pop. What selection criteria are at work? It is apparent that the types of music which have been most willingly absorbed are those which are not instantly associated with drugs, disaffection or social deviance and which, with regard to purely musical criteria, lend themselves especially well to the combination of the simple fun-giving style and the particular sort of step-dance orientation that teen pop thrives upon. One may summarize the music as being formally simple, sophisticated in production and arrangement, and artistically safe. It is designed to gratify the emotional desire for uncomplicated pleasure and romantic sentiment and to trigger the body's impulse to dance.

It will come as no surprise to see that the lyrics match the music as surely as Britney rhymes with Whitney. As with the music, there is little to distinguish the lyrics of teen pop from those of pop music generally, except perhaps a slightly narrower thematic range. In fact the themes are almost always standard regurgitations of pop music's general stock of love and romance situations: the celebration of newly discovered love, the pleasure of a secure relationship, the yearning of an unreciprocated love, or the melancholy of a broken romance. And though the last two categories are sorrowful, the emotion nevertheless comes across as a sweet sorrow, more because of the mood created by the accompanying music than because of the texts themselves. The yearning and melancholy are not depressive or terminal, merely wistful and temporary. With regard to formal aspects, the texts are consistently simple and formulaic. Rhyme is often used, which has a restricting influence on the vocabulary and the phrasing. Even when there is no rhyme, however, cliché predominates in the choice and collocation of words and in the use of images and metaphors. The following few extracts illustrate these generalizations about theme and form:

Since I met you I never had it so good
You bring the joy to my life like I knew you would.[20]

I'm thinking about your sugar lips
Got a feeling for you now that's so strong
I'm dreaming of the candy in your fingertips
Baby, don't stay away from me too long.

I've been missing you, I should be kissing you.
Honey to the bee, that's you for me.[21]

Standing on the shore
Calling out your name
I was here before
I could see your face
Only clouds will see
Tears are in my eyes
Empty like my heart
Why'd ya say goodbye?[22]

Song lyrics seldom appear to advantage when divorced from their music and it is inappropriate to judge them as a self-sufficient form of expression like poetry. Nevertheless, it would not be a judgement of value but a statement of fact to describe these lyrics as banal. They are typical of what predominates in pop and other types of popular music and not only in teen pop. They still form part of the discourse of teen pop, however, so it is appropriate to ask about the role they play in constituting teen pop. I would like to suggest that the most significant aspect is their very banality, their consistently and even wilfully uninventive and hackneyed way of giving utterance to variants of an age-old theme. Love and romance and the variant situations and stories built around them are a deeply embedded element of cultural practice, so it would be misguided to regard the perpetual recurrence of the theme itself as a sign of creative exhaustion. One should expect to keep finding it in all types and at all levels of artistic practice, but particularly in popular culture and most particularly in that which springs from or is oriented to youth and middle age. The significant banality of teen-pop lyrics lies, rather, in the expression and handling of the theme. How does this element of teen-pop discourse work in shaping the idea of teen pop and in determining the appropriate mode of conduct? I would suggest that, in tandem with the musical characteristics I have discussed, the lyrics play their part in representing teen pop as a non-cerebral fun-zone, a realm where thinking and wondering have no place. Personal, social, aesthetic and other such questions belong elsewhere, in other discourses for other times and other subjectivities. A related consideration is the fact that dance is very important in modern teen pop. So while lyrics are indispensable in a milieu where the artists are vocalists and not instrumentalists, it is necessary at the same time that they should not draw attention away from the dancing and the blithe spirit. It is enough that the texts provide a vehicle for vocal performance and suggest vaguely that love is in the air tonight.

I want to turn now to an important visual aspect of performance. When one watches a performance of teen pop, it is indeed the dancing by the singers that is the most striking characteristic. Dance is integral to the acts, whether in promotional videos, in pop shows recorded in television studios, or in live concert appearances. Given the musical and lyrical similarity I have noted between teen and non-teen pop, the element of dance is probably the main distinguishing performance element. In March 1999 I recorded a sample of three consecutive BBC *Top of the Pops* programmes and found a convincing correlation between the performers whose acts incorporated choreographed dance and those who were featured in the teen-pop magazines, whilst the pop artists whose acts did not include dance were not featured in the magazines.[23] The manner of dancing of the teen-pop artists contributes significantly to teen pop's representation of itself. Generally speaking, if the artists are a group, like Steps, B*witched or All Saints, they perform their own choreographed stepdance routine for each individual song. If they are solo singers, like Britney Spears or Tina Cousins, then they themselves dance in a choreographed routine with a troupe of backing dancers. In either case, however, it is clear that the singing and dancing are more or less equally important. The dancing routines themselves are precisely and often imaginatively choreographed. Most of them are fluid, involve much changing of position, and contain a mixture of both individual and synchronized moves. This projects an image of simultaneous conformity and individuality, much like the similar-but-distinct principle I have already indicated in the control of costume or the composition of the group photographs. Sustained, dentally enviable and seemingly authentic smiles reinforce the effect of wholesome happiness.

The dance component of teen pop offers an easily demonstrable example of how a particular discourse influences the conduct of others. In the television shows where a teen-pop group is appearing live, it is possible to observe many of the teenage members of the studio audience, when space permits, imitating the routinized movements of the artists. A similar effect is carried over into parties and discos for younger teenagers. Those who identify themselves as fans are pleasurably impelled to learn and share the dance moves of new songs as soon as they are released onto the market. Whether they are wannabe stars or just enjoy dancing and singing along with everybody else, their actions show them willingly yielding themselves to the community of shared identity defined by teen pop.

5. Some Latent Contradictions

Teen pop is a product of representational practices, but it is important not to overlook the involvement and interest of the record companies and other agencies within the industry. They foster and encourage the particular representation of teen pop that I have been describing, for it is the basis of a distinct and lucrative segment of the consumer market. Desirable images are fragile constructs, however, and vulnerable to the emergence of contradictions. The commercial representation of teen pop therefore depends on the suppression or control of anything which runs counter to it, and the agencies of the industry are predictably keen for things to be kept under control. That is why, for example, the managers of teen-pop bands tend to be much more authoritative than managers of other bands in trying to prevent their charges from doing anything that might detract from their image of wholesomeness. Nevertheless, and partly perhaps as a result of the heavy control, contradictions persist, as do the tensions involved in holding them at bay. In this final section I wish to indicate at a few instances of suppressed conflict which can be detected or inferred in the representations of teen pop.

Consider the following comment about the success of Britney Spears and the circumstances of the rise of late-1990s teen pop in the USA:

> Teen pop is driving the entire American music business at the moment. In the wake of the Spice Girls phenomenon, American record companies realised that they had no bands that teenagers wanted, and, more significantly, that teenagers' parents would allow them to listen to. Unlike rap, swingbeat or Marilyn Manson's goth metal, the Britney sound is the perfect anodyne panacea for all – innocent, non-judgemental teen pop with boundless energy, neat dance moves and just a little bit of sex.[24]

The seventeen-year-old Britney Spears is presented through interviews and feature articles as a somewhat naive and clean-living young Christian, the sort of image that would be expected to go down well with many parents of teenage and still younger fans. However, one only needs to watch the first part of the video accompanying her March 1999 hit single "One More Time" to see a contradictory image. She is dancing with a group of other 'pupils' in a school corridor, half bursting out of a blouse and short skirt that are a parody of school uniform. In another image of her "straddling the line between innocence and experience", as Andrew Male expressed it, she was photographed for *Rolling Stone* magazine (not targeted at a teen readership) wearing a bra and panties in a bedroom full of children's fluffy toys.[25] Theoretically, Britney could quit the teen-pop market and aim at an older age-group, but so long as she or her record company wish to continue capitalizing on the huge teen-pop market, her image-makers will need to play down (i.e. virtually deny) her sex appeal instead of playing it up. The other teen-pop videos I have seen are very 'safe' in respect of sexiness, and I regard the Britney Spears video only as a very mild exception. I have mentioned it, though, because it is unusual in briefly flaunting the adult sexuality of an artist whose image is packaged for a market that includes prepubescent consumers.

This and other contradictions connected with adult lifestyles face all artists and producers of teen pop. The usual strategy, especially concerning sex, is to suppress them. Hence, as I have already mentioned, the photographs in the teen magazines are never sexy or suggestive of sex. Quite the contrary. Likewise, the gossip pages will mention who is apparently going out with whom and who was seen kissing (which they prefer to call 'snogging') with whom, and the interviews sometimes refer to ideal (seldom real) boyfriends and girlfriends, but it is never said who is sleeping with whom. Sex is taboo. Getting married and having babies (selected members of Spice Girls, All Saints and Boyzone) is perfectly acceptable. And drugs are completely taboo. Cases of excessive drinking and all-night partying, on the other hand, are sometimes referred to and accommodated with a chortling sort of 'aren't they naughty?' attitude.

On the subject of sexuality, it should be apparent from my descriptions of the British teen-pop magazines (and anyone directly familiar with them will probably have realized) that the representation of the numerous teen-pop artists presupposes they are heterosexual. It became public in 1998 that George Michael was gay, but he had long ceased to count as a star for teeny-poppers. And, of course, there are other older pop stars who are known to be gay. But homosexuality was not admitted to in the teen-pop pantheon. If anyone was known within the business to be gay, then the fact was kept quiet. Then, in June 1999, Stephen Gately of Boyzone 'came out' in an interview in the *Sun* newspaper, which managed to cover four pages in its characteristic style. Some unidentified person working close to the band had threatened to sell the story, so Gately decided to anticipate it with his own declaration. That was in the national press. The question then was how the teen-pop magazines would react. *Smash Hits* made it the cover story in September 1999 and, perhaps surprisingly considering the previous taboo on homosexuality in teen-pop discourse, presented a comparatively lengthy and very supportive interview.[26] It also included a photograph of Stephen Gately's partner and referred to the letters and messages of support Gately had received not only from fellow pop artists but also, in great quantities, from fans. One might think, though it would be churlish to do so, that *Smash Hits* was forced to react the way it did since the knowledge was public and Boyzone was not a band it could afford to turn its back on. That does not alter the fact, though, that the magazine represented Gately in a very positive and friendly way. It will be interesting, however, to see whether this instance marks a change in teen-pop discourse with regard to assumptions about sexuality or whether things will go on much as before. Needless to say, the implicit or explicit representation of sexual orientation has its consequences in the positions it opens up or closes off for the teenage fan.

6. Concluding Thoughts

The title of this article includes the word 'identity', harmonizing with the title of the volume in which it appears. Yet there has been a tendency in the last twenty years or so to jettison the term 'identity' in favour of 'subjectivity' and 'subject' whenever one wishes to make clear that the human subject is not knowable as a transcendent entity but only as a decentred, amorphous product of language, discourse and cultural practice. In *Questions of Cultural Identity*, Stuart Hall sets out to restore validity to the term 'identity' without rejecting the legacy of Foucault and the concept of the subject. Identities, he suggests, are about "questions of using the resources of history, language and culture in the process of becoming rather than being: not 'who we are' or 'where we came from', so much as what we might become, how we have been represented and how that bears on how we might represent ourselves".[27] The question of identities comes into service at the points of contact between subjects and discursive practices; identities are "points of temporary attachment to the subject positions which discursive practices construct for us".[28] Hall is intent on restoring agency to the subject in view of the tendency of post-structuralist theories to represent the subject as passive. The restored concept of identity therefore gains validity wherever people who find themselves marginalized by race, gender or class, for example, need to assert their identity. In comparison with such situations, teenage identity seems to lack any urgent agenda. I would grant that there is no pressing call to talk of a history of representation which teenagers would do well to appropriate. Nonetheless, we should note in the context of teen pop that, firstly, the practice of representation is firmly in the hands of the producers of teen-pop culture (record companies, publishers, television companies, etc.) and, secondly, the discursive practices of teen pop offer subject positions which exclude or ignore conflicts and contradictions. Teen pop itself could be said to embody the suppression or evasion of problems, and I do not believe that the suddenly enforced accommodation of Stephen Gately does much to suggest the opposite. The *Smash Hits* interview with the Super Troupers from which I have already quoted concludes with the singer Billie saying: "Pop's about being cool, lighthearted, and fun. It's about enjoying being young, and being able to say that 'Those were the best years of my life.'" To which *Smash Hits* adds the endorsement, "Amen to that, Billie girl! We couldn't agree more if we tried!"[29] A forgivably unthinking sentiment from Billie, perhaps, given the heady influence of youthful stardom. But a submerged problem threatens to pop up like a pimple beneath the make-up and *Smash Hits* has either failed to notice it or has chosen to ignore it. If a teenager wishes to look back on her youth in those terms, the unspoken implication is that she soon expects life to start going downhill. Hardly an empowering thought for negotiating life after teen pop.

Notes

1 An excellent source for a much more detailed and exemplified introduction to the ideas presented in the following section, and one to which I am partly indebted, is Hall (1997a).
2 Hall (1997b: 42).
3 See, for example, Said (1984: 186-188).
4 Hayden White has written that "wherever Foucault looks, he finds nothing but discourse" (1979: 91).
5 Hall (1997b: 44).
6 I am well aware that it is not always easy for teachers who do not live in Britain to get hold of sufficient suitable materials. My 'database' of material was largely the harvest of a visit to Britain of just over two weeks, but it is possible to get direct access in or from Germany to almost every source I used. The main teen-pop magazines are *Top of the Pops* published monthly by the BBC, and *Smash Hits* published every fortnight by EMAP Metro Ltd. (The latter can be found at the press stands in some of the larger railway stations in Germany.) The main television programme is the BBC's weekly *Top of the Pops*, which features music from the British singles charts but is not dedicated to any one branch of music. It is transmitted several times a week in Germany on BBC Prime. The majority of CD albums (though not so many singles) are marketed in Germany whilst the pop videos can best be found on the various national and international television channels dedicated to pop music. Finally, though I have not analysed it in this article, the internet gives access to both the official and unofficial websites of the various bands and artists. It is important to be aware that the official websites are controlled by the performers' respective record companies and are therefore part of the marketing mix, whereas the unofficial sites are usually run by fans.
7 *Top of the Pops*, March 1999, 7.
8 *Smash Hits*, 24 March 1999, 5, 3.
9 *Smash Hits*, 10 March 1999, 9.
10 *Smash Hits*, 24 March 1999, 54.
11 *Smash Hits*, 10 March 1999, 53, 10; *Smash* Hits, 24 March 1999, 53.
12 *Ibid.*, 18-19, 67.
13 *Top of the Pops*, March 1999, 20; *Smash Hits*, 10 March 1999, 45.
14 *Smash Hits*, 24 March 1999, cover page, 12-14.
15 *Smash Hits*, 10 March 1999, 28-29. This is almost a ritual form, a formulaic procedure that has been practised by pop magazines since the early 1960s when teen pop was first institutionalized on a commercial basis and when groups like the Beatles and the Beach Boys were still new, young products firmly under the control of their record companies and management.
16 *Top of the Pops*, March 1999, 22.
17 *Smash Hits*, 24 March 1999, 12.
18 *Ibid.*

19 *Top of the Pops*, March 1999, 58.
20 "Never Had It So Good", sung by Take 5. Words and music: Full Force/Modeliste/Neville/Noeentelli/Porter.
21 "Honey to the Bee", sung by Billie. Words and music: Page/Marr.
22 "Blame It on the Weatherman", sung by B*witched. Words and music: Hedges/Brannigan/Ackerman/Caine.
23 The dancing teen-pop artists were Vengaboys, Boyzone, Steps, Britney Spears, Tina Cousins, and B*witched, whilst the non-dancing non-teen-pop artists were Cher, Blur, Stereophonics, Skunk Anansie, Beautiful South, Roxette, R.E.M., Manic Street Preachers, belated Britpop clones Travis, and Underworld. The exceptions were two soul acts: American megastar Whitney Houston, who does not count as teen pop but who had an impressive dance troupe behind her, though she herself did not dance; and young black British singer Kele Le Roc, who definitely features in the teen-pop magazines but who performed with her backing band onstage and no dancing at all.
24 Male (1999: 17).
25 *Ibid.*
26 *Smash Hits*, 22 September 1999, 58-60. I regret I have not been able to report the response of *Top of the Pops* magazine.
27 Hall (1996: 4).
28 *Ibid.*, 6.
29 *Smash Hits*, 24 March 1999, 14.

Bibliography

Hall, Stuart: *Questions of Cultural Identity*, London, 1996.

--- (Ed.): *Representation. Cultural Representations and Signifying Practices*, London, 1997a.

---: "The Work of Representation". – In S.H. (Ed.): *Representation. Cultural Representations and Signifying Practices*, London, 1997b, pp. 13-74.

Male, Andrew: "Triumph of the Shrill", *The Guardian*, 18 May 1999, G2 section, 17.

Said, Edward: "Criticism Between Culture and System". – In E.S.: *The World, the Text, and the Critic*, London, 1984, pp. 178-225.

Smash Hits, 10 March 1999.

Smash Hits, 24 March 1999.

Smash Hits, 22 September 1999.

Top of the Pops, March 1999.

White, Hayden: "Michel Foucault". – In John Sturrock (Ed.): *Structuralism and Since*, Oxford, 1979, pp. 81-115.

Claus-Ulrich Viol, Bochum

A Crack in the Union Jack? National Identity in British Popular Music

1. Introduction

British popular music and the articulation of a particular national identity – do they go together? At first sight one could be tempted to answer in the negative. Most of contemporary English-sung pop music is, after all, a commodity produced for an international mass market, which, in turn, is dominated by a small group of 'major' multinational record companies. Bands and performers are marketed globally, while the bulk of the music is geared to appeal to a young audience that seems to become increasingly global in its tastes and forms of expression. Clearly, within the concept of 'youth', in Western countries – though it is itself markedly divided along the lines of e.g. different subcultures, taste groups, fan circles, class, ethnicity and gender – national differentiations appear to have decreased in importance ever since the rise of pop/rock in the 1950s.[1] In addition to the marketing deficit that arises if a song is too much anchored in national discourse, most musicians want their music to travel, believing that one of the defining principles of 'music' lies with its universality, its potential for enhancing human understanding and transcending cultural differences. Thus, Suede, currently one of the most popular British bands, defended themselves when criticized by an English fan for having "dumbed down [their] lyrics to the point where they're patronising", by claiming that there is "a difference between dumbing down and being universal. The majority of people who buy Suede records aren't English, their first language isn't English [...;] there's a whole world out there and it's important to communicate to them as well".[2] One could think that belonging to the Anglo-American language group so championed by the dominating transnational music corporatism makes British artists especially prone to internationalize their repertoire and cleanse it of overtly nation-specific reference points.[3] But how come, then, that even self-professed universalists like Suede round off their latest album *Head Music* (1999) with a song of distinctly national content called "Crack in the Union Jack"? Admittedly, the song is rather marginalized on the album and, what is more, seems to confirm the band's general 'cosmopolitan' outlook as it mainly expresses the singer's nausea at the constant fears of national decline voiced by his "lonely" and frustrated compatriots on the radio, the news, and midday

TV shows. In view of the dreary conditions and prospects shared by the singer and the people, whose lives have apparently lost 'immediacy' and grown dependent on the media, the song suggests, there would be more pressing things to attend to than the myopic bewailing of hurt national pride ("'There's a great big crack in the Union Jack'"). To support this, the topic is given tellingly short shrift in a less-than-two-minute piece that, through its stripped acoustic sound, differs considerably from the other opulently arranged songs. Whatever the implications, it is obvious that the song has broached a discourse of national identity.

In so doing, Suede's song is actually but contributing its small share to a strong and well-established current in British music. Resolving the seeming paradox, I will try to show in this paper that a good deal of British pop music is, in fact, permeated with national discourse(s), in any case to a larger extent than its transnational character would seem to allow of. The different musics which operate under the umbrella term of 'pop' are indeed important sites where national identity is negotiated and (re)constructed, so that particular songs make use of symbols and myths that are nation-specific – activating an automatic response from members of the national community but causing difficulties of decoding for foreign listeners – to which they then give a meaningful twist, shaping them into a statement about British identity. Obviously, the world of popular music is too broad a subject to be comprehensively covered within an article like this. I will therefore have to concentrate on a selection of songs whose messages appear the most interesting and the analysis of which the most rewarding (for German students of British culture). Yet, within this vast area of British popular music, it seems that certain general currents and tendencies of constructing national identity can be perceived, which may roughly be divided into a patriotic, a multicultural, a regional, and an ironic approach. The method pursued here will be one of conventional textual interpretation – the question of (active) consumption, so fashionable in today's cultural studies of popular music, cannot be tackled here. This textual analysis pays particular attention to the employment of national symbols in the songs and their underlying cultural meaning. As such a meaning cannot simply be reduced to the lyrics of a song, I have taken care to include aspects of genre, musical texture and performance in the analysis whenever appropriate.

2. The Patriotic Discourse

I would like to take as a point of departure a discussion of Elton John's "Candle in the Wind 1997", a song that is strongly imbued with patriotic discourse and that might serve, by virtue of this, as a contrastive foil against which other more subversive popsong versions of British/English national identity may be set. A swift reworking of his 1973 homage to Marilyn Monroe, the new piano-and-vocal adaptation was written in early September 1997 on the occasion of Princess Diana's death. John's tribute to the princess, stirringly rendered at her globally televized funeral in Westminster Abbey and subsequently recorded and released, quickly became one of the biggest pop singles in history. Within a month the song, the fastest-selling single ever in the UK, stood at eight-times platinum, with worldwide sales quickly approaching the 170 million benchmark set by Bing Crosby's "White Christmas" and gallantly outdistancing another all-time big-seller, the title song of Walt Disney's *Bambi* movie. Of similar global appeal and emotional power, Diana's song, at the time, was felt to voice people's grief as well as eulogize the princess in an adequate manner. Reading the text closely now that media-driven and hysterical mass grieving has passed, however, one cannot help noticing that the song is not so much about the deceased princess, contrary to all appearances and popular belief, as about the bereaved 'nation', about the imagined community of mourners. This community, to boot, is defined in astoundingly restricted terms, especially for a text of such global appeal. By his pervasive connection of second-person singular and first-person plural pronouns to exclusively English national symbols, John makes it quite plain which nation both Diana and the mourners (apparently) belong to:

Goodbye England's rose
May you ever grow in our hearts
You were the grace that placed itself
Where lives were torn apart
You called out to our country
And you whispered to those in pain
Now you belong to heaven
And the stars spell out your name
[...]
And your footsteps will always fall here
Along England's greenest hills
[...]

Loveliness we've lost
These empty days without your smile
This torch we'll always carry
For our nation's golden child
And even though we try
The truth brings us to tears
All our words cannot express
The joy you brought us through the years
[...]
Goodbye England's rose
From a country lost without your soul
Who'll miss the wings of your compassion
More than you'll ever know

Hence, the Princess of *Wales* becomes an *English* rose; the most 'modern' and *internationally* renowned member of the *British* monarchy is seen as an emanation of the genius loci of "*England's* greenest hills", to which it is assumed she will also return after her death. Once this context is set, it is reinforced by conspicuous references to "our hearts", "our country" and "our nation[...]". Not only excluding other potential nationalities from the group of mourners, the text, being a perfect showcase for the construction of national identity, also works heavily towards homogenizing and unifying the national ingroup. This is achieved by the central position of the singer, who seems to focus the sentiments of all his compatriots and act as a kind of communicating medium ("we've lost", "we'll always carry", "we try", "[f]rom a country […] / [w]ho'll miss"), and by the role of Diana, ever-welcome projection surface for human hopes and yearnings, who comes to embody nothing less than the English themselves in this case. While the first two stanzas still concentrate on a description of Diana's character by hammering home her good-heartedness, charity, compassion and general saintliness, the attention shifts to the condition of the community from the third stanza onwards. John expresses 'national' feelings of emptiness, speechlessness, sadness and, quite strikingly, goes on to make a pledge on behalf of the nation to carry on in Diana's cheerful spirit. The country, John promises, will not be unworthy of the princess's martyrdom; in fact, it has already changed as, in mourning Diana, it betrays its newly-won emotionalism and compassion. Diana's death, one might conclude, was not in vain. It has brought about a renewal of the English national character: having left behind stereotypical reserve and emotional repression, the nation has become more human, more compassionate (a notion that was widely shared at the time, from the Prime Minister to tabloid commentators).[4]

In addition to the singer's unifying function as the mouthpiece of national feeling, Diana herself functions as an agent of national unity. With considerable religious overtones, conveyed by the song's hymn-like style (cf. "grace", "heaven", "golden child", "wings"), the late princess is built up into a redeemer who died *for* the people. In worshipping, the people become one with her and, thus, with one another. In the process, Diana evolves into a national mythical presence, a modern English patron saint. The almost incantatory lines from the chorus, "And your footsteps will always fall here / Along England's greenest hills", place her in a line with other English mythical figures. A cross between Wordsworth's Lucy Gray and the Blakean figure of Christ walking the lands of golden-age Albion, her spirit, too, is insolubly linked with the English countryside. While Lucy obviously shared a similar fate (living solitarily, dying much too young, embodying England for the speaker of the poems, and blending in with her native environment – "mountains", "bowers" and "green fields"[5] – after her death, where "some maintain that to this day / She is a living child; / That you may see sweet Lucy Gray / Upon the lonesome wild"[6]), Diana's ever-lasting presence among the green hills of England also clearly harks back to Blake's famous passage from *Milton* (1804-1808):

> *And did those feet* in ancient time
> *Walk* upon England's *mountains green*?

And was the holy Lamb of God
On England's pleasant pastures seen?[7]

Such a stylistic/thematic allusion might be understood to fulfil at least three distinct functions in asserting Englishness. Firstly, John's reference to the 'green hills' is a recurring trope of English national discourse, representing the largely nineteenth-century invention of an "idealised rural landscape in which England is figured as a pastoral Eden".[8] This is a notion that not only romanticizes pre-industrial nature but also carries strong implications of social conservatism: allusions to a mythic agrarian 'Merrie England' tend to glorify "an organic and natural society of ranks, [...] of inequality in an economic and social sense, but one based on trust, obligation and even love"[9] – a hierarchical society in which squire and labourer existed in peaceful harmony. John's national community is organic, homogeneous and, in a way, without class divisions, as Diana is revered as (and appears to be) 'naturally superior'. Secondly, her close ties with the soil – again a notion of organic wholeness –, suggested by her English birth, upbringing (as an English "child" or "rose") and final resting-place, stress the importance of ancestral links and heritage for being recognized as a member of the nation. By implication, this 'tribalism' excludes all the people who have their ethnic and cultural roots outside the 'green hills' of this community. Englishness, here, might be understood to be innate, maybe even genetic. Finally, by following 'great' English poets in style and imagery, the song calls up the English literary tradition, which in itself is considered one of the central ingredients of Englishness. According to Krishan Kumar, it was the Romantic poets who "featured significantly in the cultural definition of English nationalism", while the reading of their works, alongside other canonized texts, later came to take on the function of a "national religion".[10]

In summary, Elton John's "Candle in the Wind" might be taken as a striking example of a revitalized English patriotism that has formed and acquired stridency in the face of a continuing decline of the concept of Britishness. The English nation, here, is imagined as elect and heroic, as rooted in tradition and Christian religion, as rural and idyllic, as brave, enduring and caring, and, eventually, as loyal and monarchic. Its mythological and 'historical' framework excludes large parts of the current population of Britain and England. Presupposing an essentially monolithic, monocultural community, it does not accommodate any of the actual experiences of modern English/British society, with its undeniably multiregional, multireligious and multiethnic character. We will now turn to examples of how the latter might lead to a reshaping of British national identity in popular music.

3. *The Multiculturalist Discourse*[11]

Post-war British popular music has been shaped – apart from its ongoing cross-fertilization with US-American forms and models – to a great extent by the impact of musicians and musical styles that hail from the former colonial and imperial territories and have arrived in Britain since 1945: from early (West-)Indian influences on jazz and imports like Trinidadian calypso and Jamaican ska in the fifties and sixties, via the popularization of Indi-pop, reggae, soul and funk in the 1970s, the two-tone revival of ska around 1980, through to late-eighties' acid-house, ragga, dance-hall, and the quite recent phenomena of bhangra – a commercially fairly successful blend of North Indian folk-music, Punjabi lyrics and Western techno/dance rhythms – or house-derived drum'n'bass. But Caribbean, Indian and African musical styles have not only impinged on the character of British pop as such, they have also provided British youths with ever new subcultural formations centred around the music through which they could construct and express their particular identities. It should be expected that the attitudes these ethnically hybrid musics and groups maintain towards the idea of 'the nation' are, virtually by definition, divided rather than monolithic. Indeed, traditional notions of British identity have been undermined and criticized, either implicitly or explicitly, by the use of postcolonial forms of expression – no matter if they are practised by black rasta-influenced reggae musicians, whose songs act as an antidote against the 'Babylonian' conditions of British society,[12] or by all-white bands, in what Hebdige referred to as a "white translation of black ethnicity",[13] like the hip-hopping Stereo MCs and the recent, mega-trendy outfit Kula Shaker, who "propagate a neo-hippy Hinduism, complete with sitar and tabla atmos behind the guitars".[14] Some of these bands even address the issue of national identity head-on in their songs, calling for a more multicultural approach to British identity. A quite striking and recent example of this is the British band Dreadzone's tellingly named song "Little Britain" of 1996.

Dreadzone, a 'mixed-race' project founded in 1992, play a modern variety of dub music, a style that has its roots in Jamaican reggae and sound system recordings, i.e. the music produced for local dances or discos. It came about when already existing (and often popular) tunes were remixed in the studio so that the bass line – overemphasized, slowed down, and intricately patterned – and the drumming happened to dominate the song. This rhythmical and instrumental background, with snatches of the original tune fading in and out, would then give enough room for the DJs who operated the sound system dances to do their so-called talk overs or toasts. Later both DJs and record engineers added evermore electronic sound effects such as reverb and echo on to their multitrack recordings.[15]

Strong in the seventies and at the beginning of the eighties, the style was revived in the early 1990s by (mainly white) dance-music technicians when – together with its high-speed derivative 'jungle' developed by young black musicians – it drew more ethnically mixed audiences than ever before. Outgrowing some of its Jamaican flavour and developing into a more hybridized and metropolitan form, this modern dub has meanwhile become even more studio-based and technology-centred: its main characteristic remains a mostly offbeat drum and bass driven rhythm, yet there might also be loops and breakbeats provided by drum computers, while the toasting has either been replaced by voice and noise samples and (sometimes manipulated) vocal tracks or turned into fast rap-style singing. The tempo may vary too, ranging from leisurely fluid movement to hectic staccato-like speed. A lot of Dreadzone's songs, for instance, are slow-paced, having a meditative, ambient rhythm but there are others that are rather quick and upbeat. Their hit single "Little Britain" is of the latter kind. Released in January 1996, the song made the British top forty and was subsequently included in the soundtrack of Hanif Kureishi's latest movie *My Son the Fanatic* (1998).[16] Both the song's musical texture and its lyrics, delivered with a slight West Indian patois accent, work towards a redefinition of older constructions of Britishness:

In this green and pleasant land
We have a dream to understand
In the mountains of the mind
There is a spirit you will find
Just like the angel from above
Sent to deliver words of love
Ancient cross and Zion star
Eastern ways and praise to Jah
This is our land
This is your land
This is our inheritance
To lead you on a merry dance

In the beginning there was light
Shining path and journey bright
When the faithful pray as one
Then will the races all be one
In this green and pleasant land
We have a dream to understand
Open paradise's gate
Dance on the land and celebrate
This is our land
This is your land
Say no matter what your colour
Your race or your culture
This is our inheritance
To lead you on a merry dance

By opening with Blake's famous characterization of England as a "green and pleasant land", a phrase not only triumphantly concluding, again, "And did those feet in ancient time" but also occuring in slightly altered form in his "England! awake, awake, awake!",[17] Dreadzone apparently latch on to the patriotic tradition so lavishly celebrated in Elton John's funeral song. Echoing Blake's biblical diction, mythical imagery, and visionary tone, the song, however, goes on to tell a story of national salvation and renewal that differs considerably from both John's nostalgic partisanship and Blake's inward-looking spirituality. Although "Little Britain" likewise stresses the importance of the spiritual (cf. the "spirit" to be found “in the mountains of the mind”) and other-worldly spheres (cf. the “angel from above” and the opening of “paradise’s gate”), its ultimate message is decidedly of this world: the paradise that has to be gained – or, in Blake’s terms, the Jerusalem that has to be rebuilt – will be a (national) community in which participation and integration is independent of religious affiliations – be they (Pre-)Christian, Jewish, Muslim, Buddhist or Rastafarian –, race, ethnicity or culture. This community consists neither of a highly exclusive group of fellow-sufferers to be redeemed (and hierarchized) by a saviour figure, as in John’s text, nor of the struggling Christians striving to turn England into a pre-Fall Arcadia as evoked by Blake, but of a multicultural, tolerant and ‘enlightened’ crowd of dancing Britons taking possession of the land they live in. Traditional patriotism is replaced by an open and inclusive concept of national identity that draws heavily on modern discourses of equality and emancipation: while the twice-repeated phrase “We have a dream to understand” obviously recalls Martin Luther King’s “I have a dream”, the chorus lines “This is our land / This is your land” are redolent of Woody Guthrie’s hobo-spirited “This Land Is Your Land”. The unifying force of this community is the music itself: dub music is considered a culture of its own that transcends ethnic/religious boundaries. Performers as well as listeners of dub music share a common belief in its healing and rallying power, no matter if they favour the more mystical variety represented, for instance, by Dreadzone or the more politically outspoken version endorsed by groups like Asian Dub Foundation. According to the latter band, dub is a “community of sound” that has “the power for all the human race”, a place where “black and white” unite and come to “argue and debate”.[18] It is true, then, that the use of the central term ‘land’ remains ambiguous throughout “Little Britain” since it can either be read as a spatial metaphor for the mind that has been illuminated by this subcultural ‘dub mentality’ or be taken to refer to the concrete country/nation of Britain. However, the two meanings are in no way mutually exclusive. Dub, as a state of mind and universalist concept, is clearly linked with a national discourse here. It provides its followers with a new way of seeing themselves and assessing their national identity. It is dub culture that helps them find a positive concept of Britishness, while, at the same time, keeping in check the very significance of national sentiment in the first place. Compared to the powerful and encompassing spirit of dub music, the song suggests, Britain indeed seems to be “Little” rather than ‘Great’. The title of the song obviously juxtaposes the former ‘greatness’ of the country as suggested by its colonial history (the Empire being one of the building blocks of a common British identity of the people from the UK) with the actual ‘littleness’ in terms of cultural openness, but also with the new postcolonial situation in which Britain has to see its role greatly reduced as against the increasing influence of its former colonial subjects. Thus, Dreadzone stress Britishness rather than Englishness because it is a more appropriately ironic inversion of the former colonial situation and prevalent identity politics *as well as* due to its more inclusive character (despite all its current global and previous ideological 'littleness') that comprises the whole of the British Isles. This qualifying perspective on the country is also skilfully conveyed by the music's spheric sounds, its angelic choirs, and the imitation of seagull noises that really enforce the idea of a small, confined island that is being suffused by a larger, transcendental force.

The song's firm grounding in national discourse is underlined by its use of further national symbols. Thus, apart from being a reference to Blake's passage from *Milton*, Dreadzone's opening line is also a conspicuous allusion to the text that Blake's poem has become in the meantime. Set to music by Hubert Parry in 1916, it has ever since been identified with the choral song "Jerusalem", a morale booster in the Great War and, subsequently, a kind of second national anthem. Still very popular today, the song is probably most noted for its annual appearance at the Last Night of the Proms where it is performed, with tremendous audience participation, alongside other British imperial melodies such as Elgar's "Pomp and Circumstance March no. 1" (in the guise of "Land of Hope and Glory"), Arne's "Rule Britannia", and the sea-shanties arranged by Henry Wood, the concert series' first conductor. Here, and still more so on occasions like the annual outdoor Prom concerts promoted by the Royal Philharmonic Orchestra and held at traditional English country-house sites, Parry's hymn has come to hold a central part in a celebration of nationhood where, according to Andrew Blake,

> the lower-middle-class sings and jives along to a musical Englishness which is in some ways the analogue of the Englishness of the magazine *This England*; the music of late Empire is charged with the historicised nostalgia of heritage culture for the mainly white audiences who attend and who profess no love of things European.[19]

Even if the jingoism of Last Nights' crowds seems to have abated in most recent years, with participants tending to be slightly more self-ironic, and the number of spectators waving non-British flags apparently increasing,[20] "Jerusalem"'s long-standing connection with the Proms – an event, after all, that has managed to steer clear of any serious Asian or African Caribbean influences by either ignoring them outright or making mere tokenist concessions – has turned it into an icon of a 'great', distinctively English tradition of musical composition and performance or, as some would rather argue, a heavily romanticizing instance of imperialist reactionism. Introducing its concluding line and its overall lyrical tone into a context of modern, West Indian-influenced dance music must be recognized as highly ironic. So is the wording when Dreadzone promise to lead their audience "on a merry dance", which is suggestive of traditional English rural folk dances dating from the times of 'Merrie Old England'. This alludes to the concept of England as an idealized pastoral song-and-dance village as it was, again, conceived in the nineteenth century. The song's appropriation of British/English mythology, therefore, extends to the 'rural England ideal' so central to the construction of conventional English national identity. Yet again, subversion is not long in coming: the idea of the organic community and Morris Dancers is undermined by synthesizer sequences, drum computer sounds, and an instrumental chorus that gives a modern keyboard strings approximation of an ancient fiddle jig. The band's "inheritance" is clearly not a tradition of Old English fertility rites or harvest celebrations but rather that of the Jamaican sound system operator. Apparently, apart from opting for a redefinition of time-honoured constructions of British/English identity, Dreadzone also give notice to the traditional concepts of 'English music'. Thus, starting with a short hymn-like intro – slow, measured and distinctly classical – the song soon lapses into its quick-paced, bass-dominated dance rhythm. Dub/dance music claims its right to be incorporated into that tradition, if not to be its sole future continuation. It is striking that the song's appropriation and ironic reinterpretation of the national symbols of a pastoral, parochial, and medieval (Little) Englandism, on the one hand, as well as an expansionist and racist high imperialism, on the other, is informed by a spirit of happiness, self-confidence and, most importantly, conciliation. As such it is diametrically opposed to the more confrontational and serious lyrics of a Linton Kwesi Johnson, the figurehead of what might be called the first generation of British dub, who in his songs – like the 'classics' "Inglan Is a Bitch" (1980) or "It Dread inna Inglan" (1977) – is concerned with giving voice to the black struggle and shaping black British identity, opting for independent and separate socio-cultural development rather than 'British' unity.[21] The Rastafarian 'Babylon' – or Johnson's 'Bitch' – might not yet have become the tolerant 'green and pleasant land' conjured up in "Little Britain", but multiethnic Dreadzone no longer eschew the idea of a common Britishness, providing this notion is subjected to modernization and redefinition.

Apart from this West Indian-influenced example, a whole field of music refusing to be located within the either/or-ism of traditional national and ethnic identity has, of course, evolved in young Asian-British music, most prominently in the so-called Asian underground. Much has already been written about the famous rapper Apache Indian, who, born of Hindu Punjabi parents and raised in the multiethnic Handsworth suburb of Birmingham, expresses himself through a mixture of Jamaican patois, Punjabi and an English Handsworth youth slang on the back of rhythm tracks which owe more to dance-hall reggae than to Indian pop, for all their use of dhol and tabla drums.[22] Blending different ethnic styles in what comes across as a full cultural crossover, connecting the global with the local, Apache's music opens up new vistas of identification for young Asian Britons. Songs like "Arranged Marriage" or "Magic Carpet" (1992), for instance, take their cues from well-worn South-Asian stereotypes but develop them into ironic statements about the singer's gender role and musical tastes. Hence, taking up a cocky male teenage stance, he professes to welcome the arranged marriage as it will spare him the trouble of finding a perfect (and duly respectful) girl himself. The "Magic Carpet", on the other hand, becomes a symbol of the musical transgression of borderlines and testifies to the singer's formative dialogue with black, West-Indian culture and the emerging cultural 'triangle' that shapes his identity, spanning South-Asia, Britain, and the West Indies: "A mon a here we come pon we magic carpet / And you better watch out beca we come here fe park it / Beca me born a New Delhi but me live England / Fly way cross the sea reach the Caribbean / Over Trinidad and the little Islands / [...] Jump pon me carpet mon with them portion / Ca we can't get stop by immigration". On his well-known "For Real", then, one of those typically self-reflexive raps about Saturday nights at the dance hall and the ingenuity of the singer's innovative 'combination style', Apache raps in collaboration with the black South London reggae singer Maxi Priest, who sings parts of the lyrics in Punjabi, thereby carrying the suspension of ethnic divisions to new heights. In the wake of Apache Indian, there have followed a number of Asian artists that fuse different styles with highly syncretic results. Thus, the successful Coventry-based producer Bally Sagoo, who combines bhangra, ragga, and hip hop to create new versions of classic Punjabi folk-songs, entered the Hindi-sung track "Dil Cheez" in the mainstream charts in late 1996. Singers like Najma Akhtar blend Urdu ballad singing (the ghazal) with rock and jazz rhythms and instrumentations, while the already mentioned Asian Dub Foundation, arguably the most radical musical innovators, mix "punishing [metropolitan] break beats, rap polemic, punk attitude and traditional Indian sounds mutated by technology".[23] Here, sound system units (decks and mixers), drum machine, heavy bass and distorted, synthesized electric guitar are welded into a sound that is only vaguely reminiscent of Indian influences. This has led to the band's being criticized for their supposed lack of historical and ethnic consciousness. Their creed, however, is that "technology is [their] tradition" and that "'Asian music cannot be defined solely by its classical or folk tradition any more than 'western music' can. ADF assert that their use of samplers and sequencers, electric guitar and bass is as 'Asian' as 'sitars and tablas'."[24] Whereas all of these hybrid styles still move within the framework of alternative musics by crossing 'Asian' forms with other ethnic or with highbrow styles (e.g. jazz), there is also one band that has made it into the 'white' pop/rock mainstream. Leicester's Asian-English indie band Cornershop have managed to make a name for themselves internationally, especially since the release of their latest album *When I Was Born for the Seventh Time* (1997) and the Norman Cook dance remix of their hit single "Brimful of Asha".[25] Refusing to be pigeonholed into any ethnic slot, the band has moved from noisy hardcore, lo-fi guitar punk on to a style that, lavishly produced and orchestrated, accommodates 'authentically American' country songs (cf. "Good to Be on the Road Back Home Again"), trashy guitars, electronic rhythms, and Velvet Underground song patterns as well as a musically rather 'straight' reappropriation of the Beatles' (mock-Indian) classic "Norwegian Wood", this time sung in Punjabi. As a result, Cornershop have reached a stage of expression at which their ethnicity is still less obtrusive and more unselfconsciously mixed with other cultural traditions than in the music of the underground bands. Their identity merges into a common global identity that is necessarily fragmented and multi-faceted. One of its central components, however, remains an implied (and special kind of) Englishness to which all of the modern Asian-British bands lay claim – something that has been called "Englishness plus" by Les Back. All of their hybridized styles transgress and parody the borders of racial and ethnic exclusivity at work in the conventional construction of national identity. In their stead, a "connective supplementarity" is manifested by the music: in the case of Apache Indian this is "ragga *plus* bhangra *plus* England *plus* Indian *plus* Kingston *plus* Birmingham",[26] while for Asian Dub Foundation and Cornershop one might phrase accordingly '*plus* metropolis *plus* technology (but *minus* capitalism)' and, respectively, '*plus* Nashville *plus* punk *plus* Leicester in the days of Ford Cortina'.[27]

4. The Regionalist Discourse

The concept of regionalism, as a counterpoise to extreme national centralization and increasing supranational globalization, has now for some time been gaining force in modern British politics and cultural life. The expression of such regional or, as in the case of Ireland, Scotland, and Wales, alternative national identities has also become quite common in 'British' pop music. Early successful exponents of Celticism like the Irish bands Tir Na Nog, Clannad, or the London-Irish Pogues, with their self-ironic cultivation of the Paddy stereotype, have been followed by Scottish folk-oriented bands like Capercaillie or Runrig, who fuse Gaelic song traditions and instrumentations with rock music, and the Welsh bilingual indie band Gorky's Zygotic Mynci. All of these ensembles have turned to their (Celtic) regional musical roots, which they either reinvent or reinterpret in dialogue with modern Anglo-American forms or even attempt to reproduce as authentically as they possibly can (witness the important role of traditionals and traditional arrangements in their repertoire) in order to stress an historically inherited identity that lies outside English-dominated Britishness and to advertise the cultural and political independence of their (national) regions. In addition, there have always been bands or individual artists who have made a statement about their regional identity in interviews and through the public image they promote of themselves, while their songs' musical and lyrical texture gives little indication of regional/national distinctiveness. At the time of writing, the British music scene can boast four commercially highly successful Welsh guitar-pop groups – the Manic Street Preachers, the Stereophonics, the Super Furry Animals, and Catatonia – who are all marketed as incarnations of Welshness, although – apart from a few tracks that might be taken to deal with Welsh (provincial) life or the odd Welsh-sung B-side – the quality of their music does not differ in the least from that of other British or international bands. Thus, a recent reviewer of the Stereophonics' latest album hails the band as being "imbued with a Welshness" and "a South Wales blue-collar communality" while at the same time finding the music "bathed in monolithic rock archetypes", likening its sound and lyrics to the hard-rock style of Australian AC/DC and (the very American) Bon Jovi and Guns N'Roses.[28] Anyone vaguely familiar with the band's quite middle-of-the-road pop might have problems with bringing either verdict into line with the actual listening experience, yet the review is an adequate reflection of how the Stereophonics like to portray themselves. In a similar vein, Catatonia, whose songs have been characterized as "populist", "out-and-out pop" or "Melody FM" universals,[29] make a point of introducing themselves as "young, Welsh and feisty"[30] on their official homepage, while the singer carefully tends her "fearsome reputation as wild woman of the valleys".[31] Here again, it seems, national identity is rather part of the attitude than of the music. Not quite so, however. There is one song by Catatonia that ambiguously incorporates Welsh elements in a rather complex statement about national identity. The title track of the band's second album *International Velvet* (1998), an obvious allusion to the 1944 film *National Velvet* about the English Grand National steeplechase, consists of verses sung in Welsh and an English two-line chorus that goes "Every day when I wake up / I thank the Lord I'm Welsh". At first glance, the song appears to bluntly convey petty nationalist sentiments rather than the 'internationalism' evoked by the title. Has the band's usual flaunting of Welshness here turned into boisterous and senseless provocation? Not surprisingly, Catatonia's guitarist is reported as saying that "hopefully [the track] will get everyone to hate us".[32] Such an interpretation, however, would completely disregard the role of the music and its subtle interplay with the lyrics. In both the verses and the chorus, words and music do not fit neatly together but create a meaningful tension. The Welsh verse – in itself remarkable for English-singing Catatonia – is reinforced by lyrical markers of Celticness. The fairly impressionistic text celebrates Wales as "the land of song" and its tunes as "beauteous"; the crooning singer poses as "a shy Welsh woman" who has "the song of the lonely swan in [her] chest" and there is a mention of "the harvest", "the flame", "a feast" and "graves", which all seem to belong to a discourse of prehistoric origins.[33] Ironically, the music accompanying these lines, however, is not a version of Welsh folk but an offbeat reggae that keeps stopping and going and is played with grungily distorted guitars. The melodious and retrospective singing is undercut by a modern 'cosmopolitan' beat: Jamaican rhythm and Anglo-American instrumentation have come to be the vehicles of Welshness. Thus, a sense of regional belonging is happily (and playfully) reconciled with other, more global identities. The point made here seems to be: Welshness makes up only one part of a modern person's identity. All quaintly retrograde conceptions of it should be checked, counterbalanced, and not be allowed to gain the upper hand. This is supported by the power-chord rock chorus that carries the seemingly blatant patriotic lines. Although the musical style becomes bombastic, the tone of the singing is neither jubilant nor proud. The words are drawn out, forced; their repetition produces a schizophrenic, depressed effect. In addition, the chorus-singing coming in later is highly discordant, and eventually this mock-anthem grinds to a cacophonous halt. Compared with the light, pulsating verse, the chorus is tiresome. Sung against the grain, the words lack conviction. The chorus' jingoism is exposed as inadequate, non-viable, and – ultimately – pathological. "International Velvet" is a song that attacks narrow-minded parochialism and national/regional separatism, advocating a multi-layered cultural identity and the capability of an ironic detachment to all of its parts.

Apart from the expression of national regionalisms at UK-level, strong regional discourses can also be perceived within English popular music. Quite frequently these run along the lines of the (cultural) north-south divide. The much-hyped antagonism of 'Northern' Oasis and 'Southern' Blur in the mid-nineties[34] or the phenomenon of Northern Soul of the seventies – a youth dance culture originating in the Midlands and the English North and revolving around old rare American soul records – might testify to this.

A striking example of the employment of a particularly Northern regional discourse can be found in singer-songwriter Billy Bragg's track "Northern Industrial Town" from his album *William Bloke* (1996). Here, the Barking-born socialist makes use of a Northernness that is shot through with working-class identity in order to carry a point about the priority of regional/class affiliations over national, religious or sectarian identities. Both musically – with its vocals plus accompanying guitar-plucking – and thematically, "Northern Industrial Town" follows the tradition of the industrial working-class songs (of Scotland, Wales, and the North) that were promoted by leftist musicians and organizations as folk-music in the post-war years. Endowed with demotic authenticity and the potential for protest, folk, as the 'music of the people', seemed especially apt to convey radical political messages. Tying in with this style, Bragg's song, for instance, shows certain affinities with Ewan McColl's famous "Dirty Old Town" in presenting a 'dead' or 'dying' industrial site that determines (or rather stifles and constricts) the everyday life of its inhabitants:

It's just a northern industrial town
The front doors of the houses open into the street
There's no room for front gardens, just a two-up, two-down
In a northern industrial town

Not specifying which town he has in mind until the last stanza – the name, it is implied, is not important because this could be anywhere in the North –, Bragg goes on to depict, almost to the point of cliché, an image of traditional Northern working-class culture. Life is inevitably organized around football ("And there's only two teams in this town / And you must follow one or the other"), "payday" (when "they tear the place down"), and the public house ("With a pint in your hand and a bash'em out band"). Even stronger than in McColl's song, economic decline has fully hit the people. Living conditions are poor, social opportunities are appallingly restricted. There is mass unemployment, no money for the arts and, as expected, no consolation in religion ("Cos we're out of the black and into the red / So give us this day our daily bread"). The people hold their own, however; they are modest, tough and persistent. The singer's voice, speaking both for and about the people, carries some sense of pride and hopefulness. It is interesting to see how the particular markers of Englishness used by Elton John and Dreadzone are employed here. The green hills, mythical and pleasant in those songs, gain a material quality in Bragg's song. Yet, when they do appear in their greenness, they remain distant and hard to reach for the townspeople. Most of the time, however, they are not green and pleasant at all but rather inhospitable and threatening:

And you can see the green hills 'cross the rooftops
And a fresher wind blows past the end of our block
In the evenings the mist comes rolling on down
Into a northern industrial town

The surrounding hills, which "rise dark in the night", are associated with "mist", "wind", and interminable "rain". Thus secluded and besieged by their environment, the singer is sure that, far from dancing merrily in the old English fashion, the people would rather "dance to the rhythm of the rain falling down". One might say that here the common national symbols have been de-mythified – divested of their ahistoric glory – and then re-interpreted within the context of class mythology. The atmospheric grimness of the song is a symbol of long capitalist oppression and exploitation. Yet, when the singer finally reveals that the town he has been singing about is "not Leeds or Manchester / Liverpool, Sheffield nor Glasgow / [...] not Newcastle-on-Tyne" but Belfast, Bragg's version of Northernness takes on a new dimension. Extending the regional discourse of Northern Englishness to a part of Northern Ireland might, at first, seem like putting the case for strong 'Unionist' ties of the province with the 'mother country'. Far from any such nationalist message, on the contrary, Bragg's song is clearly a reminder that people in the Northern industrial regions of the British Isles might share a common culture and heritage and that sectarian violence and religious factionism have far too long obscured the crucial issue of class politics.

Thus, the regional discourses of both Catatonia and Bragg traverse the conventional borders of their spatial terrains. Both, too, are interlaced with other strong identities besides the place affiliation: Catatonia projects a postmodern, cultural cosmopolitanism while Bragg, more traditionally, brings the social/class identity back in.

5. The Discourse of Mock-Patriotic Englishness

I would like to conclude this overview of some national discourses in British pop music by returning once more to the (supposed/former) centre of things. We have seen that in Elton John's "Candle in the Wind" Englishness is a timeless and given value conceived in quasi-religious terms and bathed in unquestioned national symbolism. Its substance, on the other hand, remains fairly vague and utterly removed from contemporary everyday experience. It cannot come as a surprise that there are younger musicians who favour more critical and youthful versions of Englishness. One such young band that deal with (and in) Englishness are the early Blur. Up to the release of their 1997 U-turning, American-flavoured and self-titled album the group styled themselves as an archetypal English band, mainly in defiant and loud-mouthed opposition to US-American music and culture. Spurned by American audiences, frustrated by the domination of transatlantic grunge music, and then pushed into a battle for the ascendancy of the short-lived, media-driven yet elusive phenomenon of 'Britpop',[35] the band expressed their Englishness at various levels. For one, their own approach to music drew heavily on a distinctly English musical pop heritage, namely the late-sixties sounds of the Beatles (in their Magical Mystery phase), the Kinks, and the Small Faces. Apart from similarities (and sometimes more than that) in song structures, harmonies, vocal quality and sound production, there was also a perceivable orientation towards the lyrical styles of those bands. Thus, it has been noted that Blur, apparently more than any other 'Britpop' group, "often created vignettes or small scenarios out of southern English suburban ordinariness"[36] that recall the lyrics of Ray Davies or Steve Marriot and Ronnie Lane. Critics have not only debated about the extent to which Blur's music and lyrics were indebted to earlier English models, but they have also argued over the cultural and nationalist significance of this harking back to the 'golden years' of 1967/68. Some commentators have maintained that the values behind Blur's retrospective sound and style – like that of Britpop in general – were essentially conservative and reactionary, with the music itself figuring, in museum-fashion, as "a symbol of England's former greatness" or a celebration of a white "outer-suburban, middle-class fantasy" that is informed by "petty nationalism" and negates the experiences of a modern multicultural British society and music scene.[37] The band's style of clothing, publicity shots and promotion material (especially the video clips) seemed to point in a similar direction: the cover of the second album *Modern Life Is Rubbish* (1993) is graced by a painting of the English world-record-holding steam locomotive Mallard while the booklet of the third, *Parklife* (1994), centres round the theme of greyhound-racing, featuring a number of photographs from the ground and a playlist that is layouted in the manner of a racecard. On the whole, Blur's pre-1997 music, lyrics and image appeared to merge into a kind of nationalistic-patriotic supertext that one critic described thus:

> Spitfires, greyhounds, foaming pints of ale, The Shipping Forecast, The Small Faces, The Beatles, XTC, the white cliffs of Dover, DMs, Fred Perrys, the District Line, Portobello Road, sugary tea, *Quadrophenia*, Club 18-30, bank holidays, a nobly streamlined steam locomotive rushing along the tracks of London and North Eastern Railways ... As Blur navigated the 'Parklife' and 'Modern Life is Rubbish' albums, they verged on becoming some rock Routemaster offering a guided tour of British nationhood.[38]

Critics accusing Blur of unqualified English reactionism – the band does move within a discourse of Englishness rather than "British nationhood" after all –, however, cannot hold their ground after a closer reading of the band's texts. Peter Bennett has already pointed to the modern subject matter of their songs, which is merely delivered, at times, in a retrospective guise.[39] Moreover, although the band might have had in mind a critique of the Americanization of culture and, hence, by implication highlighted their native way of life (apart from some explicitly jingoist anti-

American interview statements), English culture is never dealt with in a celebratory, glorifying mode. Blur, on the contrary, like playing with conventional imaginings of Englishness, in their songs as well as in their self-projection. This is illustrated, for instance, in their two promo photos "British Image nos. 1 and 2",[40] the first of which shows them in a defiant yob posture complete with mastiff, whereas the second finds them stiffly draped around a living-room settee having a 'cuppa' tea and exuding unbearable sophistication and effete upper-class snobbery. There are other pictures in which they play out the stereotype of the faceless City clerk or, as on the back cover of *The Great Escape* (1995), impersonate conformist, latter-day computer yuppies. As far as the music goes, we can say that here too, Englishness is ironized and held at bay critically – and this is not only because of some recent 'corruption' of English culture through 'detrimental' foreign influences. What is criticized is not the modernization of culture as such but rather the stubborn adherence to old concepts (of national culture) which then opens up a grotesque discrepancy in people's everyday experiences. Two of these central English myths the band wryly comments on are the country ideal – which we have already encountered in a more sublime context in John's song – and the cultural institution of the English Sunday.[41] In their song "Sunday, Sunday" (1993), the day of collective national recreation and commemoration, of family gatherings and the Sunday roast holds none of the traditional values usually associated with it. The feeling of community – familial or national – appears to be legislated, forced upon the individuals; it is a coerced construction of the nation by virtually defunct, meaningless rituals. In contrast to that, Sunday is exposed as the day on which everyday suburban tedium and inertia come to a head and petty bourgeois narrowness is most oppressive:

> Sunday, Sunday here again in tidy attire
> You read the colour supplement, the TV guide
> You dream of protein on a plate, regret you left it quite so late
> To gather the family around the table, to eat enough to sleep
> Oh, the Sunday sleep
> Sunday, Sunday here again a walk in the park
> You meet an old soldier and talk of the past
> He fought for us in two world wars and says the England he knew is no more
> He sings the Songs of Praise every week but always falls asleep
> For that Sunday sleep
> [...]
> And Mother's Pride is your epithet, that extra slice you will soon regret
> So going out is your best bet, then bingo yourself to sleep
> Oh, the Sunday sleep

The humdrum ritualization of this Sunday experience – emphasized through phrases like "again", "every week", "always" – is borne out by the listing of stereotypical activities: dressing in one's Sunday best, watching telly, reading the Sunday papers, the Sunday walk and bingo, eating and, most importantly, sleeping. Sleep is both the apex and the embodiment of Sunday boredom, but it is also one way of escaping the drabness, symbolizing that irrepressible urge to get away from the enforced community which is a constant presence in the song (other attempts are reading the "*colour* supplement", the TV guide, dreaming, going for a walk, or generally "going out"). Everything that might inspire the feeling of togetherness, such as communal activities or communication, is conspicuously absent. The integrative function of the communal Sunday lunch is lacking too: lunch is a travesty of the traditional meal, a mere "dream of protein on a plate" and slices of mass-produced toast. Moreover, Sunday has lost its spiritual or religious meaning, it is completely secularized. Cherishing the national past, which is an essential part of the traditional religious value of this day of rest, lies with the old soldier who is too weak to see it through and too much of a cliché to go beyond the trite statement that everything used to be better in former times. Hence, the only attempt at communicating and establishing a vital link with tradition remains abortive. The soldier's "Songs of Praise" have the same flimsy affective-emotional impact on the member of the younger generation as the tradition-faking brand name of "Mother's Pride". Obviously, Blur do not long for a re-Christianization or a traditional revalorization of the Sunday. Instead, the satire is poked at those who hold on to the empty shell of a reactionary idea: the singer is clearly not taken in by the hoax of this national myth that the addressee, the "you" in the song, still tries to uphold, regretting "to have left it quite so late / To gather the family around the table" despite the blatant failure of this plan. The band's ironic detachment can also be gauged from the musical texture which with its jolly upbeat rhythm – once trenchantly called the "chimney sweep" style by Oasis' singer Liam Gallagher[42] – and its joyful horn section seems to convey a naïve happiness at the arrival of yet another Sunday – a musical message that takes the side of the simple-minded 'you' character in the song and stands in sharp contradistinction to the actual grimness of the occasion.

It is a similar irony that informs the jaunty tune of the no. 1 hit single "Country House" off *The Great Escape*. Here we are told the story of a City businessman who has come to riches and social esteem (by not always legal means), moving to the countryside in order to, on the one hand, get away from city life and, on the other, fulfil the socially desirable ideal of converting money into a luxurious country lifestyle, thereby living out the centuries-old myth of a rural England. Just like the English

Sunday, however, the rural idyll is another version of Englishness which does not work out the way it should:

City dweller, successful fella
Thought to himself
Oops I've got a lot of money
I'm caught in a rat race terminally
[...]
Caught up in the centuries anxiety
It preys on him, he's getting thin
Now he lives in a house, a very big house in the country
Watching afternoon repeats
And the food he eats in the country
He takes all manner of pills
And piles up analyst bills in the country
It's like an animal farm
Lots of rural charm in the country
[...]
Oh, it's the centuries remedy for the faint at heart,
A new start

Rural England, the song suggests, is a sham, a projection foil for upper-middle-class and upper-class fantasies of Englishness. There is no ancient remedial power connected with it. The corrupt and stress-ridden city dweller gone country gent still needs the TV set, drugs, and psychoanalysis for his spiritual well-being. Moving from the "rat race" to an (Orwellian) "animal farm" is indeed like leaping out of the frying-pan into the fire. This is not realized by the character in the song who keeps on believing in the clichéd notions of the "rural charm", "morning glory" and reinvigorating qualities of country life. Yet, if, paraphrasing Stanley Baldwin, England still is the country, and the country still is England, Blur paint a dour picture of both. The 'country', first and foremost, emerges as nothing but an ideological concept that serves as social cement, as an unreachable elysium for the masses that cannot afford to move there but feel they do have a share in it by being part of the English nation, while the actual place is used as a playground by those who have enough money to turn it into private property.

In conclusion, it should be made clear that Blur is by far not the only white guitar-based (pop/rock) act that reflects on British/English national identity. The scenes of 'English' relationships, commuter routine and suburbia portrayed by female-fronted Sleeper or the recently more politically committed lyrics of Gene, which deal with the band's disillusionment with New Labour, are only two further examples.[43] What is more, the very national myths tackled by Blur – the park/country life and the Sunday –

are also taken up by other English groups. When the threesome indie project Black Box Recorder released their debut album *England Made Me* in 1998, the title song, expressing a "moral bankruptcy allied to an English middle-class upbringing" similar to Graham Greene's 1935 novel of the same name,[44] dealt with the kind of person the English garden/countryside brings forth, which is, in this case, a withdrawn, private yet relentlessly cruel psychopath who, although travelling all his/her life "never got away / From the killing jar / And the garden shed". Another song, "Hated Sunday", evokes an atmosphere of total seclusion from the outside world, which, although at first seeming reassuring, turns out to be in fact deadly paralysis and a spurious and hypocritical attempt at glossing over the rotten and "disturbing" real conditions of (English) life. Family relationships have here, for instance, come down to the obligatory phone call: "Your sister calls / She's in hospital / [...] Your brother calls / He wants money". The sarcastic chorus of "It's good to be in England on a Sunday / Dear old dismal England on a Sunday", delivered with morbidly fragile vocals by the singer Sarah Nixey, verges on the macabre, going far beyond Blur's still more optimistic, less embittered approach to the English Sunday.

Notes

1 For a definition of popular music and a discussion of its relationship with 'youth' see Shuker (1994: 6-10, 226-227).
2 Quoted in Oldham (1999: 23).
3 On the cultural dominance of the Anglo-international repertoire and the corporate industries see Negus (1996: 173-174).
4 There have been critical musical responses to this assertion (and to the related exploitation of the idea of a new, compassionate but also 'cool' Britannia by Prime Minister Tony Blair). On their latest release *Cruel Britannia* (1998), the ska oldtimers of the Selecter, for instance, criticize New Labour for their social imbalances and attack the general callousness and (limousine liberal) hypocrisy of British society ("The bed was so rosy / The talk was all cheap / [...] All fun and sushi / Dressed up so sweet / [...] You can't deny / It's all a lie ... Goodbye / Cruel Britannia"). The Selecter's social criticism even extends to the cover of the album (which contrasts a quite optimistic picture of the "Empire Windrush" with an image of a British West-Indian sleeping on the ground in front of a brick wall, destitude and homeless as his piece of cardboard states) and the selection of cover versions that include the social protest reggae classics "Better Must Come" (which was already instrumentalized in Jamaican politics in 1972) and "What a Confusion" (with passages like "Man will soon start eating man / Cost of living rising / While poverty flowing / [...] The fat is laughing while the meagre is crying").
5 Wordsworth (1975: 48): "I Travelled Among Unknown Men" (1801).

6 Wordsworth (1975: 48): "Lucy Gray; or, Solitude" (1799).
7 Blake (1971: 488; my emphases).
8 Giles & Middleton (1995b: 22). Rooted in the nineteenth century, the identification of 'England' with 'rural England' has held constant appeal throughout the twentieth century. It seems to have been particularly strong in the inter-war years (cf. Stanley Baldwin's 1924 speech "England is the Country, and the Country is England") but is still going strong today, as could be witnessed in 1993 when John Major conjured up the image of an eternal white middle-class England of warm beer, village cricket and spinsters cycling to evensong. See also Lunn (1996: 86-87; 97-98).
9 Howkins (1986: 80).
10 Kumar (1995: 91-92).
11 Considering the controversies over the concept of 'multiculturalism', it seems important to clarify how the term is understood here. It does not denote the kind of simple cultural tokenism Salman Rushdie once criticized for "being little more than teaching the kids a few bongo rhythms [and] how to tie a sari" (Rushdie 1991: 137) or the 'white colonization' of non-white musical styles that is actually often practised in popular music when a mainstream song, in order to make it sell, is spiced up with some 'exotically' ethnic embellishments. Multiculturalism has also been identified to stress, in an essentialist manner, difference, exclusion and separation rather than similarity and integration (see Quadflieg 1994: 154-155). Here, however, in connection with the concept of national identity, which in itself always strives to create (or feign) homogeneity, the term is merely used to refer to constructions of the nation that, on the one hand, allow for ethnic and cultural diversity, and, on the other, result from authentic and sincere hybridizations of different ethnic experiences. The outcome of such constructions might well be inclusive and, more than likely, non-essentialist.
12 An example would be the black British reggae band Steel Pulse from the seventies, whose songs, as on their first album *Handsworth Revolution* (1976) for instance, centred on the familiar Rasta theme of 'tribal war in Babylon', using Jamaican reggae mythology in order to criticize black living conditions in Britain. 'Babylon', in Rastafarian discourse, stands for oppressive and corrupt Western society, which enslaved and forcefully exiled (Caribbean) Africans from their homeland.
13 Quoted in Negus (1996: 108). Hebdige originally used the phrase to describe the appropriation of reggae and ska rhythms by white (punk rock) bands such as the Clash at the end of the seventies.
14 For a story of British pop that does justice to these postcolonial influences see Andrew Blake (1997: 76-119; here: 106).
15 On the early development of dub see Hebdige (1987: 82-89).
16 As would be expected of a dub song, there is more than one version of "Little Britain": the single with vocal track and lyrics is featured on the soundtrack of Kureishi's film (*My Son the Fanatic*, 1998), while there is also an instrumental version of the song on Dreadzone's second album *Second Light* (1995).
17 See Blake (1971: 489, 796).
18 These quotations are taken from two songs of Asian Dub Foundation's third album *Rafi's Revenge* (1998), "Black White" and "Dub Mentality", which explicitly deal with the purpose and the values of the dub movement. The band,

founded in 1993 by five young men of Indian and Pakistani descent, see themselves as a music collective that tries "to agitate, educate and organize" young, particularly Asian, people, stressing self-empowerment and self-sufficiency and trying to instil an awareness of historical issues as well as of social/racial injustice ("Asian Dub Foundation. Biography").

19 Blake (1997: 199).

20 Here, the 1999 Last Night might be taken as a case in point for this new tendency. "Rule Britannia", delivered by a Jamaican-born soloist with Union Jack headband, was greeted frenetically not only by audiences in the Royal Albert Hall and in Hyde Park, but also in Swansea, one of the new sites of Proms in the Park live transmission, where the crowd sported a host of Welsh dragon flags.

21 At a time of massive racial discrimination, police violence, the sus-law, and so-called 'race riots', the rather militant overtones of Johnson's dub poetry were hardly surprising. With a Black Panther background and influenced by Marxism, Johnson spoke up for the self-assertion and self-empowerment of British ethnic minorities, rallying these to collective political action. In the songs, the relation between minorities and host society, on the whole, remains one of 'us' and 'them', 'England' is seen as foreign and hostile. "It Dread inna Inglan" is a case in point: [...] right now, / African / Asian / West Indian / an' Black British / stan firm inna Inglan / inna disya time yah / far noh mattah wat *dey* say, / come what may, / *we* are here to stay / inna Inglan" (Johnson 1991: 21; my emphases). Compare this with the carefree and inclusive "This is our land" of "Little Britain".

22 Apache Indian's style, soon termed 'bhangramuffin', draws on a derivative of bhangra folk and the reggae-derivative ragga (which was identified as *the* principal musical form of the expression of blackness at the beginning of the nineties, and, provoking moral outrage due to the sexual explicitness of a lot of its songs, was adopted by other subcultural youth groups). The degree of accomplished fusion of both musics can be guessed from the fact that Apache's first record "Movie Over India" (1990) topped both the British reggae and bhangra charts.

23 "Asian Dub Foundation. Biography".

24 *Ibid.*

25 Band leader Tjinder Singh described the scope of the record thus: "Something for everyone: from country to brunch with hip-hop, cricket on the lawn with Punjabi folk music and square-dance before dinner with the most righteous of beats" ("Cornershop: *When I Was Born for the Seventh Time*").

26 Back (1995: 12).

27 A much more thorough account of recent South Asian musical production in Britain is, of course, given by Sharma, Hutnyk & Sharma (1996a). Theirs is a committed attack on hegemonic, eurocentric scholarship that is seen to fetishize and exoticize marginality, celebrating otherness and hybridity in an attempt to evade matters of epistemic and racial violence, social inequality, and radical politics (that would deserve the name). Trying to avoid that pitfall, I think it is important to mention that large parts of Asian dance artists do not content themselves with – and should not be reduced to – musical gestures of hybridity or mere symbolic 'subversions' of dominant cultural codes. Politics, anti-racism, and the furthering of community-centred consciousness are high on the agenda, not only with such outspoken groups as Fun^Da^Mental, ADF

or Hustlers HC, and much of the music's fundamental "capacity to implode [...] contemporary cultural racisms constituted through exclusionary narratives of nationhood" (1996b: 6) arises from its direct (lyrical and thematic) antagonism to liberal multiculturalism (see interview with ADF's Chandrasonic in the present volume).

28 Wilkinson (1999: 78-79).

29 See the reviews of their second and third albums: Wilkinson (1998: 77); Cigarettes (1998: 39); Perry (1999: 80).

30 "About Catatonia".

31 Cigarettes (1998: 39).

32 Quoted in Wilkinson (1998: 77).

33 Here, I have to rely on the translation provided on the internet at www.durandal.easynet.co.uk/catatonia/international_velvettab.html ("Lyrics of Catatonia"). The original lyrics are: "Deffrwch Cymry cysglyd gwlad y gân / dwfn yw'r gwendid / bychan yw y fflam / Creulon yw'r cynhaeaf / ond per yw'r dôn / 'Da' alaw'r alarch unig / yn fy mron [...] / Darganfyddais gwir baradwys Rhyl / Gwledd o fedd gynhyrfodd Cymraes swil".

34 This phoney, media-induced 'battle of the bands' (stylized into an antagonism of "self-conscious southern pop stars versus bluff northern rock realists") culminated in the summer of 1995 when Blur's and Oasis' new singles were simultaneously released to top the single charts, and Blur's victory even made the evening news (Moy 1999: 76).

35 For a short introduction to 'Britpop' see Moy (1999), for a detailed discussion Bennett (1998).

36 *Ibid.*, 18.

37 These verdicts by Mark Fisher and Jon Savage are quoted *ibid.*, 17, 22.

38 Wikinson (1997: 80).

39 See Bennett (1998: 19).

40 These are reproduced in Wilkinson (1997: 81).

41 Taken Blur's retro-ness at this stage, it is hardly surprising that their song about the English Sunday has a precursor (with which it shares similarities in its rhythmic quality, 'circus' sound, and singer's pose) in the Small Faces' classic "Lazy Sunday" off the seminal *Ogden's Nut Gone Flake* (1968).

42 Quoted in Harris (1997: 98).

43 Prominent examples include Sleeper's "In-betweener" from *Smart* (1995), with a couple's life revolving around "[k]eeping the rain off her Saturday hairdo" and "cleaning his car on his pebbledash driveway", "Feeling Peaky" from *The It Girl* (1996), featuring a couple that is caught in the rat race with "monday morning fiction on the tube then sorting out the daily mail", or "Rollercoaster" from *Pleased to Meet You* (1997), introducing the anaemic suburbanite Mr Morgan, whose "flowers in [the] garden / Make a lovely display". Gene, on their latest offering *Revelations* (1999), abandon the usual universality of pop in favour of an outright topical record that not only voices severe political criticism of the Labour Party and the former left in songs like "Mayday" – where "Bevan spins round in his grave" and the "[p]eople need to see / The new enemy" –, but also comments on the general face of Britain and its 'national character' after 1 May 1997 in a song like "Love Won't Work", which – in the style of the Selecter – is highly sceptical of the alleged gain in humanity

and compassion ("Now we've entered / New Britannia / Lord don't tell me / Love won't work / […] Now I come first").

44 Giles & Middleton (1995a: 7).

Discography

Apache Indian: "Magic Carpet". – On *No Reservations*, 1993, Island, 731451411229.

Asian Dub Foundation: "Black White", "Dub Mentality". – On *Rafi's Revenge*, 1998, London Records 90/FFRR, 731455600629.

Black Box Recorder: "England Made Me", "Hated Sunday". – On *England Made Me*, 1998, Chrysalis, 724349390720.

Blur: "Sunday, Sunday". – On *Modern Life Is Rubbish*, 1993, Food/EMI, 077778944225.

---: "Country House". – On *The Great Escape*, 1995, Food/EMI, 724383523528.

Bragg, Billy: "Northern Industrial Town". – On *William Bloke*, 1996, Cook/Cooking Vinyl, 711297150025.

Catatonia: "International Velvet". – On *International Velvet*, 1998, Blanco y Negro/Warner, 639842083423.

Dreadzone: "Little Britain". – On *My Son the Fanatic. Original Soundtrack Recording*, 1998, MCI, 5032697000105.

Gene: "Love Won't Work", "Mayday". – On *Revelations*, 1999, Polydor, 731454711920.

John, Elton: "Candle in the Wind 1997", 1997, Mercury/PolyGram, 731456810928.

Johnson, Linton Kwesi (Poet and the Roots): "It Dread inna Inglan". – On *Dread Beat and Blood*, 1990 ([1]1977), Virgin, 077778731726.

Selecter: "Cruel Britannia", "What a Confusion". – On *Cruel Britannia*, 1998, Snapper, 636551281225.

Sleeper: "In-betweener". – On *Smart*, 1995, Indolent/BMG, 5016555600720.

---: "Feeling Peaky". – On *The It Girl*, 1996, Indolent/BMG, 743213647722.

---: "Rollercoaster". – On *Pleased to Meet You*, 1997, Indolent/BMG, 743215335122.

Suede: "Crack in the Union Jack". – On *Head Music*, 1999, Nude/PolyGram, 5099749424395.

Bibliography

"About Catatonia", http://www.catatonia.net/old_browsers/index.html.

"Asian Dub Foundation. Biography", http://www.asiandubfoundation.com/bio.html.

Back, Les: "Fe Real: Apache Indian. Combination Style and Dance-Hall Culture", *British Studies Now* 6, July 1995, 11-13.

Bennett, Peter: "Britpop and National Identity", *Journal for the Study of British Cultures* 5, 1998, 13-25.

Blake, Andrew: *The Land without Music. Music, Culture and Society in Twentieth-Century Britain*, Manchester, 1997.

Blake, William: *The Poems of William Blake.* Ed. W.H. Stevenson, London, 1971.

Cigarettes, Johnny: "Review of Catatonia: *International Velvet*", *NME*, 31 January 1998, 39.

"Cornershop: *When I Was Born for the Seventh Time*", http://www.wbr.com/cornershop/wheniwasborn/cmp/biography.html.

Giles, Judy & Tim Middleton: "Introduction". – In J.G. & T.M. (Eds.): *Writing Englishness 1900-1950. An Introductory Sourcebook on National Identity*, London, 1995a, pp. 1-12.

---, ---: "The Ideas and Ideals of Englishness". – In J.G. & T.M. (Eds.): *Writing Englishness 1900-1950. An Introductory Sourcebook on National Identity*, London, 1995b, pp. 21-25.

Harris, John: "Review of Blur: *Blur*", *Select*, March 1997, 98-99.

Hebdige, Dick: *Cut 'n' Mix. Culture, Identity and Caribbean Music*, London, 1987.

Howkins, Alun: "The Discovery of Rural England". – In Robert Colls & Philip Dodd (Eds.): *Englishness. Politics and Culture 1880-1920*, Beckenham, 1986, pp. 62-88.

Johnson, Linton Kwesi: *Tings and Times. Selected Poems*, London, 1991.

Kumar, Krishan: "'Britishness' and 'Englishness'. What Prospect for a European Identity in Britain Today?" – In Nick Wadham-Smith (Ed.): *British Studies Now Anthology. Issues 1-5*, London, 1995, pp. 82-96.

Lunn, Kenneth: "Reconsidering 'Britishness'. The Construction and Significance of National Identity in 20th-Century Britain". – In Brian Jenkins & Spyros A. Sofos (Eds.): *Nation and Identity in Contemporary Europe*, London, 1996, pp. 83-100.

"Lyrics of Catatonia", http://www.durandal.easynet.co.uk/catatonia/international_velvettab.html.

Moy, Ron: "Britpop". – In Peter Childs & Mike Storry (Eds.): *Encyclopedia of Contemporary British Culture*, London, 1999, pp. 75-76.

Negus, Keith: *Popular Music in Theory. An Introduction*, Cambridge, 1996.

Oldham, James: "The Fan-ish Inquisition", *NME*, 8 May 1999, 22-24.

Perry, Andrew: "Review of Catatonia: *Equally Cursed and Blessed*", *Select*, May 1999, 80.

Quadflieg, Helga: "Across Borders, beyond Borders. Perspectives of a Multicultural Society", *Journal for the Study of British Cultures* 1, 1994, 149-172.

Rushdie, Salman: *Imaginary Homelands*, London, 1991.

Sharma, Sanjay, John Hutnyk & Ashwani Sharma (Eds.): *Dis-Orienting Rhythms. The Politics of the New Asian Dance Music*, London, 1996a.

---, ---, ---: "Introduction". – In S.S., J.H. & A.S. (Eds.): *Dis-Orienting Rhythms. The Politics of the New Asian Dance Music*, London, 1996b, pp. 1-11.

Shuker, Roy: *Understanding Popular Music*, London, 1994.

Wilkinson, Roy: "What Have We Done …?", *Select*, March 1997, 78-88.

---: "Review of Catatonia: *International Velvet*", *Select*, February 1998, 77.

---: "Review of Stereophonics: *Performance and Cocktails*", *Select*, April 1999, 78-79.

Wordsworth, William: *William Wordsworth. Selected Poems.* Ed. Walford Davies, London, 1975.

Merle Tönnies, Bochum

Problematic Youth Identities in Contemporary British Drama

As the sociology of literature began to recognize in the 1970s, theatre is especially suitable for examining constructions of identity because it highlights the creation and adoption of roles that – according to sociological role theory – form the basis of everyday human interaction.[1] Thus, it does not come as a surprise that notable works of contemporary British drama use the medium to examine issues of identity in a context where they gain particular prominence, namely as young people try to define their own roles in their immediate environment and in society at large. In the plays under consideration, this process is made more difficult by severe social problems which the young characters have to cope with. From among the various 1990s dramas dealing with youth identities, the present study will focus on an especially notorious one, Mark Ravenhill's *Shopping and Fucking*, which was premièred at the Royal Court Theatre Upstairs in September 1996, then went on a tour of the UK and transferred to the London West End (Gielgud Theatre) in June 1997.[2] This play will be examined against the background of two works from the previous decades, both of which were first produced at the Royal Court: Nigel Williams's classic *Class Enemy* of 1978 and the now perhaps less well-known but award-winning *Road* (1986), the first play of Jim Cartwright, whose 1990s dramas are almost as (in)famous as Ravenhill's and Sarah Kane's.[3] Through this comparative 'historical' perspective it will become possible to ascertain how the conditions and responses of youth as perceived by the playwrights have changed over the decades.

1. Dismal Conditions

Although Williams's play is set in South London and Cartwright's in a small Lancashire town, both locations satisfy every single criterion of a 'bad neighbourhood' in a similar manner.[4] The residents are so poor that long trousers, meat (*CE*, 42, 62), new clothes, sufficient heating or their favourite shampoo (*R*, 36) are all equally out of the question for them, and the surroundings are characterized by extreme squalor: Just as in the "Road" with its broken sign and derelict houses Carol complains, "Nowt's nice around me" and expresses her fervent wish "to be clean" (*R*,

82), so the attempt of Racks's father to introduce a little beauty into his environment ends with his geranium guarded "[l]ike a fuckin' bunker. Like a tank cemetery" to keep the sordidness of the outside world from claiming it (*CE*, 29). Before the hyperbolic image, the whole absurdity of such an endeavour is already obvious from the complete inability of Racks's mates to understand why one would want nice-looking surroundings anyway. Gang leader Iron goes even further by rejecting the whole idea of brightening up one's surroundings as hypocritical "lipstick" (*CE*, 30). Violence, on the other hand, is accepted by the characters as a natural element of their world: "you go ter ver winder ter watch ve ambulances go past or ter check up 'oo's bin stabbed on ver pavement dahn below" (*CE*, 27). The elimination of the fourth wall in *Road*[5] is partly designed to make the audience see drunken fighting – in a similar vein – as no more than a half-comic, half-annoying interlude when Marion and Brian pursue each other in the theatre building. Most of the young characters' homes do not provide any shelter from this atmosphere of misery and aggression. Nipper's father drinks and is incontinent, while Iron's parents have regular fights under the influence of alcohol and Snatch's father has thrown him out, so that he now has to live in a hostel. Interestingly enough, the parents of Skylight, the most positive and constructive figure in *Class Enemy*, at least seem to have a functioning relationship though even here misery is not excluded: they are both blind. It is thus only logical that the lads refuse to go home as an alternative to staying at school: "Thass why." (*CE*, 15) In *Road*, such broken homes are not only described but dramatized: Carol and her alcoholic mother insult each other, Eddie and his father do not seem to be on speaking terms, Chantal's mother expressly announces that she is not worried when her daughter is chatting up men in the audience, and twelve-year-old Linda has to clean up after her drunken father and Marion, the woman he has picked up.

Against this background Cartwright's metaphor is almost over-explicit when he has blood from Marion's injured thumb drip on Linda's face (63). Psychoanalytic implications aside, it is already as obvious as possible to the audience that young people growing up under such conditions will hardly ever have the chance to leave the "Road". In *Class Enemy*, this idea is echoed by Iron: "What we need is a ticket out of 'ere" (11), i.e. there is no way they can get away through their own effort. The plays are thus pervaded by a sense that there is no future and that life can therefore be no more than an empty routine. The exact forms the playwrights' critical impetus takes, however, differ in the two works. As the setting makes clear, Williams's focus is on education, first of all in its institutional context. From this perspective, his work is a scathing attack on the authorities, who give up on the unteachable group and simply leave them to their own devices, hoping that they will drift into the streets and thereby become the police's business (75-76). Iron logically continues this train of thought when he tells Sweetheart he was already abandoned when he came to an understaffed school with absolutely no resources or indeed when he was born in an area where it was clear that no-one cared for him (46). But even when the formal requirements of 'education' are met, this does not mean that the authorities are accepting their responsibility, as is shown when the lads parody some of the teaching they have received:

> NIPPER: 'How do you feel that your environment affects you?' [...] 'Do you feel that the urban environment situation leads to poverty and despair in the Inner City?' [...]
> IRON: [...] Never even fuckin' taught us anyfing. Jus' 'urban' 'iss an' 'urban' that an' fuckin' essays abaht woch yoo done lars' Sat'day. I don' call *that* ejucation. (7-8)

Thus, they are neither satisfied with sociological rhetoric – which of course sums up the situation accurately – nor with attempts to focus on their everyday concerns. In addition to the lads' own perspective, the play makes the spectators see for themselves how little help this 'teaching' has been: Whenever the characters try to express something beyond routine communication and therefore want to use Standard English instead of their socially marked South London dialect, they quite literally lack words, so that Sweetheart is "trembling with the effort" to continue (21; see also Snatch, 54) and Racks and Skylight, who are slightly more articulate, involuntarily reproduce linguistic clichés of advertising and advice manuals (25, 62-65). All of them are thus extremely ill-equipped for finding their own voices and defining a place for themselves in society (which is exactly what teaching should enable children to do), and they seem to be at least subconsciously aware of this defect.

Apart from an accusatory element, their repeated protestations that they "don' know nuffink" (54, see also 19, 81) therefore betray a desperate thirst for knowledge, which is personified in Sweetheart's fantasy of the ideal teacher walking towards their classroom and also comes to the foreground in Iron's suggestion that they teach each other. Paradoxically, of course, they have at the same time constantly been destroying all chances of acquiring knowledge, as Sweetheart inadvertently demonstrates: he would like to hear the rest of the story of Antony and Cleopatra, which was begun by a teacher before they hit him with a hammer (46). This paradox may be partly explicable by their dissatisfaction with the teaching provided, but it also has wider implications. Iron attacks Sweetheart's 'teaching' on the grounds that he has provided nothing but "facts": "Where was ver fuckin' knowledge in woch yoo said? Were was sunning ter give us a lit'l lift up eh? A lit'l 'elp eh?" (21). Genuine "knowledge" would thus go beyond practical skills to helping them to make sense of their situation: "the queschion we all wanner answer i.e. Why Are We 'Ere An' 'Oo's Fault Is It?" (37). Although he only admits it openly in a moment of extreme distress, Iron knows that such answers do not exist ("No one got knowledge. Ain't no fuckin' knowledge to be 'ad nowhere in ver wide fuckin' world", 81), which makes him reject all attempts to impart knowledge as hypocritical – just like trying to make the surroundings look more beautiful. In the play, Nipper and Skylight demonstrate that Iron's experience of meaninglessness is no exception. In an involuntary parody of National Front discourse Nipper's 'lesson' shows the attractiveness of straightforward 'explanations' in a world that makes no sense and has constantly made him feel excluded from everything (42). The extreme simplicity of his 'theory', however, at the same time allows the more intelligent Iron to see through its absurdity very easily and to mock Nipper in an implicit appeal for independent thought instead of ready-made ideas: "Let the lad talk. Facts. Figures. Less give 'im a chance. I mean 'e's obviously bin 'finkin' abaht vis fer a long time" (40). Skylight is similarly proof against racist ideology though his main defence is his warm humanity, which cannot accept such distinctions ("Blacks is people ain't they?", 39) and directly makes him consider the consequences for the West Indian member of their group, Snatch.[6] It is this basic approach to life which makes Iron beat up Skylight violently as he cannot bear his optimism. Skylight, however, continuously refuses to recognize that the feeling of senselessness which he shares with Iron could be more than a stage they have to pass through. He sticks with his belief that someone will come very soon and "they might be the bes' we' ad [*sic*] yet. [...] We might never argue when vere 'ere. We might jus' know. An' 'oo's ter know – they might come on wiv' so much fuckin' knowledge we won't be able ter move fer knowledge. We'll 'ave arrived" (81-82). However, the author ends the play neither with Skylight's hope nor with Sweetheart's dream of the teacher on his way to them but with the bell which announces that school is over. He thus seems to uphold Iron's rather than Skylight's point of view; the bell after all means that – contrary to Skylight's belief – no teacher will come at least on that day, so that on a deeper level 'knowledge' in the sense of a meaningful existence is at best deferred indefinitely.

With Cartwright, the lack of perspectives for young people takes a classic form from the perspective of Marxist-oriented social theory: unemployment.[7] In the town in which the play is set having lost one's job is an everyday experience shared by all age-groups. This widening of scale compared with the special case of the notorious 5K in *Class Enemy* also manifests itself in the use of a regional accent instead of one that in the first place signals a distinct London underclass. As Eddie puts it, "England's in pieces. [...] My town's scuffed out. [...] Don't weaken, or you're Dole and Done" (*R*, 81), and Clare even has visions of someone losing "the last job on earth" (45). Marion's clichéd 'advice' to Linda that "whatever it is [what Linda wants to be when she grows up] luv, stick at it and you'll get there" (64) thus turns into keenest sarcasm. The young people in the play are hit particularly hard because besides all the obvious aspects, a job for them meant a continuous, structured way of learning to live their lives (see Clare, 36) – just what education should provide but is already shown to be failing in by Williams. The young characters of *Road* consequently share the desperate longing for a sense in life which manifests itself in the earlier play, and like Williams's lads apart from Nipper, they have come to realize that ready-made ideologies (in this case communism) are no help: "[t]here's not one thing to blame" (39). At the same time, they are equally unable to respond like Skylight and Sweetheart with hopes and dreams of how the situation is going to improve. This is even true on a very personal level: Whereas with Racks the wish for a meaningful existence takes the form of the old romantic dream of the ideal partner waiting for him somewhere out there (*CE*, 13), Joey cannot even transcend the feeling of emptiness in his real, functioning relationship with Clare. On the whole, Cartwright's adolescents seem to be much more thoroughly disillusioned than the adults, so that Linda for instance does not even bother to answer Marion's question about her career plans, as she has understood that choice and personal fulfilment have long become impossible. From among the attitudes shown by Williams, it is thus Iron's – authorially approved – determination to face up to meaninglessness that is closest to *Road*'s young characters and calls for more detailed comparative study.

2. Young People's Reactions

Iron's most pronounced characteristic is the immense tension which makes everything he says and does both hectic and aggressive. He is desperately trying to stay in control, and as there are so many important circumstances he cannot influence, he clings to what can be controlled, i.e. the other lads – and his own feelings. Iron only allows himself to react with either derisive laughter or anger, which becomes especially obvious through his increasing viciousness when something threatens to take down his defences by arousing his interest (like Snatch's window story) or pity (like the situation of Skylight's parents). Showing one's feelings is, of course, often seen as a weakness in an adolescent male context, but for Iron there is more at stake. If he abandoned his pose of superiority and distance from events, senselessness might suddenly have a full emotional impact on him, which would be unbearable. This renders Iron unable to establish a relationship on any but the most superficial terms. Characteristically, the cohesion of his gang depends on a hierarchy of physical strength[8] and a shared opposition to the rest of the world, particularly to those in authority like teachers, whose appearance immediately makes the lads forget all internal differences. It is thus logical for Iron to conclude, "[m]y frien's are the cunts 'oo 'ate my enemies" (68); any form of mutual understanding would constitute a dangerous opening up in Iron's situation, as Skylight realizes: "none of us ever told each ovver nuffink" (66). At the same time, however, Iron is constantly suppressing his wish to express and share feelings, as becomes obvious to the audience – if not to the lads – when Skylight describes the gang leader as having no feelings (32, 66). Tellingly, Iron's most violent outburst occurs after Skylight has pronounced him unable to respond emotionally to music (79-80); by smashing up the classroom Iron tries to cover up the "desperate longing to be liked" made explicit in the stage directions (81) and to re-assert his superiority over the events.

In the first place, Williams thus presents violence as an eruption of the unbearable tension caused by conflicting impulses in the individual in the face of a dead-end situation. In addition, Iron's exhaustive list of people "'oo put us in this dump" (including lollipop men, 48-49) and whom he 'fights' in the final scenes of the play demonstrates his conviction that senselessness is not simply a given but society has somehow failed him by allowing such a situation to come about, so that violence becomes his way of fighting back. This also includes revenge for being excluded from both material possessions and rights, a mechanism personified by Snatch, who starts breaking windows when he realizes that his ethnic origin will always prevent him from becoming a full member of the dominant culture represented by the shop decorations. His urge to continue with this activity on an ever increasing scale and the subsequent switch to writing his name on walls at the same time point to an underlying wish to be acknowledged and recognized by society as an individual. Iron sums up these interrelated responses when he explains to the teacher that "ve on'y 'fing we don' lay waste to is ours. An' nuffink's ours. You ain't given us nuffink an' wot you give us you take away at your convenience" (75). Seen positively, this reasoning means that the vicious circle of violence might be broken once the authorities allowed the lads to feel they had some responsibility and a share in society's goods.[9] Given Iron's overall violent tension, it is, however, still doubtful whether such a strategy would work with Williams's lads – and quite apart from that, the audience know for sure that nothing along these lines will ever be tried in the world of *Class Enemy*; the Master only replies, "You're not fit for ownership Herron" (75).

In Cartwright's play, the young characters' response to meaninglessness undergoes a shift in focus. They are much more courageous than Iron in letting emptiness have its full impact on their lives, even though they realize that this is only possible in exceptional states of mind. Joey and Clare go on a hunger strike to reach beyond everyday reality, while Eddie and Brink introduce Carol and Louise to the practice of hard drinking accompanied by Otis Redding's music "[t]o stop going mad" (82), to find release from pent-up tension. Tellingly, Brink uses this moment of a consciously induced loss of control to describe that he "always keep[s] tight in front of people", i.e. his starting point is similar to Iron's situation but he manages to go beyond it by acknowledging his feelings. Alcohol, which interestingly enough does not play any role for the characters of *Class Enemy*, thus has slightly more positive connotations for the adolescents in *Road* than for the adults, for whom it provides nothing but temporary oblivion. Indeed, rational considerations aside, one almost feels that the young people's chant of "Somehow a somehow, might escape" at the end of the play might build up energy that could really change something, perhaps if more characters and – in keeping with the play's tendency to break down the fourth wall – also the spectators joined in. After all, in contrast to Skylight and Sweetheart's dreams in *Class Enemy*, this moment arises from facing up to senselessness first: Carol for instance states explicitly that she wants to break away from the routine of meaningless one-night stands that characterizes their and their parents' usual idea of a night out. Moreover, the experience in *Road* is a shared one which posits community as a potential counter-value.

The characters of *Road* thus do not worry so much about getting their own back from society; indeed, Joey cannot even answer Clare's question if they are protesting (after all the usual purpose of a hunger strike) in any definite way (36). Violence consequently plays a much smaller role for the adolescents in this drama, again in contrast to the parent generation. Even Skin-Lad, whose fighting practice on stage initially recalls Iron's sparring, ends up describing how he has embarked on a spiritual quest and turned Buddhist. Characteristically, this search for meaning moves far beyond Iron's longing to find out how the dismal situation in which he finds himself came about; while clearly missing their normal working routine, the young characters of *Road* at the same time have got an inkling that maybe such an existence where "[t]hey rush you from the cradle to the grave" (41) does not make any more sense than their present lives. What they have lost can thus suddenly appear as a kind of gain, "a standstill" where one can at last ask the questions otherwise lost in the daily hustle and bustle. Although the search for the meaning of life is, of course, an almost clichéd project for young people, their acute suffering is conveyed to the audience as Joey and Clare are even prepared to die in this venture. Ironically, the "message or [...] sign" (44) Joey has been waiting for indeed seems to get through to him immediately before his death – but it only consists in the realization that there is no solution. Aware of the audience's tendency to ignore such depressing conclusions, Joey anticipates their response by the tongue-in-cheek observation that they will add "a 'maybe'" (46) to his statement anyway. He thus gives the pessimistic ending of the first act the same status as the potentially positive result of the second act's spiritual search (see above), and the play as a whole is kept both more balanced and vaguer than Williams's more straightforward diagnosis of Iron's psychological set-up.

3. A Shift towards Consumer Identities

In 1990s drama about youth issues, the dismal conditions in which Williams and Cartwright show young people to be growing up stay virtually the same. However, these surroundings recede into the background of the audience's attention. In *Yard Gal* and Enda Walsh's Irish play *Disco Pigs* (1996), for instance, the problems of surviving among poverty, drugs and violence in Hackney and in a boring, fairly run-down Cork neighbourhood only provide the backdrop for the relationship between the respective two characters on stage. The development of their feelings for and treatment of each other rather than their response to the conditions in which they find themselves are the focus both of the play and of their own interest. In a similar manner, Ravenhill's *Shopping and Fucking*[10] examines the two intersecting hetero-/homosexual 'eternal triangles' formed by Lulu/Robbie/Mark and Robbie/Mark/Gary respectively. As the title indicates, these relationships are presented as being influenced by pervasive commercialization rather than by unemployment, violence, squalor and the lack of perspectives, all of which are nevertheless still present. Thus, the play can almost be said to mirror the shift that has occurred in critical theory from analysing society in terms of production in the Marxist tradition (where unemployment would loom large, as in *Road*) to a concentration on consumption, the sphere of commerce, as a paradigm for social relations.[11] Against the background of the recurring jingle of coins (23, 24, 32, 40, 41) and in a world where individual choice can only be understood to refer to the selection of products (12, 26), feelings can no longer be what they used to. Already Louise in *Road* bewails their replacement by "profit and loss" (83), but in Ravenhill's play this development is dramatized on an unprecedented scale. Most obviously, Lulu and Robbie's telephone sex business and Gary's work as a rent boy can only flourish because there are "so many sad people in this world" (50), because 'normal', non-commercial forms of interaction are no longer working. In his private life, Gary is looking for a more personal relationship, and his dream of the right person somewhere "out there" (63) has distinct romantic overtones. However, he can still describe his preference for sexual domination and violence instead of loving tenderness only in terms of a financial transaction: "I want to be owned" (54). Commercialization is thus not simply the opposite of meaningful contact but is always included in any relationship. This becomes most obvious with Lulu, Robbie and Mark: They have ritualized the memory of their first meeting into "the shopping story" (2), the designation of which refers both to Lulu and Robbie's activity when Mark spots them and to the way they come into contact. After a stereotypical love-at-first-sight recognition that they are meant for each other, Mark buys the couple at a bargain price from their previous owner, who has grown tired of them, and this leads to a conventional ending of living happily ever after. Through this intermingling of business and romance, the drama demonstrates to the spectators that it is no longer possible to differentiate between 'genuine' feelings and affections professed in return for payment.

Throughout, the commercialization of feeling is epitomized by the drugs the characters both take and sell. In contrast to the role of alcohol in *Road*, they neither stand for temporary oblivion, nor for transcending everyday life in search of meaning, but pinpoint the issue of genuineness. Thus, Robbie insists that selling Ecstasy means spreading happiness which is as "real" as the "planet" itself (17-18): 'real' feelings and artificially induced ones no longer belong to different categories for him. In accordance with his higher level of awareness, Mark at least questions this equation and wants to find out whether "there are any feelings left" because "for so many years everything [he has] felt has been ... chemically induced". He is therefore wondering – together with Gary – whether even without drugs what they feel might not be caused by coffee, cigarettes or still more obscure influences (31-32). The difficulty of identifying 'real' feelings is only increased by Mark's realization that relationships work like drugs for him, in other words, that he tends to get addicted to people and "to define [himself] purely in terms of [his] relationship to others" (30), losing his sense of self in the process. Ironically, the only way for him to establish a stable identity thus consists in transforming relationships into pure "transactions" where the money paid and received makes it clear that it "doesn't actually mean anything" (16, 22). Thereby sex becomes just another product to be consumed and commercialization reigns supreme, eliminating all chances for genuine feeling.

The loss of the 'genuine' is also represented metaphorically by the microwaved ready meals which are consumed so often on stage that Michael Billington's review of the first production calls their "vile smell" "the chief sensory impression left behind" by the play (1996: 6). Pre-packed in plastic containers with cellophane covering and specifically designed for long-term storage, such convenience food is the epitome of mass-produced artificiality as opposed to the natural freshness of home-cooked meals. Typically, Lulu describes their food as offering access to "all the tastes in the world", which previously could only be sampled by invading the respective countries (59). Industrially produced "tastes" and genuine ones are thus all the same to her, and the characters quite literally internalize commercial artificiality throughout the play. Robbie, however, refuses to eat his meal at one point because "it doesn't taste of anything" (*ibid.*), i.e. he has a rare moment of insight into what essential elements are missing in their lives. His apparently foolish failure to sell the Ecstasy provided by Brian can thus be seen as a desperate attempt to break out of the vicious circle of commercialization by handing out "happiness" for free. Quite apart from Brian's retaliation, however, this venture is doomed to failure from the start because refusing to sell the drugs still does not make the feelings induced by them any more 'real'; the atrophying effects of commercialization are thus still making themselves felt.

This points to a general dilemma in the world of the play: Even though sensing at some points that they have lost something, the characters have no clear idea of what this might be, and even the author does not oblige the audience by creating an unequivocal counter-concept of genuineness. As opposed to the virtual sex Gary predicts for the near future (20), the actual sexual encounter between Gary and Mark draws blood – a fairly conventional metaphor for affecting someone genuinely. In the age of AIDS, however, blood simultaneously signals danger, prompting Gary to protest immediately that he is not infected (24). Similarly, after Robbie has been beaten up, Lulu is busy disinfecting his wound, explaining that "with blood[...] [i]t might get infected" (32), and when Lulu has witnessed the stabbing in the Seven-Eleven, she is aghast that some of the victim's blood has splashed on her face and frantically tries to wipe it off to get "clean" again (27). The use of this adjective is significant in two ways. Firstly, it clearly has positive connotations (one may want to recall Carol's wish "to be clean", *R*, 82) and thus makes the spectator realize why it would be very hard for the characters to step out of the polished world of artificiality into messy reality again – even if they could do it. After all, secondly, 'clean' also denotes 'free from drugs' and is indeed employed in this sense later on in *Shopping and Fucking* (71), so that the word can be taken to refer to both the genuine and the artificial at the same time, thereby taking the confusion of concepts to its limits. Ravenhill plays on this slippage even further by introducing the figure of Brian. He professes to stand for genuine feeling and pure beauty when he presents to Lulu and Robbie the video of his son playing cello, which moves him to tears and which he specifically distinguishes from the (commercialized) music in supermarkets or discos (43). At the same time, however, the audience knows that this person is a drug dealer, and the playwright takes great care to foreground the ensuing ironies: After an inquisitorial examination,

Robbie has to admit that the handkerchief he has offered to Brian for wiping his eyes is not "clean" (44). Brian rejects it indignantly and uses his own "pristine" one (45), thus personifying the stereotype of the drug dealer who washes his hands of the effects of his wares and – in the context of the play – mixing antiseptic artificiality with his demonstration of 'natural' feelings. More directly, Brian himself reveals the non-commercial "purity" (*ibid.*) of the son's musical talent as fundamentally dependent on his own commercial efforts and submits Lulu and Robbie to the educational test of earning the money they have lost – not because he wants it but because he wishes them to learn that "[m]oney is civilization. And civilization is [...] [m]oney" (85). This scheme seems to be especially successful with Robbie: when Lulu disconnects the phones because she can no longer bear the complete take-over of their private lives by commercial sex, Robbie accuses her of not wanting to live (58). Apart from his understandable fear of Brian, this also shows to what extent he has already assumed the role of 'adopted son' which Brian is constantly holding out to him: "We're making money. [...] We're gonna be all right. [...] We've been working. We're making money. We're good at it aren't we?" (50, 56) From wanting to rebel against commercialization, Robbie is thus co-opted into the system, and it is more than likely that he and Lulu will accept Brian's offer to join his all-embracing project for making money, ostensibly in order to create "purity" in some future generation (87). In a final ironic twist of concepts, this venture will move from drugs to something 'purer': TV shopping as the distilled essence of commerce.

Despite Brian's victory and the intermingling of categories, however, 'real' feelings prove more resilient than both the characters and most of the reviewers seem ready to believe.[12] Mark is significantly not turned on by shopping, as Gary at first suspects, but by Gary's presence, and after trying to reduce this response to purely physical attraction, he then admits that "there's an attachment" (53). Gary in his turn denies that he feels anything for Mark, but even he strikes a blow against commerce when replying to Robbie's question "You on special offer?" that Mark does not have to pay him (61). The 'eternal triangle' constellation of characters in itself focuses on surviving feelings: Lulu is clearly jealous of Robbie's relationship with Mark, while Robbie goes mad to the point of physical violence because of Mark's love of Gary, and even Gary – for all his claims of aloofness – has his share of jealousy when Mark relates a sexual encounter with a woman (73). Ironically, jealousy is, of course, generally understood to be closely linked with the wish to 'own' someone, and it thus does not seem to take the characters very far away from the mixture of feelings with commercial relations. However, in the play it can also draw the two categories apart, if only momentarily. This becomes especially obvious when Lulu expresses her belief that she and Robbie will be better off on their own[13] by telling Mark, "You don't own us. We exist. We're people" (5), thus expressly rejecting their ritualized ownership story. In this context, the pre-packed meals acquire another metaphorical function: As Lulu explains, "[i]t's actually very difficult to share them actually [*sic*] because they're specifically designed as individual portions" (60). The commercial layout thus forms an ideal pretext for isolating oneself – as Lulu demonstrates twice when she feels that Mark is intruding upon her relationship with Robbie (18, 60). However, after apparently capitulating to the impossibility of sharing, she later offers to fetch some means of changing the pre-arranged portions, and in the final moments of the play Lulu, Robbie and Mark are seen feeding each other in a picture of mutual care and understanding that overcomes all industrially designed separateness. Characteristically, Mark presents a variation on the "shopping story" immediately before this scene in which at some point in the distant future, he buys an attractive mutant in the usual "transaction" (88) – and then sets him free, even risking that he might not survive. Lulu seems to welcome this elimination of ownership from personal relations, and Robbie grudgingly grants that "[i]t's not bad" (*ibid.*). Thus, it seems that if all the characters agreed to do "the best [they] can do" (*ibid.*), there might still be a chance for 'real' feelings – even if only in the future and (as the continuous presence of 'synthetic' food suggests) although it might not be possible to get rid of all traces of artificiality at once.

4. Story-Telling as a Strategy for Young People?

Apart from concentrating more closely on relationships and on the influence of commerce and consumption, 1990s drama on youth issues differs from earlier examples through an increase in the importance of narratives within the plays. Most obviously, both *Yard Gal* and *Disco Pigs* consist only of stories told and partly enacted by the respective two characters.[14] *Yard Gal* differentiates more clearly than *Disco Pigs* between the time levels of the events and of the narration, but characteristically this does not create a distance from the stories for the audience. On the contrary, the play calls for an intimate staging – as in the German première at Grillo-Theater Essen in 1999 – where the two women's stage presence draws the spectator into the poignancy both of their shared past and of their subsequent separation. Such story-telling belongs to a completely different category than the narrative sections in *Road*: Scullery's presentation of "'JOEY'S STORY'" is a classic Epic Theatre technique, and the Professor's records of personal episodes from the Road create a similar distance from the events through the recording business (22-24). It is thus rather the much more muted narrative elements in *Class Enemy* that can be seen as precursors of the 1990s plays, as they involve the audience in experiences relived by the characters. The lads show surprising creativity when relating and enacting events or imagined occurrences in the group (e.g. 6, 12-13) and are strikingly unimpaired by the linguistic limitations that trouble them when they are called upon to 'teach' on their own. However, whereas in *Class Enemy* joint story-telling is at best a way of momentarily rising above the situation in a glorification of the group's exploits, the young people of *Yard Gal* and *Disco Pigs* use it for coming to terms with their lives and creating an identity for themselves.[15] It thus seems at least possible that the feeling of meaninglessness which troubles Iron could be overcome through a shared narrative which 'made sense', even though this point is never addressed explicitly in these two 1990s plays.

It is Ravenhill's drama which brings the connection to the foreground not only of the spectators' but also of the characters' minds. Although – in contrast to *Yard Girl* and *Disco Pigs* – the plot as a whole unfolds directly before the audience instead of being narrated and enacted by the characters, it is pervaded by stories on a very large scale. In a whole row of scenes one of the characters relates to another what has happened to him/her – Mark to Robbie when he comes back from his treatment, Lulu to Robbie and vice versa when they have each been involved in violent incidents and Gary to Mark about the authorities' inability to stop his stepfather's abuse. In all of these cases, there is not simply one straightforward narrative but the addressee constantly introduces his or her own versions of a possible sequence of events which are then rejected or accepted by the speaker. It thus seems as if the characters' lives consisted of an intricate web of potential stories and 'actual' incidents represented only one of these options. The situation becomes even more complex when one considers imaginary occurrences like Lulu, Robbie and Mark's "shopping story" and Mark's Fergie story: they have exactly the same status as accounts of actual events in the play,[16] so that telling one's life becomes at least as important as living it. This point is made explicit in an almost literal paraphrase of Jean-François Lyotard's famous thesis about "incredulity toward metanarratives" in the postmodern age (1984: xxiv):

> ROBBIE: I think we all need stories, we make up stories so that we can get by. And I think a long time ago there were big stories. Stories so big you could live your whole life in them. The Powerful Hands of the Gods and Fate. The Journey to Enlightenments [*sic*]. The March of Socialism. But they all died or the world grew up or grew senile or forgot them, so now we're all making up our own stories. Little stories. It comes out in different ways. But we've each got one. (64)

The feeling of meaninglessness, which troubles especially young people in *Class Enemy* and *Road* and can no longer be assuaged by "big stories" like National Front ideology or communism, would thus loom large in *Shopping and Fucking* as well, if the characters were not constantly proving themselves true postmodernists by telling and enacting their individual "[l]ittle stories".

This is particularly true for the "game" (65) near the end of the play, in which Robbie, Lulu and Mark undertake to 'realize' Gary's dream of the "bloke" who will come and take him away (63-64). The narrative proceeds in a mixture of telling and performance, and it inadvertently blends with the "shopping story" of the three 'assistant narrators'. However, even though Gary does not recognize the "fat bloke" of this story, its overall drift is so close to his own that he can fill in the term "transaction" without any difficulty (77-78) – another demonstration of how central a factor commerce has become in the characters' world. Indeed, the whole process of helping Gary to make sense of his life is itself a "transaction", as Robbie makes clear from the start: "Pay me and you'll get what you want" (64). Interestingly enough, though, when Robbie hands Gary over to Mark, he repeats the motif from the "shopping story" without the financial element. It thus seems as if Robbie realized that – despite his earlier protests and his offer of tenderness instead of violent sex – Mark is naturally suited to the part Gary wishes to have played and that in the interest of getting as close as possible to the "pictures in [Gary's] head" (76), they have to change places immediately. And it turns out that he is right. Whereas Gary did not respond at all to Robbie, he accepts Mark as the embodiment of his father he has been longing for: "I know who you are. So finish it" (81). At this point, however, it becomes obvious that the characters' expectations do not match. For Gary, a fictional story alone does not suffice; he pushes young people's desire for 'making sense' to its limits: "I thought you were for *real*. Pretending isn't it? Just a story" (83, my emphasis). He wants his dream to be 'realized' not simply in performance but by crossing the boundary between fictionality and 'reality'. His phrase "there's only one ending" (83) equates the two realms: taking the term 'life story' as literally as possible, the desired ending of the story would at the same time end his life. Such a 'realization' scares Robbie and Lulu, but characteristically Mark is prepared to play the role to the very end in both senses, so that the spectators know it is "for real" when Mark is seen to start telling Gary's story again at the end of Scene 13.[17] This ending of the "game" retrospectively gives a deeply sarcastic edge to all declarations of the power of narratives, as well as presenting the complex relationship between the artificial and the genuine in the play from yet another angle. For the audience, it is therefore finally doubtful whether story-telling can at all be a strategy for young people to 'make sense' of their lives. At the same time, the potential optimism of the last moments of the drama pointed out above comes to look hollow when the spectators remember how the characters have managed to pacify Brian and to (re)create this idyll.

All in all, *Shopping and Fucking* can be seen to examine key issues of its time with regard to their implications for young people. Compared with *Class Enemy* and *Road*, there are definite shifts in the focus of the audience's attention and in the characters' behaviour. The dramatists' method of representing the problems that interest them is, however, comparable in all three instances: Ravenhill's play has been said to deal with an extreme, untypical section of society or to resemble a "clever, [...] disturbing cartoon",[18] by which the critics either censure or applaud the uncompromising intensity and concentration of the work. In exactly the same way, Williams and Cartwright focus on groups which as such may not be representative of 'youth' in the 1970s and 1980s but which pinpoint difficulties young people of the decade typically had to struggle with. Rather than constituting an exceptional case as to method, *Shopping and Fucking* thus continues to work with a quality of drama that makes it especially well-suited for the treatment of problematic identities quite apart from role theory: its ability to draw the spectators into the action and to affect them much more directly than a written account would do, which one could lay aside at will. In pursuing this strategy, all three dramatists touch upon or infringe taboos of their decade for the sake of intensity, so that in this 'historical' perspective, Ravenhill's play loses much of its 'shocking' singularity and it becomes easier to examine the wider issues involved – which are unsettling enough in themselves.

Notes

1 See especially Goodlad (1971: 39-40) and Burns (1972: 1-2).
2 Since then the play has also been performed at the Queen's Theatre London, and it went on another UK tour in 1998.
3 *Road* won the Samuel Beckett, Drama Magazine, George Devine and Plays and Players Awards and was adapted for BBC Television in 1987. It was called "the most significant and original new English play to appear in London for a long time" by Michael Ratcliffe (1986) and "the play of the year" by David Nathan (1986).
4 References to the plays will be included in the text, preceded by "*CE*" or "*R*" where necessary.
5 The Royal Court productions of the play intensified this characteristic of the script through promenade-style performances that placed the spectators on stage together with the actors.
6 The optimistic implications of Iron and Skylight's reactions to racist ideology are curiously absent from Bernhard Reitz's detailed analysis of this aspect of the play (1995: 109-129).

7 The playwright himself was unemployed at that time (see Shorter 1986). Robert Gore Langton calls the younger characters of the play "supremely convincing" (1986: 25).

8 SWEETHEART: I can do Racks Nipper can do me Skylight can do Nipper and Iron can do ver lot of us. (32)

9 For this point see Rebecca Prichard's *Yard Gal* (1998) where Boo concludes: "[w]e liked it [a squat the girls tried to make a little more homely] 'cos it was ours" (31).

10 References to the play will be included in the text. Apart from Gary, who is fourteen, the characters are not given a fixed age in the play. In the original production, which Out of Joint prepared in close collaboration with the author, they had a "quasi-innocent youthfulness", but even in the Gielgud version where they were "by no means kids" (Macaulay 1997: 19) the play still showed them as engaged in a quintessentially adolescent search for their place in society and a stable identity. This preoccupation clearly includes Ravenhill's work among 1990s British youth drama.

11 See especially Baudrillard (1998) and Jameson (1991).

12 An exception is Billington (1996: 6).

13 See also "LULU: [...] Wish we could go back to before. Just you and me." (29)

14 This has prompted Michael Billington's half-sarcastic comment that for Prichard, 'plot' "is more a description of the action" than Aristotle's "imitation" (1998: 14).

15 Andreas Rossmann has called this strategy "Erzählen als Versuch der Selbstbehauptung" (1999: 41).

16 With regard to the Fergie story, Robbie repeatedly insists on being told the truth. However, the other characters dismiss these questions as irrelevant, and Robbie himself is obviously motivated by a jealous desire to vent his anger on Mark rather than any real wish to know about all the details; indeed, he finally settles for an almost parodistically inaccurate account (70).

17 The threat of the 'real' is not only felt by Robbie and Lulu but has also found expression in critical responses (see e.g. Billington 1996: 6). After all, transferring Gary's story from the fictional to the 'real' within dramatic illusion brings it one step closer to the audience's reality.

18 The first point is Billington's (1996: 6), the second Macaulay's (1997: 19).

Bibliography

Baudrillard, Jean: *The Consumer Society. Myths and Structures*, London, 1998 [French original: 1970].

Billington, Michael: "Effing Blind Cynicism", *The Guardian*, 3 October 1996, 6.

---: "*Yard Gal*. Royal Court Theatre Upstairs", *The Guardian*, 13 May 1998, 14.

Burns, Elizabeth: *Theatricality. A Study of Convention in the Theatre and in Social Life*, London, 1972.

Cartwright, Jim: "Road". – In J.C.: *Plays One*, London, 1996, pp. 1-89.

Goodlad, J.S.R.: *A Sociology of Popular Drama*, London, 1971.

Jameson, Fredric: *Postmodernism, or, the Cultural Logic of Late Capitalism*, London, 1991.

Langton, Robert Gore: "*Road*", *Plays and Players*, August 1986, 25.
Lyotard, Jean-François: *The Postmodern Condition. A Report on Knowledge*. Tr. Geoff Bennington & Brian Massumi, Manchester, 1984 [French original: 1979].
Macaulay, Alastair: "Thrills at a Price", *The Financial Times*, 30 June 1997, 19.
Nathan, David: "Review of *Road*", *The Daily Mirror*, 20 June 1986 (quoted from *London Theatre Record*, 4-17 June 1986, 651).
Prichard, Rebecca: *Yard Gal*, London, 1998.
Ratcliffe, Michael: "Review of *Road*", *The Observer*, 15 June 1986 (quoted from *London Theatre Record*, 4-17 June 1986, 647).
Ravenhill, Mark: *Shopping and Fucking*, repr., London, 1998.
Reitz, Bernhard: "'Ver Blacks Done It'. Zur Thematisierung von Rassismus und Gewaltbereitschaft in den Dramen Barrie Keefes und Nigel Williams'", *anglistik & englischunterricht* 57, 1995, 109-129.
Rossmann, Andreas: "Unter die Haut. Prichards *Yard Girl* im Theater Essen", *FAZ*, 20 February 1999, 41.
Shorter, Eric: "Review of *Road*", *The Daily Telegraph*, 31 March 1986 (quoted from *London Theatre Record*, 26 March - 8 April 1986, 313).
Walsh, Enda: Disco Pigs *and* Sucking Dublin. *Two Plays*, repr., London, 1998.
Williams, Nigel: *Class Enemy*, repr., London, 1995.

Gerd Stratmann, Bochum

'Absolute Beginners' and Their Heirs in Contemporary British Novels

The hectic succession of competitive and ever-changing youth (sub)cultures, accelerated by the greedy impatience of a global media market, has made any generalization on 'youth' at the turn of the twenty-first century virtually impossible. The elements of the *bricolage*[1] of a given 'young' fashion, music style or behavioural pattern are being modified and replaced at a breathtaking rate. It frequently seems to take only weeks before a cultural innovation has become the victim of commercialization.

Thus it is with a certain nostalgia that we look back to the fifties when the teenager was 'invented' as a distinct identity with a whole set of comparatively well defined identity markers. The general excitement and/or indignation which accompanied this process (especially in Britain) must sound, to the more cynical observers of today, almost touching. Separated by nearly half a century, the respective concepts of youth, then and now, do not seem to have much in common. Still, as the following examples may demonstrate, it is instructive to remember some of the roots of the present confusion. A comparison between the respective representations of youth – in this case: of influential novels on youth – discloses conspicuous contrasts, but also unexpected continuities.

As Osgerby and others have pointed out, one may discover, long before the fifties, even in Victorian and Edwardian Britain, "in incipient form, the key facets of social and cultural life that we now label 'youth culture'".[2] Such a cautionary statement, however, appears to be almost misleading. The earlier phenomena were local and transitory. The fifties, on the other hand, saw a revolutionary development: a set of new identity constructions conquering, on a national scale, practically all fields of culture, not only the media, popular music, fashion, advertising, but also the more ambitious cinematic, dramatic and narrative forms of representation. One contemporary text stood out as possibly the most complete and prophetic attempt to describe the emergence and the far-reaching claims of a new type of youth culture in the fifties: the novel *Absolute Beginners* by Colin MacInnes (1959).

The protagonist, an affluent photographer of 19, does not doubt for a moment that he belongs to the first generation of teenagers – a blessing which was denied even to his elder brother:

> The trouble about Vernon [...] is that he's one of the last of the generations that grew up before teenagers existed [...]. Even today, of course, there are some like him, i.e., kids of the right age, between fifteen or so and twenty, that I wouldn't myself describe as teenagers: I mean not kiddies who dig the teenage thing, or are it. But in poor Vernon's era, the sad slob, there just weren't any: can you believe it? Not any authentic teenagers at all. In those days, it seems, you were just an over-grown boy, or an under-grown man, life didn't seem to cater for anything whatever else between. (37)[3]

This pride – of belonging to the first generation, of having lived through "the dawn of creation when the teenage thing was in its Eden epoch" (110) – becomes a leitmotif of the book, contributing to the meanings of the title of *Absolute Beginners.* As the father of the nameless narrator (an amateur historian) summarizes, the recent past, i.e. the thirties, was not only an age of poverty and fascism:

> It was a terrible time for the young [...]. Nobody would listen to you if you were less than thirty, nobody gave you money whatever you'd do for it, nobody let you live like you kids can do today. (35)

It was a time, in other words, when the young could not yet claim a recognized identity. The novel gives sufficient space to the narrator to develop his specific identity construction, a construction which appeared to be mainly based on three distinctive features: firstly, the combination of a relative economic independence with minimal social or political responsibilities; secondly, a *bricolage* of identity signals, i.e. an eclectic set of fashion and music elements; and, thirdly, the downgrading or invalidation of other markers (especially class, but also political or sexual orientation, national or ethnic origins, gender).

After Abrams's influential study *The Teenage Consumer* (1959) it became a commonplace to explain the first youth cultures of the fifties by pointing to "a newly affluent body of young people patronizing a youth market of unprecedented scale".[4] As we have learnt in the meantime, the sensational figures offered by Abrams were "grossly simplified",[5] even distorted. This however seems almost irrelevant in our context: that the teenagers of the fifties owed their self-confidence and their 'visibility' to their spending power was an indispensable part of the new mythology. The hero of *Absolute Beginners* repeats it again and again:

> This teenage ball had a real splendour in the days when kids discovered that, for the first time since centuries of kingdom-come, they'd money, which hitherto had always been denied to us at the best time in life to use it, namely when you're young, and strong [...]. (10)

Most of the adult characters of the novel seem to disapprove of teenagers with spending power, not excluding the protagonist's mother ("You've too much spending money, that's your trouble! ... All you teenagers have", 40). This is, as the narrator explains, motivated by pure envy – and by the realization that the attempts to deprive minors of practically all legal rights and responsibilities have backfired in the most grotesque manner:

> You made us minors with your parliamentary whatsits [...]. That also freed us from responsibility, didn't it? Because how can you be responsible if you haven't any rights? And then came the gay-time boom and all the spending money, and suddenly you oldos found that though we minors had no rights, we'd got the money power. [...] You majors find the laws you cooked up have given you all the duties, and none of the fun, and us the contrary, and you don't like it, do you. (40-41)

By sociological standards, this diagnosis was less than realistic. Most of the money in teenage hands was, as all experts agree, the hard-earned money of apprentices and working-class lads, young people, in other words, who *did* have responsibilities and duties and only limited time for fun. This distinguished them from the freelance photographer who tells us the story of *Absolute Beginners*, and his friends who owe their income to similarly irregular forms of self-employment, working as high-class pimps, song-writers or singers, journalists or writers.

Thus, what the anonymous narrator's voice offers is not a realistic assessment – it is a construction. But it was, in the fifties, a construction of tremendous influence. The space inhabited by youth culture (as it is constructed in *Absolute Beginners*) appears to lie outside society and its obligations, to be dominated by a hedonistic freedom, creativity and "fun", but, on the other hand, to produce and demand money and thus to form a market of its own.

One immediately recognizes that this curious self-contradictory construction inspired a number of subsequent youth cultures: a space outside the jurisdiction of social responsibilities and norms, but at the same time a market-place where "fun" generates money and costs money. It would be the same space as that found by Jim Dixon and Charles Lumley at the end of their respective novels, *Lucky Jim* (1953) and *Hurry on Down* (1955). These two proverbial Angries are finally admitted to a world where they earn more than enough money without being dependent on society any longer. They have found, as Charles Lumley explicitly pronounces, "neutrality" at last – in London, i.e. the classless world of arts and the media, of entertainment and fashion. This idea of an island where one could enjoy affluence, fun and creativity without paying the price of social or financial dependence was, of course, utopian. But is was also powerful, decisively contributing to the new identity formations of young people.

One of the reasons why money became such an important part of those constructions was the expenditure demanded by the respective "drag":

> I had on precisely my full teenage drag that would enrage him [i.e. his elder brother] – the gray pointed alligator casuals, the pink neon pair of ankle crêpe nylon stretch, my Cambridge blue glove-fit jeans, a vertical-striped happy shirt revealing my lucky neck-charm on its chain, and the Roman cut short-arse jacket just referred to … not to mention my wrist identity jewel, and my Spartan warrior hair-do […]. (32)

Hebdige has taught us to read such subcultural outfits as 'texts'[6] in which signifiers (taken from vastly different sources) work together according to certain syntactical rules and semantic functions. The composition described in the quoted passage exemplifies some of the principles Hebdige discovered in subcultural self-fashioning: the blending of dramatically contrasting elements (like the crêpe nylon socks and the warrior hairdo), the multi-cultural and androgynous ambiguities, the narcissistic emphasis on the body, the variety of exotic connotations etc. As the context of the quote illustrates, some of the most important 'meanings' of teenage drag were negative: i.e. signifying the refusal to adapt to mainstream dressing codes, the resolution to 'enrage' non-members by being provocatively different.

Thus, *Absolute Beginners* may be read as an introduction to the syntax and semantics of certain sections of contemporary teenage culture. Especially when it comes to picking and integrating the kind of music to go with the new identities, the novel sounds almost didactic. The narrator teaches the reader to distinguish between the outfits of the "trad. boys" ("skiffie survival[s], with horrible leanings to the trad. thing") and the "modern jazz creation" (65). Teenager identities are thus defined by their music styles and fashion items. As to the protagonist's own taste, he doesn't mind a musical bricolage of "ancient English, or modern American, or wierdie minority songs from pokey corners" (139), but insists that the songs should be "about the scene, about us and now".

> And though Zesty caught all the necessary US overtones, […] the words he thought up were actually *about* the London teenage kids – I mean not just 'Ah luv yew, Oh yess Ah du' that could be about anyone, but numbers like *Ugly Usherette*, and *Chickory with my Chick*, and *Jean, your Jeans!*, and *Nasty Newington Narcissus* which all referred to places and to persons which the kids could actually identify round the purlieus of the city. (110)

Again the list provided ironical comments on teenage subculture and the forms in which it expressed itself: its self-reflexive, narcissistic tendencies, its obsessive cross-references (the songs celebrating the jeans or the blue suede shoes), its eclectic predilections.

Finally, and most importantly, *Absolute Beginners* demonstrates again and again that youth culture did indeed create a new barrier (between the young and the adults), but on the other hand invalidated older forms of social departmentalization and discrimination:

> But the great thing about the jazz world, and all the kids that enter it, is that no one, not a soul, cares what your class is, or what your race is, or what your income, or if you're boy, or girl, or bent, or versatile, or what you are – so long as you dig the scene and can behave yourself, and have left all that crap behind you, too, when you come in the jazz club door. (64)

The narrator finds that this ideal of an alternative young culture has been betrayed by the commercial "exhibitionists and moneylenders" (*ibid.*), which is why he changes over from the more popular teenager places to the jazz clubs. But he and his friends – "Spade-crazy" Suzette (14), the homosexual Hoplite ("I think this game of putting everyone you meet in precise sexual categories, is just a bit absurd", 124), the ex-Deb, the Jew Mannie Katz, Mr Cool (half Caribbean, half English) – they all demonstrate their belief that while the wall between mainstream adult society and the young is higher than ever, the differences in class, gender, race, sexual orientation have lost their importance among the young. The narrator, with his working-class background and his handsome income, does not feel any class loyalties:

> I do *not* reject the working-classes, and I do *not* belong to the upper-classes, for one and the same simple reason, namely, that neither of them interest me in the slightest, never have done, never will do [...], I'm just not interested in the whole class crap that seems to needle you and all the tax-payers [...]. (38-39)

This conviction that the new culture of the young implied classlessness was, of course, shared by many commentators of the fifties. Political theorists and social critics of the New Left discussed the issue of classlessness in the pages of *The Left and Universities Reviews*,[7] the scholarship boys in many of the 'Angry' novels considered themselves classless, and at the end of the fifties advertisers and columnists began selling Swinging London and its new elite of young achievers as classless.[8] But it was in the context of early British youth cultures that this axiom claimed a most central importance – which was, in a sense, amazing. The Teddy Boys, for instance, were (in spite of their Edwardian outfit) definitely working-class boys who did not at all believe in the crossing of borderlines. This is why the protagonist of *Absolute Beginners* does not include them in the new teenage movement; for him they have, on the contrary, skipped the teenage stage completely: "The truth is, Ed, […] you've tried to be a man without having been a teenager. You've tried to miss out one of the flights of stairs." (45)

The example shows that our hero finds it difficult to fit all contemporary realities into his model of teenage culture. The book ends with his painful disillusion: when the Notting Hill race riots break out teenagers – "Teds, semi-Teds … you know … local hooligans" (147) – play a central and disturbing role in many of the incidents. Still, there remains the hope, on the last page of the novel, that while there were always "horrors as well as felicities" (217), the young were the only group promising to overcome those petrifications of class, gender, and race.

Absolute Beginners owes its fascination to its prophetic precision – it outlined, long before the discipline Cultural Studies had begun its astonishing career, let alone its debate on identities, a new type of identity construction which turned out to be the prototype of a long line of successors and variants. This British Ur-teenager was defined by his (only rarely: her) consciousness to be a new phenomenon, by his claim to be independent of all social obligations and norms, while at the same time producing and consuming on the growing 'fun' market, by his use of music styles and fashion elements as identity markers, and, finally, by his attempts to invalidate or neglect other markers (especially class, political and sexual orientation, race) in favour of age group.

This construction revealed a number of contradictions and unrealistic elements. In practice some of the first youth cultures were demonstrably under the spell of a marked machismo, and certainly not free from racist or homophobic impulses. Still, that prototypical construction was an important factor during the subsequent metamorphoses.

Looking at some of the more recent novels on the young in contemporary Britain and their 'signifying practices', one might find the differences more striking than the similarities. The selection is, of course, anything but representative – but all of the titles have proved to be bestsellers and/or met with critical acclaim. The titles are: Hanif Kureishi's *The Buddha of Suburbia* (1990), Karline Smith's *Moss Side Massive (*1997), John King's *Headhunters* (1997), and Tim Lott's *White City Blue* (1999). Kureishi's and Smith's novels point to one of the most obvious new developments: Youth cultures have multiplied – the idea of one monolithic identity concept of youth invalidating, for instance, other concepts based on ethnic origins has become difficult to maintain. The X Press, which published *Moss Side Massive*, specializes in Black literature (including its series "Black Classics"), and consequently it will surprise nobody that the two youth gangs fighting their deadly battles in Smith's novel are without exception non-white. Kureishi's books and films present protagonists of Asian origin, but concentrate on the no-man's land between two cultures, one of them English, the other Pakistani. *White City Blue* (winner of the 1999 Whitbread First Novel Award) is, in this respect, as onesidedly white as Smith's novel is black; in other respects, however, it is the most conscious and uncompromising farewell to the older patterns. The novel tells the story of four youngsters (male) who suddenly discover that their little subculture with its rituals, its machismo, its unconditional concept of mutual loyalty has robbed them of their freedom to develop. When the group disintegrates, the protagonist Frank Blue will be able, after all, to discard his obsessive lying and found the family he has been longing for; Nodge, who has all the time suppressed his homosexuality can finally come into the open; Colin becomes a fundamentalist follower of Jesus, and Tony, who used to dominate the group, is now unmasked as a cheap bully and a failure. This study – "a hilarious (but horribly true) account of male friendship"[9] – can be read as a celebration of adulthood after the distortions and enforced conformity of youth. Similarly, *Headhunters* confronts the reader with the self-styled "Sex Division", a highly ritualized, "lager-soaked" group of five young men who have made the pub the headquarters of their sexual campaigns;[10] and again the respective 'happiness' of the ending for the five characters is defined in terms of becoming an adult.

Still, there are interesting echoes of MacInnes. All of the selected novels structure the space in which the (young) identities are developed around the familiar dialectics of social non-responsibility and the market mechanisms of fun and style. Practically all the protagonists and subcultural groups at the centre of the respective novels refuse to be controlled by the social rules of adult society. They either find their independence in eccentric niches, e.g. the arts or popular culture (Charlie and Karim in *The Buddha of Suburbia*), in the hermetically sealed world of gang criminality (*Moss Side Massive*) or in the hedonistic and drunken excesses of bloodbrotherhood. All of them are shown as consumers (of lifestyles, drugs and entertainment), but if they work in 'normal' forms of employment this is never visualized. There is, however, a puzzling difference between the 'post-colonial' authors and their 'English' colleagues: While Kureishi and Smith never leave the charmed circle of 'neutral' space (Charlie and Karim, and the survivors in *Moss Side Massive*), not even at the end of the respective stories, King and Lott, who see the circle as dominated by a kind of black magic, allow some of their protagonists thc liberating experience of breaking the restrictions of youth.

As could be expected, the principles of bricolage have become less prominent in the later novels. Authors writing in the eighties and nineties have already seen an endless sequence of subcultural fashions and styles, all of them immediately commercialized after a short spell of exciting novelty. For many of their characters nostalgia is more tempting than invention – "heavy bass taking [them] back to when they were kids into reggae, dub, punk".[11] Thus the elements going into their self-fashioning are either slightly repressive and escapist, or mainstream and traditional (football, golfing etc.). Again it is Kureishi and Smith who are nearest to the excitement of the fifties. Charlie is a highly inventive master of self-stylization, theatrical, playful, eccentric. And Smith's two gangs (The Piper Mill Posse and The Grange Crew) are almost fetishists when it comes to cars, sun glasses, hairdos or furniture. The reason is obvious: the youngsters of Asian or African origin have, again, to invent their identities, not because they are young, but because they have to integrate their two worlds into a new synthetic construction. It goes without saying that this makes their respective 'blends' of identity markers less tentative and more purposeful than in the case of the 'absolute beginners' – more purposeful but also more fragile:

> On stage [Charlie] wore black leather, silver buckles, chains and chokers, and by the end of the performance he was bare-chested, thin and white like Mick Jagger. [...] He appealed to the people who had the most disposable income, gays and young people, especially girls. [...] But the menace was gone. The ferocity was already a travesty [...].[12]

This clearly sounds like a more cynical version of Hebdige and MacInnes.

A very similar contrast is observable when the competing identity parameters (class, gender, ethnicity) come into focus. King and Lott seem to illustrate that these markers are having, in the nineties, a disturbing comeback. Their young characters are disgustingly male, suppressing everything which might render their image dubious. The members of the "Sex Division" are hunting after women (as a 'lay' gets them four points in their continuing competition); but the dream achievement (ten points) is awarded to those who successfully shit into a lady's handbag. This, intended as a grotesque satire on the obsessions of overgrown English boys, obviously misfires – but the success of the book is an indicator for the cultural changes since the fifties.

Kureishi's protagonists, on the other hand, appear to be the much more credible heirs of these fictitious teenagers and jazz cats of the fifties. True to his famous praise of hybridity,[13] his youngsters in *The Buddha of Suburbia*, but also in *My Beautiful Laundrette* learn to cross all boundaries and unite opposites which seem mutually exclusive. Like so many teenagers in *Absolute Beginners* they are British *and* Pakistani, "versatile" (used by MacInnes to denote bisexuality),[14] playful and professional, outside society, but lucratively catering for an audience which pays for the fun. All of them are 'young Londoners' – which could be called the formula of the resulting synthesis. But 'youth' is no longer the uncontested identity marker, Kureishi being on the whole more interested in the specific mixtures of ethnic ingredients.

Finally, all of these – extremely different – cases seem to play down the category of class. This impression, however, is partly misleading. It obviously applies to Kureishi who in fact demonstrates how his young heroes manage to escape the social pigeonholing practised by their elders (whether English-suburban, or, as in *My Beautiful Laundrette*, Pakistani-entrepreneurial). Neither are there class differences in Smith's closed world of black warfare. But the two 'white' novels both have a central character who is more educated and financially better off than his chums – and in both cases he leaves the charmed circle to start the solid life of middle-class (or yuppie) adulthood. Constructions of youth are still an important factor, for the music industry or for advertising. But in the hierarchy of culturally important identity markers it has lost its priority – and much of its excitement.

Notes

1 Hebdige (1979: 102-106).
2 Osgerby (1998: 6).
3 Numbers in brackets refer to the pages of MacInnes (1959).
4 Osgerby (1998: 25).
5 *Ibid.*, 26.
6 Hebdige (1979: *passim*).
7 E.g. Hall (1985: 57-58).
8 See e.g. Booker (1969), Stratmann (1987).
9 Thus the reviewer of the *Cosmopolitan*, reprinted on the blurb of the Penguin edition.
10 Introductory advertisement in King (1998).
11 *Ibid.*, 29.
12 Kureishi (1990: 247).
13 See Kureishi (1986).
14 MacInnes (1959: 64 *et al.*).

Bibliography

Abrams, Mark: *The Teenage Consumer*, London, 1959.
Booker, Christopher: *The Neophiliacs. A Study of the Revolution in English Life in the Fifties and Sixties*, London, 1969.
Hall, Stuart: "In the No Man's Land", *ULR* 2, 1985, 57-58.
Hebdige, Dick: *Subcultures. The Meaning of Style*, London, 1979.
Lott, Tim: *White City Blue*, Harmondsworth, 2000.
King, John: *Headhunters*, London, 1998.

Kureishi, Hanif: "The Rainbow Sign". – In H.K.: My Beautiful Laundrette *and* The Rainbow Sign, London, 1986, pp. 7-38.
---: *The Buddha of Suburbia*, London, 1990.
MacInnes, Colin: *Absolute Beginners*, London, 1959.
Osgerby, Bill: *Youth in Britain Since 1945*, London, 1998.
Smith, Karline: *Moss Side Massive*, London, 1997.
Stratmann, Gerd: "'Classlessness' – Die kurze Karriere eines Klischees (1955-1965)". – In Günther Blaicher (Ed.): *Erstarrtes Denken. Studien zu Klischee, Stereotyp und Vorurteil in englischsprachiger Literatur*, Tübingen, 1987, pp. 363-372.

Martin Brüggemeier / Horst W. Drescher, Mainz

A Subculture and Its Characterization in Irvine Welsh's *Trainspotting*

Trainspotting by Irvine Welsh is one of Scotland's best-known novels of the 1990s. It depicts the life of a group of young drug addicts who live in one of the poorest Edinburgh quarters. One of the novel's most important features is that it is composed of forty-three originally independent episodes. These episodes deal with very different aspects of the junkies' everyday lives: the consumption of drugs, the different ways of acquiring drugs and money (which, in many cases, involve crimes), the relationships between the group members (who, depending on the situation, help or abuse each other), sexual adventures, social advancement and decline, and finally the (usually abortive) attempts to overcome the addiction. Each of the episodes has its own narrator (a first-person narrator in most cases) and thus also its own specific language. The novel, therefore, is not a one-sided presentation of drug addicts and their environment; the stories are told from a variety of perspectives, and the drug addicts are characterized from insiders' and outsiders' points of view.

This essay analyses the socio-cultural context in which the novel is embedded as well as the important role that language plays in it as a means of characterization. Finally, some comments will be made on the problems of rendering the socio-cultural features and the specific language of *Trainspotting* in a German translation of the novel.

1. On the Edge of Society

The young people in *Trainspotting* are on the margins of society for various reasons. First of all, they belong to the lowest social stratum. They live in housing estates in Leith, a formerly independent city that became part of Edinburgh in 1920 and then suffered from a long period of economic stagnation. Like many inhabitants of these housing estates, the junkies in the novel are either unemployed or live on occasional odd jobs.

Irvine Welsh has lived in the Leith housing estates and was a heroin addict himself,[1] which enables him to draw an extremely realistic image of the drug addicts' lives. Part of this type of realism lies in the use of typical working-class, youth and drug scene slang – including the breaking of linguistic taboos – and the description of sex and violence. This kind of social realism was not accepted by large parts of the readership, and *Trainspotting* has often been criticized for dealing with negative aspects of society which are part of everyday life in the streets and the neglected housing estates and should not be themes of entertainment literature.[2]

Welsh directly contrasts the environment in which the young people in *Trainspotting* grow up with the tourist attractions for which Edinburgh is known. One example of this can be found in the chapter "The First Day of the Edinburgh Festival": When Mark Renton, the novel's main character, is smeared with excrement after recovering an opium suppository that has fallen into an extremely dirty toilet, he realises that it is the first day of the Edinburgh Festival, the town's big annual cultural event. In a later chapter, Edinburgh Castle, one of the city's famous tourist attractions, is compared with the gasworks at West Granton, which represent the poorest of the town's housing estates.[3]

In addition, the young people in *Trainspotting* are marginalized because they belong to the subculture of young drug addicts which rejects many of the generally accepted values of society. The social conditions under which such a form of youth culture can develop are described by Irvine Welsh as follows:

> Nowadays, younger working-class people grow up in a society where the main institutions of socialization, where kids learn morality – the family, the community, the trade unions and the churches – have been emasculated by the promotion of consumerism and the market economy. Nowadays young people grow up exploring a psychoactive terrain, stimulated by computer technology and advertising. For the rampant consumerism of the Eighties had other outcomes: Certain drugs, once the preserve of a bohemian elite, found their way into mass culture.[4]

This statement summarizes many aspects of today's society which are dealt with in *Trainspotting*. An important theme of the novel is the young junkies' attitude towards established values and conventional morality, with the subculture of drugs being characterized as a counterculture to conventional society. Even in their own families, the socialization of these young people is unsuccessful in many cases. Many of the drug addicts in the novel come from broken families. Francis Begbie's father, for instance, is an old alcoholic who has never cared for Francis and who has had relationships with various women (263-264), and Spud Murphy's grandmother was married to several men, from whom she separated when she had had enough of them (125-126). The young people in *Trainspotting* not only live outside traditional family structures – they have no opportunity to learn the traditional values connected with them, such as faithfulness in a relationship. The community cannot provide young people with such values either since it is characterized not only by broken families but also by alcoholism and violence – even among adults. Other institutions which could provide moral values play no such role in *Trainspotting*. The church, for instance, is only mentioned in connection with a funeral ceremony, and the only person who shows religious feelings is a little girl who hopes that her dead father has gone to heaven (294-295).

Furthermore, the subculture depicted in *Trainspotting* rejects the ideals of consumerism. Mark Renton expresses this attitude by commenting on the marketing slogan "Choose life", which propagates a consumption-oriented lifestyle, as follows: "Well, ah chose no tae choose life. If the cunts cannae handle it, it's thair fuckin problem." (188) But what he chooses instead of life is not death but the subculture of drugs with its special norms and values. This subculture, however, is also consumption-oriented in a certain way, although it does not practise the consumerism of the middle classes which aims at finding secure jobs and acquiring status symbols. Instead, it lies in the excessive consumption of drugs, which, to the junkies in the novel, is primarily a means of having fun. The fact that fun is the most important element of drug-consumption is expressed by Renton as follows: "Take yir best orgasm, multiply the feeling by twenty, and you're still fuckin miles off the pace." (11)

Besides the "choose life" attitude of the middle classes, the youths in *Trainspotting* reject many generally-accepted norms of conventional society. This applies, for instance, to the relationships between the group members. True friendships are extremely rare; instead, it is not unusual for the junkies to humiliate each other, and violence among group members is not uncommon either. The most violent of the protagonists is Begbie, who sees himself as the leader of the group. He practises what he calls "the discipline ay the basebaw bat" (147), often gives harsh orders to his mates and attacks those who do not obey him – not only verbally, but also physically. He often beats up strangers without cause, and he even kicks his pregnant girl-friend to the ground. Besides, he is not willing to take responsibility for the child after birth; as he himself puts it: "Nae cunt gits fuckin lippy wi me, bairn or nae fuckin bairn." (112-113) The general attitude of the group members towards each other is also expressed through the use of (sometimes abusive) nicknames. Simon Williamson, for example, is only called Sick Boy by his mates because, as Renton puts it, he is "just one sick cunt" (3). But Renton himself is often referred to by a nickname that he dislikes: the Rent Boy.

However, Begbie is not the only character in the group who uses violence. In fact, all its members consider violence to be acceptable in certain situations. Sick Boy, for example, shoots a bull terrier to cause it to bite its owner, who is a skinhead (179). The most prominent example of this kind of violence, however, can be found in the chapter "Eating Out": Kelly, another group member, who works in a restaurant, is insulted by some guests, a group of business students with upper-middle-class English accents, whereupon she mixes excrement, urine and rat poison into their food. She comes to the conclusion that "under certain circumstances, morality is relative" (305) – an attitude which she shares with the other members of the group. The junkies' attitude towards sexuality is also extremely different from the views generally accepted in society. In most cases, the protagonists have promiscuous sexual relations, and the novel contains various rather detailed descriptions of sexual practices, among them oral and anal sex. Some of the protagonists have steady boy- or girlfriends, but these relationships do not normally last long.

With regard to the systems of values which are presented in *Trainspotting*, it is important to mention two general characteristics of the novel. First, the life of the drug addicts is not described from a one-sided point of view. With the narrative point of view changing from chapter to chapter, the various social groups in the novel as well as their attitudes towards each other are presented from an insider's point of view. *Trainspotting* depicts not only the drug addicts' attitude towards the middle classes but also outsiders' attitudes towards the drug scene, which are often contemptuous as well. The drug addicts' way of seeing drug-consumption primarily as a way of having fun is not understandable for outsiders, who view it mainly as a way of destroying one's own life. Ironically, and partly as a result of this multiplicity, the drug addicts are particularly despised by those who consume other drugs such as alcohol or stimulants. Secondly, it must be mentioned that *Trainspotting* does not convey a moralizing message in any form. Instead, the presentation of the events in the novel is neutral and objective due to the continuous change of the narrative points of view.

To sum up these points, it can be said that the protagonists of *Trainspotting* are on the edge of society mainly for two reasons: firstly because they live in a part of town which is rather low on the social scale, and, secondly, because they are part of a subculture which radically contradicts the norms and values of society. This circumstance, however, has been, to some extent, chosen by these young people.

Another important aspect of the novel is the Scottish socio-cultural context. Themes related to it are those of Scottish national and cultural identity, England's influence on Scotland (which is related to the rivalry between Catholics and Protestants and the conflict in Northern Ireland) and the Edinburgh-Glasgow rivalry.

Due to Scotland's historical development, negative attitudes towards England and the English are not uncommon in Scotland. With the Union of Crowns (1603) and the Union of Parliaments (1707), Scotland lost its independence as a nation. Besides, English culture has had a major impact on Scotland since that time and before. England is therefore seen, in some ways, as a colonial power. Resentment against the English – which, however, does not necessarily go along with feelings of Scottish patriotism – is also widespread among young people. Mark Renton expresses such an attitude in this interior monologue:

> It's nae good blamin it oan the English fir colonising us. Ah don't hate the English. They're just wankers. We are colonised by wankers. We can't even pick a decent, vibrant, healthy culture to be colonised by, No. We're ruled by effete arseholes. What does that make us? The lowest of the fucking low, the scum of the earth. The most wretched, servile, miserable, pathetic trash that was ever shat into creation. Ah don't hate the English. They just git oan wi the shite thuv goat. Ah hate the Scots. (78)

The statement reflects not only contempt for the English but, even more so, the fact that Scotland – according to Renton – is unable to maintain its cultural independence, which makes it even more contemptible since it is losing its specific national identity. Indirectly, Renton's statement is also a call for a new cultural independence for Scotland which could raise the country's prestige.

"Victory on New Year's Day" is one chapter of the novel in which this ambiguous attitude towards the Scottish nation is dealt with. Moreover, it expresses the typically Scottish mixture of national sentiment, religion and football. The protagonist of the chapter is Stevie, who has moved from Edinburgh to London and who has come to his home town to meet his mates. At a New Year's Eve party, they sing Irish folk songs such as "Off to Dublin in the Green", which express love of one's country and also Irish Catholic contempt for the British Crown and for Protestants. The youths at the party sympathize with the IRA and are fans of the football club Edinburgh Hibernian, or 'Hibs'. The supporters of this club are Catholics, and fights between them and the Protestant fans of Hearts of Midlothian, the other Edinburgh football club, occur quite often, for example at the traditional New Year's Day matches of the two clubs. To belong to a particular religious denomination and to support a particular football team also means to express a certain political attitude, i.e. sympathy either for the IRA's fight for independence or for the unionists. This is also expressed in the way in which football fans of both sides attack each other verbally. In various instances in the novel, Hibernian fans are called "Fenians" by Hearts supporters. This nickname refers to the 'Fenians', a nineteenth-century Irish revolutionary organization, a predecessor of the IRA. The Hibernian fans, for their part, use the derogatory term "Huns" for the Hearts supporters.[5]

The reason why supporting Irish political movements is important for many people in Scotland is that they relate the ideals of these groups to their own situation, i.e. Scotland's position in the United Kingdom. In *Trainspotting,* Stevie, who now sees himself as a Londoner rather than an Edinburgh person, has an ambiguous attitude towards this kind of support. On the one hand, he still regards Scotland as his home country and therefore sees himself as part of the group of friends. On the other hand, he detests the IRA's terrorist activities and the hatred between supporters of different football clubs.

"Victory on New Year's Day" is not the only chapter of the novel that deals with such problems. The chapter "Bang to Rites", for instance, is set at the funeral of Billy Renton, Mark's brother, who has been killed while serving in the army in Northern Ireland. Here, Mark meets some members of his father's family who are Glasgow Protestants. They support the radical Orange Order and are proud of Billy having died for his mother country. Another theme of this chapter is the Edinburgh-Glasgow rivalry, which expresses itself in the use of derogatory terms as well. A common example is the word *Weedjie* (derived from *Glaswegian*), which is often used in combination with other swearwords. Another one is *soapdodger*, a Scottish slang word which normally refers to someone who is not particularly clean but which is used by Mark Renton as a synonym of *Glaswegian*.

One can say that the people in *Trainspotting* are not primarily on the edge of society because they are inhabitants of Scotland. They are part of a disadvantaged group in British society, however, because they have lost part of their national identity and because they are exposed to (sometimes violent) clashes between people with pro-independence and unionist attitudes. Alan Freeman summarizes the situation in the novel as follows: "Inhabitants of society's periphery, the trainspotters may be citizens of the world, but they live in a decentred city, in a peripheral nation within a fading imperial state. In all ways, they are on the edge. They are shadows cast by the social mainstream [....]."[6]

But there is another way of describing the situation of the junkies, namely with reference to the novel's metaphorical title. The first point of similarity between trainspotting, a typically British hobby which consists in collecting the numbers of the trains that one has seen, and the life of drug addicts is the similarity of attitudes which each of them inspires. It has been emphasized that "drugs are a hobby as useful or as useless as trainspotting".[7] Trainspotting is a real passion of those who do it; for outsiders, it might seem nothing but a waste of time. As has been explained before, attitudes towards drugs are quite similar in this respect. The second point of similarity can be seen in the chapter "Trainspotting at Leith Central Station", in which Renton and Begbie are standing in the closed-down central station of Leith. When Begbie's drunken father comes along and asks them whether they are trainspotting, Begbie says yes.

Here, trainspotting really means waiting for trains that will not come. It symbolizes the hopelessness of the junkies' situation and their low chances of advancing in society.

2. Language as a Means of Characterization

One of the most prominent features of *Trainspotting* is the use of very different stylistic registers. Freeman explains this use of language as follows:

> In the twentieth century we have learned that language, rather than a window upon the world, is a structure within it, and our notion of reality is ordered, in important ways, in accordance with the rules of language: the *system* of language in this view is a paradigm for the codes by which we live.[8]

Since language usage reflects the social norms according to which a language user lives, Freeman uses the term *grammar* to refer to both linguistic and social sets of rules. This view should be kept in mind when analysing the use of stylistic registers in *Trainspotting*, the function of which it is to characterize social groups as well as individuals. The most important stylistic features are the use of Scots and of vulgarisms, but even Standard English is often employed for the purpose of characterization.

Scots was originally the general language of the Scottish Lowlands but was replaced by English in the course of the centuries. Today, many people consider Scots not to be a language of its own but a form of spoken English, or even bad English.[9] Scots is therefore used primarily in spoken language. This attitude towards the language is also reflected by the fact that, in literature, it is hardly ever used for third-person narrators.

The most important feature of the Scots used in *Trainspotting* is the spelling, which is fundamentally different from English. It corresponds to the spelling traditionally used in written Scots and, in many cases, reflects phonetic differences between Scots and Standard English. Many words are similar to their Standard English equivalents so that they can be understood even by those who do not speak Scots, for example *o, fae, nixt, eftir, boatil* and *goat* (in Standard English: *of, from, next, after, bottle* and *got*). Distinctly Scots grammatical forms and lexical items are less frequent than these renderings of Scots pronunciation. Examples are the negation suffix *-nae* and the words *wee, bairn, ken* and *greet* (in Standard English: *small, child, know* and *cry*). At least in Scotland, the forms and lexical items used in *Trainspotting* are generally known; besides, they are perceived by language users as being part of the Scots tongue, and most of them signal a rather low social prestige. This status of the language is also visible in the way it is used for the different narrators and characters.

Scots is used exclusively for first-person narrators and in direct speech, which is typical of contemporary literature; moreover, the characters who speak Scots are usually members of the lower social classes. The novel's protagonists, for instance, use Scots in their conversations as well as in their function as first-person narrators. Some of them, however, are able to adjust to different communicative situations by switching between Scots and Standard English. Mark Renton, for example, uses Standard English without Scots elements during a job interview (64-65). Similarly, Sick Boy occasionally switches to Standard English in order to impress his numerous female acquaintances.

The ability to perform this kind of code-switching is one of the major differences between these two characters and most of their friends, as for example Begbie and Spud. Moreover, it reveals certain important aspects of their characters. Sick Boy, although a junkie, often tries to create the impression of being a smart, educated person like his role model, Sean Connery *alias* James Bond. In the case of Renton, the use of Standard English shows that he has a relatively high level of education – after all, he has passed his A-level examination and studied history at Aberdeen University for one year. More importantly, his ability to switch to Standard English and thus to adjust to different situations hints at his possibility of escaping from the subculture of drugs and advancing socially. In fact, he is characterized as the only member of the group who could be able to live outside the drug scene. He makes various attempts to get off his drug habit, and when he leaves Edinburgh to work in London, where he does not have contact with heroin users, he even succeeds in living without the drug. However, he only quits his group of friends at the end of the novel, after stealing the money they have all earned in a major heroin deal. He could certainly have left the group earlier, but the reason for his remaining in the drug scene lies in the attraction that the scene and its specific lifestyle have for him. Furthermore, by leaving for Amsterdam, one of Europe's main drug centres, he still has the option of going on living within the drug subculture.

There are various chapters in the novel in which the use of certain forms of language reflects the social role relationships between the characters involved. In the chapter "Courting Disaster", where Renton and Spud appear in court on theft charges, the judge uses a language which Renton finds "patronising" (165) and which shows that he has a high level of education and that his position is clearly superior to that of Renton and Spud. The two defendants react differently in this situation. While Renton is able to use an equally educated language, Spud's speech is marked by youth slang expressions and incomplete sentences. The language is decisive for the impression that the two defendants create: while Spud is sentenced to ten months in prison, Renton is put on probation. The chapter "Searching for the Inner Man" provides an example of a different kind of language usage. In a conversation with a psychiatrist, Renton, intending to emphasize what social class he belongs to, uses his usual linguistic style. Besides Scots, this style is characterized by youth slang expressions and vulgarisms on the one hand and expressions belonging to a more educated language on the other.

One further important characteristic of the language in *Trainspotting* is the frequent use of vulgarisms. In contemporary English, many lexical units "are used with such monotonous regularity that they have lost their disturbing connotations".[10] In *Trainspotting*, where various characters use vulgarisms excessively, many of these words have lost not only their original connotations but also their original meaning. While some vulgar words (e.g. *shite*, a Scots variant of *shit*) are used in their original meaning relatively often, others are used in a much broader sense. The adjective *fucking*, for example, is mainly used as an intensifier expressing annoyance, and the word *cunt*, in most cases, refers to despicable persons.

It must be emphasized that, in *Trainspotting*, the use of certain linguistic patterns is more important than the semantically correct use of the vulgarisms.[11] An example of a word used in this way is *cunt*. In the chapter "Grieving and Mourning in Port Sunshine", the members of a card school are waiting for their mate Granty, who is carrying the entire card school money with him, and are wondering whether he has been mugged. One of them remarks: "Nae cunt wid try tae mug Granty. He's the kind ay cunt thit mugs cunts, no gits mugged fae them." (97) The following day, when they learn that Granty has died, one of them repeatedly calls him "one ay the nicest cunts you could hope tae meet" (100). The word *cunt* here has different meanings and functions. The expression *nae cunt* is synonymous with *no one* but has a negative connotation. In the expression "the kind ay cunt thit mugs cunts", it has a neutral meaning. This expression characterizes Granty as a tough person, and obviously, the speaker does not consider mugging to be particularly loathsome. Finally, in the expression "one ay the nicest cunts", the word even has a positive connotation. Here, it is obviously used as a synonym of *bloke*. With this use of vulgarisms, people express that they belong to a certain subculture. The taboo words are chosen because they create the impression of coarseness and because their use is provocative. In this context, sexual vulgarisms are particularly important because of their strong shock effect, and they are often chosen because of this very effect and not because of their actual meaning. In *Trainspotting*, this kind of language usage marks the members of the social underclass and the subculture connected with it.

The most striking example of this use of swearwords is the language of Begbie. For him, they have the function of intimidating people. When he shouts out his orders, he uses the word *fucking* to place special emphasis on them, for example in the chapter "There Is A Light That Never Goes Out". Here, Begbie orders his mates to have a full cooked breakfast, but Renton, as a vegetarian, protests. While Begbie uses the words *fuck* and *fucking* in almost every sentence, the others do not use them at all. Begbie has the last word in this discussion, saying: "Because ah fucking sais, that's fuckin how!" (272) This utterance shows that Begbie's vulgarisms can be understood as threatening gestures towards his mates, whom he considers inferior. Another example of Begbie's speech shows that *fucking* is also used as a general expression of disapproval. Begbie has woken up with a terrible hang-over and now has to hurry to catch his train to London. As the first-person narrator, he describes the situation as follows: "Ah make straight fir the fuckin fridge. [...] Huvtae fuckin watch the time, but. [...] She's still fuckin sleeping whin ah go back ben the bedroom." (109) Begbie uses *fuckin* for all persons and things that surround him in order to lay the blame for his miserable state on them.

Begbie is another person in the novel whose character is largely reflected in his language. Not only is his language typical of his social stratum and subculture; his permanent use of vulgarisms also hints at his extremely low level of education. He did not finish school, ending up in a vocational class for pupils with special needs, and at one point, he says that he despises people who talk about literature because he sees this as an expression of arrogance.

The language of Spud is also very revealing because it has some characteristics that go beyond those discussed so far. Besides Scots and specific youth slang expressions, syntactic incoherence characterizes Spud's language. He frequently uses gap-fillers such as *like, likesay* or *ken*, and his speech is interrupted by numerous breaks, which are represented graphically by three dots. Furthermore, unlike his mates, he uses many slang words which have their origin in American pop culture (e.g. *cat/catboy* and *man*). These expressions, which Spud often uses as interjections, reflect his identification with this culture and with some of its representatives such as the musician Frank Zappa. In fact, Spud's entire language can be considered a reflection of his character. Like his speech, his personality is incoherent. He is described as an unassertive person who belongs to the group of junkies but who does not share their norms and their patterns of behaviour in all points. For instance, he occasionally commits burglaries and thefts, but he despises the violence of the other group members as well as cruelty to human beings and animals (cf. 159-160). Another characteristic which distinguishes him from people like Renton or Sick Boy is his inability to adjust to different situations. His only stylistic register is his typical incoherent youth slang so that, for instance, he says to a personnel officer at a job interview: "You're the man, the governor, the dude in the chair, so tae speak, likesay." (66) Here, Spud's inability to switch from the group-specific language to Standard English causes a major communication problem, with the personnel officer occasionally failing to understand him and having to ask for clarification. Moreover, this inability also shows that he is a prisoner of his social situation, which is marked by heroin addiction, alcoholism and criminality, and that he is not able to improve it.

Finally, the languages of youth and drug subcultures have to be mentioned. The novel's protagonists use youth-specific terms such as *gig* or *heavy* (the latter referring to sounds) as well as drug-specific terms such as *gear, works, cold turkey* or *shooting gallery.* Although such words are understood by outsiders, they are normally used only by the members of the respective subculture and therefore serve to create a certain distance between the subculture and the rest of society.

The major role that linguistic registers play in the characterization of people – and groups of people – in *Trainspotting* is obvious. With the presentation of Scots as a social dialect, the social situation of the different characters is underlined, and the extent to which the characters use Scots reveals their social status and roles as well as their prospects of social mobility. Vulgarisms are used mainly because of their provocative character. More importantly, the characters' language patterns indicate various factors which influence their attitudes. On the one hand, the protagonists use distinctly Scots elements in their language; on the other hand, they are also influenced by a largely international youth and pop culture, which can be seen most clearly in the Americanisms in Spud's language.

3. Translation and Translatability

It has been argued that *Trainspotting* is a novel which unites typically Scottish elements with subcultural features not limited to Scotland. Due to various characteristics of the novel (linguistic features, references to Scottish culture), translators of *Trainspotting* are faced with different kinds of translation problems. In the following, selected examples will be discussed – some of which are also revealing with regard to the differences and similarities between youth subcultures in Germany and Scotland.

Today, most literary translations are "exoticizing translations",[12] i.e. the situation and function of the source text is preserved in the translation, whose readers are introduced to characteristic features of the source culture so that an 'exotic' effect is created. Because such cultural characteristics must remain understandable for the readers of the translation, various problems can arise from the 'exoticization'. An example of these problems is provided in the chapter "Victory on New Year's Day". For readers of the source text, it is obvious that the participants in the party sympathize with the IRA, a point which is expressed mainly through the lyrics of the folk songs they sing. Since pop and folk songs in English normally remain untranslated, the lyrics of those songs are rendered in English. The readers of the target text, therefore, can only understand that the youths are IRA supporters if they have a certain knowledge of English.

Another problem is the comprehensibility of names related to the source culture. The translator has to decide whether such names require additional explanations in the target text. In *Trainspotting*, many of these names refer to parts of Edinburgh or to streets and buildings in the town. All of these names should be familiar to people who know Edinburgh fairly well, but even for English-speaking readers who are not familiar with the town, the knowledge of these names cannot be presupposed. Their translation, however, remains largely unproblematic because, in many cases, sufficient explanation is given in the source text. For instance, when the "Royal Mile" is mentioned in connection with tourists looking for Edinburgh Festival venues (29), it is obvious that it must be a major tourist sight, and when West Granton is first mentioned, it is said that some particularly ugly council estates can be found there (115).

The transfer of the novel's linguistic diversity, however, presents major problems. For example, the Scots in *Trainspotting*, which reflects the low social prestige that the language has today, is rather difficult to translate. There are some German working-class dialects whose status is similar to that of Scots, but using any German dialect in a novel set outside Germany would have a bewildering effect on the reader. So Peter Torberg, the German translator of *Trainspotting,* chose to translate the Scots forms and lexical items by colloquial elements, obviously intending to avoid regional or dialectal forms. *Nich* (instead of *nicht*) and *nix* (instead of *nichts*) are examples of such colloquial forms which often occur in the translation of passages originally written in Scots. Other forms of this kind are contractions typical of a (slightly careless) colloquial pronunciation, for example *ham* (instead of *haben*) and *bleim* (instead of *bleiben*).[13] Besides these renderings of colloquial pronunciation, Torberg uses words which are common in speech but normally not used in writing. *Boatil*, the Scots variant of *bottle*, for instance, is sometimes translated as *Pulle*, the use of which is restricted to informal speech. However, lexical items are not the only means of rendering Scots in colloquial German. Torberg also deliberately uses certain grammatical and syntactical characteristics of informal speech. An example of such grammatical characteristics is the use of the preposition *wegen* with the dative instead of the genitive case. The following translation provides an example of distinctly colloquial syntax:

> Ah'm fucking brassic until the rent cheque hits the mat the morn. (99)

> Ich bin total pleite, und der Scheck für die Miete landet erst morgen auf meiner Fußmatte.[14]

The translation of a subordinate clause by a main clause hints at the fact that, in German, subordinate clauses are far less common in speech than in writing.

One final translation problem is the rendering of Scots in the lyrics of pop songs. In "Victory On New Year's Day" and other chapters, people sing pop songs using their customary Scots pronunciation instead of Standard English. In the German translation, such quotations of songs are written in Standard English. Thus, the meaning of the lyrics is understandable for readers with sufficient knowledge of English, but part of the original atmosphere which is created by the very use of Scots is lost inevitably in the translation. This is, in fact, a general problem inherent in the German translation of *Trainspotting*. The main characters in the novel are given a distinctly colloquial language style. Yet, much of the novel's typically Scottish character is lost in the translation since the typically Scottish language cannot be rendered in German.

Other translation problems arise from an important aspect of the language of subcultures, namely the use of numerous vulgarisms. There are two reasons for these problems: firstly, the above-mentioned 'monotonous regularity' with which such words are used and, secondly, many English four-letter words are sexualized, while the most frequently used German ones are scatological. A German translator therefore has to choose four-letter words which are not unusual in German slang (translating *fucking* by a sexualized word would, for instance, be inappropriate in many cases), and, more importantly, he must reduce the large number of such words occurring in the original.

While many English taboo words have lost their shock effect because they are used rather often, this is not the case with German words of this kind. Torberg therefore often uses what Ieva Zauberga calls "softening", i.e. replacing a taboo word by a target language word which is stylistically neutral or more acceptable.[15] For example, the word *cunt*, which is a highly taboo word in English, is often translated into German as *Arschloch*. Not only would the use of a stronger taboo word seem unrealistic in many cases – it is actually difficult to find a stronger, perhaps sexualized four-letter word which might be used in the same way (the literal German translation of *cunt*, *Fotze*, is only used as an extremely rude swearword for women). Besides such softening, Torberg reduces the total number of taboo words, as a result of which many of these words are not translated at all. This can be illustrated with the following sentences already quoted above: "Nae cunt wid try tae mug Granty. He's the kind ay cunt thit mugs cunts, no gits mugged fae them." In the German translation, it reads: "Granty überfallen, das würd keiner wagen. Der überfällt selbst, der wird nich überfallen."[16] The word cunt is left out in each case. Although, in the first sentence, one could have found a (slightly 'softened') slang equivalent for *nae cunt* (*kein Arsch*), rendering cunt by a German slang word in the second one might have been inappropriate, especially because *cunt* is used in a neutral rather than a negative sense here, namely as a synonym of *person*.

The above-mentioned translation problems are closely related to the fact that there are differences in the language use of certain subcultures and social strata in German and in English. There are, however, many terms and expressions from youth and drug scene slang which are known in Britain as well as in Germany and which, for this reason, are taken over in the German translation. Examples are *gig*, *speed* (referring to stimulants), or the expression "heavy techno-sounds" (137), which is composed of words commonly used by German-speaking youths as well. Such translations hint at the international character of today's youth culture: With British and American pop music being fashionable in Germany as well, many English expressions related to it have found their way into the German language. But not only the music scene is largely internationalized; the numerous English expressions in German drug slang hint at the fact that fashions in the area of drug-consumption are also largely influenced by Britain and the United States.

4. Conclusion

Of the various aspects of youth culture depicted in *Trainspotting*, many are distinctly Scottish, while others outline the international character of this subculture. To the protagonists of the novel, their Scottishness is very important in certain ways. They see England as a sort of colonial power, and they have a clear position concerning the issue of Scottish independence. Moreover, they use Scots, the vernacular of their region, as often as they can, and they see English as a form of language reserved for educated or upper-class people. Foreign readers will be struck by another typical characteristic of the youth culture in Scotland and the rest of Britain: the regularity with which sexualized four-letter words are used.

The novel also presents various aspects of youth culture which are not restricted to Scotland. The characters' idols, such as Sean Connery, Frank Zappa and Iggy Pop, are famous world-wide, and many of them are not from Britain but from the United States. This global youth culture influences young people's taste, ideals and language in many countries. But it is not only youth culture that is universal. The social problems presented in the novel – unemployment, addiction, the break-up of families and the diminishing importance of traditional norms and values and with it, for instance, more widespread promiscuity – are phenomena which can be observed in many countries. The same applies to the development of drug counter-cultures. In many countries, drug addicts are part of subcultures in which taking drugs is seen as a way of having fun and which consciously reject the traditional values of society. For these reasons, *Trainspotting* is an interesting novel to read not just for young people in Scotland, although reading the original might be difficult for many non-native speakers of English due to the predominant use of non-standard language. Many people, therefore, will probably prefer to read a translation of the novel, by which, as the German translation shows, much of the original's atmosphere is inevitably lost.

Notes

1 "*Trainspotting* by Irvine Welsh" (1997).
2 Cf. Kravitz (1997: xxii).
3 Cf. Welsh (1994: 115-116). Further references to this edition will be included in the text.
4 Welsh, "Irvine Welsh on *Trainspotting*".
5 It must be remarked that these nicknames are not only used for football supporters but for Catholics or Protestants, respectively, in general (cf. Knight 1992: 73).
6 Freeman (1996: 254).
7 Jacobs (1996). My translation.
8 Freeman (1996: 251-252).
9 Cf. Low (1985: 162-163). For information on the low social prestige of distinctly Scots forms and lexical items, see Sandred (1983).
10 Zauberga (1994: 141).
11 Cf. Freeman (1996: 255).
12 Cf. Nord (1988: 103).
13 Welsh (1997: 177).
14 *Ibid.*, 107.
15 Cf. Zauberga (1994: 141-143).
16 Welsh (1997: 105).

Bibliography

Freeman, Alan: "Ghosts in Sunny Leith. Irvine Welsh's *Trainspotting*". – In Susanne Hagemann (Ed.): *Studies in Scottish Fiction. 1945 to the Present*, Frankfurt, 1996, pp. 251-262.

Jacobs, Peter: "De chaos van kicken en afkicken. De literaire sensatie van *Trainspotting*", *De Standard*, 21 August 1996 (quoted from http://194.7.235.55/dsfiwelsh2.html).

Knight, Lorna: "Glasgow Slang". – In Claudia Blank (Ed.): *Language and Civilization*, Frankfurt, 1992, pp. 69-75.

Kravitz, Peter: "Introduction". – In Peter Kravitz (Ed.): *The Picador Book of Contemporary Scottish Fiction*, London, 1997, pp. xi-xxxvi.

Low, Thomas John: "Is Scots English? Or is Scots no juist orra English?" – In Manfred Göbel (Ed.): *Focus on Scotland*, Amsterdam, 1985, pp. 182-187.
Nord, Christiane: "Loyalität statt Treue. Vorschläge zu einer funktionalen Übersetzungstypologie", *Lebende Sprachen* 2, 1988, 100-105.
Sandred, Karl-Inge: *Good or Bad Scots? Attitudes to Optional Lexical and Grammatical Usages in Edinburgh*, Uppsala, 1983.
"*Trainspotting* by Irvine Welsh" (review), *Concrete Soup. Book Reviews*, 1997, http://www.qmw.ac.uk/~english/cbl/projects/cs/Bookreviews.html.
Welsh, Irvine: *Trainspotting*, London, 1994.
---: *Trainspotting*. Tr. Peter Torberg, München, 1997.
---: "Irvine Welsh on *Trainspotting*", http://www.criterionco.com/catalog/trainspotting/indepth/linders/liners.html.
Zauberga, Ieva: "Pragmatic Aspects of the Translation of Slang and Four-Letter-Words", *Perspectives. Studies in Translatology* 2, no. 2, 1994, 141-148.

Jürgen Neubauer, Frankfurt

Critical Media Literacy and the Representation of Youth in *Trainspotting*

When the lights dim, the hard beat of Iggy Pop's "Lust for Life" pulses through the theatre and has the audience rocking in their chairs. To the images of two detectives chasing two pale and scruffy young men, Mark Renton and Spud, through the streets of Edinburgh, a voice begins to intone a creed of youthful non-conformism:

> Choose life. Choose a job. Choose a career. Choose a family. Choose a fucking big television, choose washing machines, cars, compact disc players and electrical tin openers.

With the detectives at his heels, Renton is hit by a car, roles over the hood and grins at the viewer in a close-up. The scene changes to a bare interior, Renton injects and sinks to the ground. As his head hits the bare and dirty floor, the voice-over continues:

> Choose good health, low cholesterol and dental insurance. Choose fixed-interest mortgage payments. Choose a starter home. Choose your friends.

The scene shifts to a soccer pitch. Renton, Spud and several of his friends, completely out of place in their shabby street-clothes, are engaged in a match with a professional-looking team. They try to make up for their lack of talent with excessive unfairness. The voice continues:

> Choose leisurewear and matching luggage. Choose a three-piece suite on hire-purchase in a range of fucking fabrics. Choose DIY and wonder who the fuck you are on a Sunday morning. Choose sitting on that couch watching mind-numbing, spirit-crushing game shows, stuffing junk food into your mouth. Choose rotting away at the end of it all, pishing your last in a miserable home, nothing more than an embarrassment to the selfish, fucked-up brats you have spawned to replace yourself. Choose your future. Choose life.

The scene returns to the interior. Several young men and one woman are getting ready to shoot up and the voice, which is Renton's, asks:

> But why would I want to do a thing like that? I chose not to choose life: I chose something else. And the reasons? There are no reasons. Who needs reasons when you've got heroin?[1]

After this bleak statement, the movie *Trainspotting* has begun, the music ebbs away, we are left watching Mark and his friends shoot up one after another.

1. Youth and Media Culture

A riveting opening sequence, in which beat, images, cuts, and voice-over are woven together to a fast-paced, 'cool' aesthetic, not at all unlike an MTV music video, and with a significant impact on a range of recent motion pictures.[2] Yet also an opening which may result in a profound sense of unease, not the least in parents and educators, exactly for the hip manner in which it packages rather shocking images of irrational violence and drug abuse in a cool and immensely pleasurable aesthetic. An opening that illustrates the new and complex relation between young people and global pop culture, which is on the one hand a source of pleasure, yet on the other narrows down the possibilities of participation in democratic public life and generally limits the imaginable ways of being-in-the-world with very clear-cut norms of what it means to a 'good' member of the community. An opening, finally, that permits me to think about the possibilities young people might have of reclaiming the terrain of popular culture and representing themselves, the pedagogical interventions that might support such reclamations, and the new forms of literacy required for kids to launch their own interventions.

Trainspotting is paradigmatic of the way youth is represented in contemporary media society. But with 'representation' I do not simply refer to fashionable aesthetic conventions like the format of MTV clips, the violence or the heroin chic which *Trainspotting* taps into. By 'representation' I mean the totality of social processes in and around motion pictures, their production and consumption, and the public discussions about youth through which it is taken up. Throughout the 1980s and 1990s, popular culture, of which *Trainspotting* is a part, has become an increasingly important public sphere, i.e. a site where socially relevant issues are negotiated and struggled over. Representation is therefore never just a question of entertainment, but always thoroughly political, because it challenges or affirms the ways in which we see and treat youth.

In this sense, movies like *Trainspotting* perform a pedagogical function in that their representations to some extent teach viewers in all kinds of social classes, age cohorts and geographical locations, what it means to be young, a member of the working class, male and unemployed, or simply a consumer of postmodern media culture.[3] In the words of Henry Giroux, popular culture is the medium through which children and teenagers fashion their individual and collective identities and learn, in part, how to narrate themselves in relation to others. [...] In fact, they [films] are powerful educational sites where children and adults are being offered specific lessons in how to view themselves, others and the world they inhabit. In this sense, such films must be seen as a serious object of social analysis by anyone who takes education seriously.[4]

As co-educators or "teaching machines"[5] movies like *Trainspotting* become a pedagogical problem for parents, educators and other cultural workers, who are often at a loss how to address popular culture.

Stuart Hall has developed a model he calls the "circuit of culture" to describe the importance of popular culture as a public sphere. This model is a useful heuristic device to understand the complex ways in which movies like *Trainspotting* participate in the processes of 'identification' in a global media age, and it also helps to envision pedagogical interventions.[6] To begin at a random point in the circuit, *Trainspotting* is a product of a market economy. Within the logic of profit, the producers produce representations that target particular audiences and assume potential viewers with a certain identity. The representations are also created within a particular cultural climate, or more specifically, regulatory discourses of public opinion as well as institutions like jurisdiction, education or social security. These representations are then taken up within the context of consumer culture, i.e. they come almost with in-built instructions on how and how not to use them. To come full circle, the representations of youth, the way they are produced, distributed and consumed feed back into the identities of young people themselves, i.e. the ways in which they see themselves and their possibilities for participation and agency within various social contexts. They also feed into the way in which society and its institutions treat youth.

I have tried to give a cautious description of the circuit of culture: Stuart Hall does not imply that representations automatically reproduce the identities that were assumed at the outset. Kids are not cultural dopes. At every point in this circuit, things can go away, representations can be taken up creatively with completely unintended results. And this is where possibilities for critical pedagogical interventions begin.

In the following pages, I will situate *Trainspotting* in this circuit of culture and raise three questions: Firstly, I will ask what especially male teenagers in America, Sweden or Germany find attractive about representations of the degraded lives of Edinburgh junkies. Secondly, I ask how youths are constructed in popular representations, what forms of agency are offered or denied to them, both in the representations themselves and the ways in which young people can engage with them. Finally, I want to raise the question of cultural literacy: what does it mean to

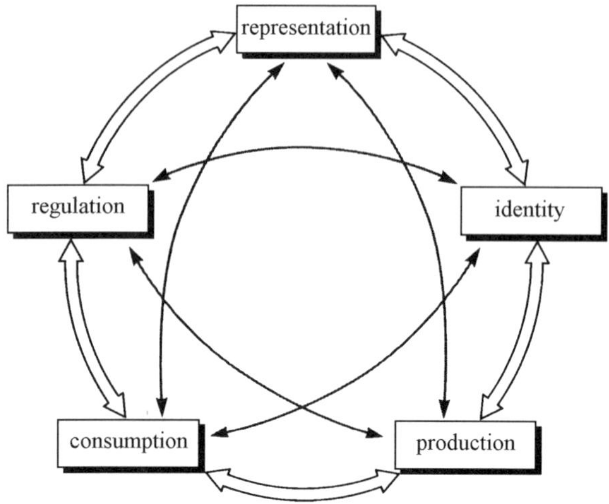

be a critical agent in a postmodern media society, where popular culture has created a new public sphere? What do young people have to learn in order to decode movies like *Trainspotting*, how can they become critical agents, and what can parents, educators and other cultural workers contribute in this process? This implies a broader investigation into the possibilities of subjectivity and democratic public life in global, corporatized media society.

2. Trainspotting *as Popular Event*

The story of *Trainspotting* is quickly told. In loosely connected episodes, the movie parades a group of friends, or rather fellow addicts, in the housing schemes of Edinburgh. The protagonist and commentator is college drop-out Mark Renton, who is always half-heartedly trying to break the habit and finances his addiction with petty theft; when caught in the opening sequence, he is temporarily put through a compulsory methadone programme. His friend Spud Murphy, on the dole, is sentenced to a year in jail in the same trial. Tommy, originally the athlete of the group, discovers the needle when his girlfriend leaves him; he quickly deteriorates, is infected with HIV and dies of a haemorrhage. Sick Boy is a fashionable 'cat' and Casanova who wears trendy suits and shoes with special heels to hide his gear in the manner of his idol James Bond. Begbie, finally, detests junkies; he is an alcoholic hooligan, always ready to stick his boot, knife or glass into unsuspecting bystanders. On the margins of the movie, there is Allison, one of the very few female character in the movie, whose baby Dawn dies of sudden cot death while Mark and his friends shoot up next door. The individual episodes serve to illustrate the characters, their almost exclusive concern with themselves and the habit, and their group interaction or lack of it. The focus is mainly on Renton and his constant oscillation between withdrawal and high. In keeping with this vicious circle, the plot does not develop, until Renton moves to London about three quarters of the way through the movie. His friends follow and are eventually involved in a drug scam, which earns them £16,000. Renton manages to steal the money and gets away, dreaming of breaking the habit and moving, of all places, to Amsterdam.

Teenage audiences made *Trainspotting* a surprise success at the box office – not only in Britain, but in the US as well, where non-American movies are notoriously unsuccessful and where even the modified Edinburgh accent initially caused considerable consternation among distributors. In Germany, Italy, and Japan, teenagers streamed into dubbed versions, despite the fact that the language is arguably one of the major attractions of the movie. For young audiences all over the Western hemisphere, the movie rapidly attained cult status. On a very basic level, young viewers began to some extent to model their behaviour on that seen in the movie, for instance by repeating hip lines, or by imitating gestures like the 'tapping' of the vein of the opening scene. More importantly, these audiences were targeted by and bought the huge array of merchandise that now surrounds any major movie, like the two sound track albums, T-shirts, key-rings, posters, stickers and mugs, to name only a few. Through them, the movie has also entered the vast and expanding internet sub-culture, as young viewers began to put images and text fragments on their homepages.[7]

The adult public responded vociferously, and was largely divided into two camps: one greeted the movie with a chorus of disgust at the appalling moral decay of Generations X and Y and accused director Danny Boyle and author Irvine Welsh of celebrating drugs. The other indulged in celebrations of the tough, gritty realism and praised the movie for offering an authentic slice of 'life as it really is' in the slums and present day youth culture. One of the more prominent critics of the movie was Bob Dole, Republican candidate in the 1996 US presidential elections, who, obviously without ever having seen the movie, berated it as an instance of the nihilism of young Americans.[8] For him, the movie snugly registers with a conservative American drug policy associated with Nancy Reagan's 'Just Say No' campaign, as well as the American war on drugs, which represents drug use not as a social problem, but an issue of personal choice and 'character'; this policy has little sympathy with individual users, who are criminalized and treated as juvenile delinquents.[9]

At the other end of the popular political spectrum are typical 'enlightened' readings like that of Elizabeth Young, who seems to confuse present-day Britain with a Dickensian themepark and praises Welsh for his

> unparalleled ability to represent *the real lives of most people in Britain today* – the lives of poor accommodation, indifferent health, scams, deals and fantasies of escape, long days with the curtains drawn and the video on, with the dope and the Carlsberg and the speed or the smack.[10]

For her and numerous other liberal critics, the movie seems to hold the promise of participating (slumming would be the better word) in a dangerous and exotic lower-class world.[11]

Neither of these responses, typical as they are of what Stuart Hall calls "regulatory discourses" of youth, is nearly adequate in its analysis of the movie or of youth culture. Though they appear to be at opposite ends of the political spectrum, both use a simplistic notion of 'representation' which assumes that movies like *Trainspotting* authentically 'reflect' the lives and choices of young people in Edinburgh and elsewhere. But the movie does no such thing. Rather than *reflect* reality, the images of the movie *enact* versions of reality as refracted through the conventions of consumer culture. In other words, they *construct* identities; their aesthetics and the way in which they are circulated teach certain possibilities of being and acting in the global media age. Both Dole and Young miss that these representations emerge within complex contexts of consumption and production of consumer culture in the way Stuart Hall describes. They entirely miss the reasons for the popularity of *Trainspotting*, which I would locate *not* in an impossible authenticity, but in a pop aesthetic.

3. Trainspotting *and the Subcultural Critique of Consumer Society*

The single most obvious reason for the popularity of the movie is that its characters offer powerful points of identification for young viewers, whether they come from Edinburgh's working class or white American suburbs. The movie deliberately employs the well-known registers of subcultural social protest which has acquired a 'hip' status. This protest rejects the blessings of consumer society and develops its very own rituals of resistance in which style, clothing, music, or drugs are of central importance.[12]

The opening voice-over (as well as the entire movie) sends up normative versions of happiness and ways of being-in-the-world. It burlesques the post-war compromise in Britain and other industrialized nations of the West, where the working classes accepted material wealth as a substitute for more radical forms of redistribution and self-determination. Since the 1980s and the rule of Margaret Thatcher in Britain, Ronald Reagan in the US and Helmut Kohl in Germany, it has become clear that this compromise was no more than a ruse. Punk was one of the subcultural responses to the new climate of social Darwinism and the spiritual vacuity of the society of stock owners. For the young men in the movie, all of them from Edinburgh's urban and suburban working classes, the expectations of consumer culture are now a sham, its promises ridiculously unattainable. The post-industrial society has relegated them to the margins; they have become part of the 'superfluous' or 'problem' populations. Their culture, like that of punk and the numerous other subcultures to follow it, is to some extend an attempt to find meaning and happiness outside the dominant norms and regulations.

Welsh points out that in the culture of touristy Edinburgh in particular, working class youths have little or no voice. Not only that, 'schemies' are literally "taken out of existence" and "out of range of resource allocation for vital services like health and housing".[13] Welsh likes to present his own work as a corrective and challenge to that dominant culture:

> Now most British city centres that escaped the ugliness of 1960s redevelopment look nice, but such places are not for the schemies. They are for yuppie incomers, shoppers and tourists. The 'city' (the city centre) is this alliance of new and old bourgeois, new and old puritans, and so therefore must its 'art' be. It has to be 'life-affirming', or, more accurately, reaffirm those liberal middle-class values that everything and everyone is jolly, decent and wonderful. Fuck that for a laugh; if we're truly a diverse multicultural society, and we are, let's have some diverse, multi-cultural art and art criticism.[14]

This chimes in with a popular reading of the movie which emphasizes the aspect of subcultural resistance. In this reading, the 'life' Mark Renton chooses not to choose in the opening voice-over is the bourgeois, puritan, yuppie life. Middle-class dreams of happiness are spiritually draining and degrading, and even if they were not, they are simply unattainable to Renton and his friends. The 'art' Welsh produces, be it the novel or the movie, is meant to represent and return a voice to the marginalized subculture of working class youth. Welsh's writing shows the dark underside of the new prosperity, it represents a part of society that has been silenced, it even attempts to empower those it represents.

The gestures of refusal made by the characters in the movie have an immense appeal to young people, who often feel marginalized and alienated by the values of their parents whether or not they share this particular background. The movie aims at a 'real' life and 'real' experience beyond the tepid conformism of the dominant culture that is so often experienced as threatening and coercive. The movie offers a language, gestures and rituals that seem to articulate protest in a particularly powerful way and empower those who employ them. Drugs, violence, music, and clothing all in various ways act to create a "great symbolic barrier"[15] between mainstream culture and various subcultures; they offer a new identity and a sense of belonging.

For viewers across the globe, *Trainspotting* offers up subculture for vicarious participation: even if one does not belong to the subculture itself, the movie still provides styles which can act as symbolic boundaries. The deliberate appropriation of punk aesthetics, the shocking and surreal images of squalor, the use of punk songs like Iggy Pop's "Lust for Life" or Blondie's "Atomic" as well as club tracks like Underworld's "Born Slippy" or Blur's "Sing" amplify these identifications with a 'cool' life style. The discontent with the narratives of progress and material wealth, still strong among young people throughout the West, finds its outlet in a pleasurable punk *Gesamtkunstwerk*.

4. Critiquing Subcultural Romanticism

Of course, this is only one half of the story. While a description of the movie as a form of subcultural resistance to dominant models of being-in-the-world may not be altogether wrong, the alternatives it offers are neither attractive, nor are they real alternatives. Most problematic is of course the blatant celebration of drug abuse as legitimate or maybe even the only way out of repression and marginalization.[16] The charge is a serious one, and therefore no attempt to address *Trainspotting* pedagogically can ignore the accusation that the movie celebrates heroin.

Asophisticated reading may of course be able to reject any such accusation as a piece of disingenuous conservative propaganda. Such a reading can appreciate the ironies and subtleties with which Welsh and Boyle use the drug culture to burlesque and savagely critique hegemonic consumer culture. To return to the opening of the movie, the ironic juxtapositions of text and images make it quite clear that drug abuse is merely another form of consumption, and that, conversely, consumer culture is nothing more than a different form of socially acceptable narcotic. But the subtle irony and social criticism are more or less lost on most viewers, and most young audiences would seem to respond to the movie on an entirely unironic level. Like the rest of the movie, the opening scene holds up a kind of gratification to kids that far exceeds the shallow pleasures of one's parents: where adults are stupid enough to pursue those petty pleasures of welfare capitalism, heroin is the only true big bang, a form of pleasure entirely inconceivable in the terms of hegemonic common sense.

The moments of the celebration of drugs, clustered around the beginning of the movie, are quite intense and memorable. "Take the best orgasm you've ever had, multiply it by a thousand, and you're still nowhere near it"[17] – thus one of the most popular lines in the movie. Of course the movie also shows the other side of heroin abuse in the pain of Renton's withdrawal, his near o.d., the constant threat of AIDS from shared needles, and the social decline and death of his friend Tommy, and a classroom discussion of the movie can certainly address the contrast. But the line sticks. It seems to have developed a life of its own and has floated through the channels of popular culture into the CD-booklet, onto posters and web pages. There it has become entirely divorced from all context and criticism the movie may once have held; the celebration of heroin becomes the sole message.

In an interview with Ben Thompson in *The Independent on Sunday* Welsh himself acknowledges but by-passes his responsibility when he says:

> One thing that does concern me is that young kids are passing *Trainspotting* around at school now. They're reading it in the same way that kids used to read Richard Allen's 'Skinhead' books, and you can't stop them doing that because kids will get into anything that they think might annoy their parents. But sometimes I think 'It's got f---all to do with you, you little c---. *Stay there*, grow up, do your own thing.'[18]

Clearly, the responsibility is not with the kids, but with a book and a movie which deliberately address the sense of rebellion in kids only to leave them with a self-destructive, albeit coolly staged alternative. Any pedagogical approach to the movie, in classroom situations, youth clubs, the home or any other formal or informal pedagogical setting would have to address this problem of drugs.

But my concern here is less with drug use as such, or with the movie as a possible incentive to try heroin. More problematically, Welsh's use of substance abuse as a form of resistance to consumer culture enacts the very logic of choice which it seems to criticize. Like many romantic celebrators of subcultural resistance, Welsh overlooks the involvement of subcultures in consumer culture, and the popular heroin chic of the nineties in particular.[19] In the mid-nineties, Kate Moss was the incarnation of Calvin Klein's new heroin chic. Ultimately, for the viewers across the globe, the heroin aesthetic of *Trainspotting* derives its 'authenticity' not from a comparison with the 'real' situation of junkies in Edinburgh, but from the similarities with the tormented looks of the emaciated model. In return, Calvin Klein appropriated the gestures of the movie for his 1996 advertising campaign: in one of the adverts, Vincent Gallo imitates the pose of Mark Renton on the movie posters, doubled up, streaming with perspiration, staring ahead, obviously in pain.[20]

This is not to deny that there is a large population of heroin addicts on the margins of Western cities. It is merely to point out that for the majority of viewers, the movie has little or nothing whatsoever to do with those 'real' junkies; for them, the heroin chic of *Trainspotting* is indistinguishable from Calvin Klein's models. While the novel may well have been an attempt to give voice to and empower marginalized groups in Edinburgh, for the majority of viewers the movie comes perilously close to an advert for the right kinds of clothing and make-up.[21] Therefore, the forms of agency Welsh envisions are extremely limited. Taken literally, heroin is a form of self-destruction, not liberation. Taken as an aesthetic of the fashion industry, the movie represents subjects exclusively in the terms of the very consumer culture it chastises, and it is here that I see the greatest problem of the movie, and the greatest need for pedagogical intervention.

5. Representations of Resistance in Popular Culture

In *Trainspotting*, drug use is a form of hyper-real consumption, consumption to end all consumption. The subculture depicted in the movie, as well as the movie itself (staged as subcultural event), is not a form of radical resistance to, but to some extent an integral part of global consumer culture.

Renton can only envision liberation from the logic of consumption as itself a form of consumption, even though the neoliberal reduction of agency to choice and his experience of the emptiness of a community based on commodity exchange are at the very heart of his alienation. In another voice-over about half-way through the movie, Renton describes his own consumption of drugs in terms of choice from a catalogue, which provides an odd commentary on the voice-over of the opening:

> We took morphine, diamorphine, cyclozine, codeine, temazepam, nitrezepam, phenobarbitone, sodium amytal dextropropoxyphene, methadone, nalbuphine, pethidine, pentazocine, buprenorphine, dextromoramide, chlormethiazole. The streets are awash with drugs that you can have for unhappiness and pain, and we took them all. Fuck it, we would have injected Vitamin C if only they'd made it illegal.[22]

And the reasons? There are no reasons, except the performance of resistance-as-lifestyle. The drug market is no different from the drug store; ultimately the movie celebrates resistance as the radical freedom of consumer choice. Therefore it does not come as a surprise that at the end of the movie, Renton marches off into a clean future, ironically choosing all the consumer goods he chose not to choose in the prologue:

> I'm cleaning up and I'm moving on, going straight and choosing life. […] I am going to be just like you: the job, the family, the fucking big television, the washing machine, the car, the compact disc and electrical tin opener, good health, low cholesterol, dental insurance, mortgage, starter home, leisurewear, luggage, three-piece suite, DIY, game shows, junk food, children, walks in the park, nine to five, good at golf, washing the car, choice of sweaters, family Christmas, indexed pension, tax exemption, clearing the gutters, getting by, looking ahead, to the day you die.[23]

While this final rap-like voice-over is of course highly ambiguous and continues to ironize the choices of bourgeois life, it no longer questions the ideology of consumer choice itself. For those who miss the mild irony, it becomes a straightforward endorsement of the 'normalcy' of John Major's classless middle-class society. The merchandise that accompanies the movie encourages the process of incorporation into market ideology: one of the many posters featured a grinning and altogether pleased Renton captioned by "I'm cleaning up and I'm moving on, going straight and choosing life. I am going to be just like you." Here, the irony that may have been implicit in the ending of the movie is completely obliterated. The "you" projects a movie theatre full of perfect consumers who, after having eaten the last morsel of their cinema popcorn, go out to buy the poster. In the words of Alan Sinfield, "the film cancels Renton's leftish rebellion, making Thatcherite selfishness the 'natural' way, on or off heroin, to live".[24]

By analogy, the kind of resistance expressed by the kids who watch the movie is restricted to the consumption of a certain kind of product which has connotations of danger and social taboo. Resistance is exhausted in the purchase of the right T-shirts, soundtracks, posters and key rings, in wearing the right kind of old-fashioned nicki, baggy pants, nail polish or make-up, listening to the right music, going to the right rave at the right club, and, not to be forgotten, watching the right movies. Resistance has become a life-style choice, and one that is easily targeted by the marketing departments of the global entertainment, beauty and garment industries.

In other words, the representations of resistance are part of the very culture of greed and egotism that is allegedly chastised in the movie. This becomes most apparent in the social interaction of the protagonists. When Renton, Sick Boy and Spud find that Baby Dawn has died, they leave the mother alone for fear they might be caught by the police. There is a constant sense of distrust among the 'friends', especially towards Begbie and Sick Boy.[25] Of course it is insufficient to blame this egotism on the alleged moral decay of the twenty- and thirty-somethings, as Bob Dole or Margaret Thatcher would. Renton and his friends merely repeat the lived reality of entrepreneurial individualism that destroys all social bonds and reduces friends and family to acquaintances and associates. This cold logic of competition and greed allows Mark Renton to betray his friends in the final episode of the novel and to run off to Amsterdam with the £16,000 they have collected after their drug scam in London.[26]

Just as problematic as the representations themselves are the cynical conclusions drawn from them, not the least by Welsh himself. In an interview with Jennifer Berman in *The Bomb*, he mouths the platitude that Thatcherism systematically smashed "[t]he old routes of radical social change"[27] and institutions of solidarity. According to this surprisingly nostalgic and defeatist view, public life has disappeared, "[t]he only ways that young working-class people can get together are raves and parties".[28] The fashionable cynicism of statements like these illustrates the crux of *Trainspotting*: for Welsh, popular culture is not a space where alternative forms of solidarity can be invented, it is merely a space for narcissistic hyper-consumption. He suggests that the only alternative to the 'spirit-crushing' realities of consumer culture is the consumption of counterculture, either in the form of drugs, or, vicariously, in the commercial representations of subcultural resistance in texts like *Trainspotting*. For most audiences of the movie, particularly those of the suburban middle classes all over the UK, Europe and the US, cultural struggle would therefore be exhausted in the imitation of the signs and gestures of a decontextualized subcultural lifestyle.

However, critical educators cannot accept this as the last word on social transformation; they cannot yield to the fashionable rhetoric of the 'death of the social' and its rebirth as an acid house party. They have to question the rampant neoliberal egotism that pervades Welsh's counterculture. There are indeed kernels of hope, especially in *Trainspotting*'s critique of consumerism, but these have to be taken up differently, they have to be reinserted into a political discourse that re-imagines public life and new forms of agency.

6. Towards Critical Media Literacy

Trainspotting has given us much to think about in terms of its representations of agency, solidarity and consumerism, but the initial set of questions has yet to be tackled: how can the texts of popular culture be approached in an educational context? What do teenagers and cultural workers have to know to decode these texts? What kind of critical literacy is required beyond the traditional concepts of reading and writing? How can people become critical agents in a world that is increasingly negotiated through popular culture? How can *Trainspotting* be approached in a way that mobilizes its radical and critical potential without at the same time renewing its fatalism? In the remainder of the essay I want to offer not so much an answer, possibly in the form of a 'teachable' lesson plan, as a frame, a starting point for discussion.[29]

To avoid misunderstandings, a few words on critical media literacy are in order. The critical media literacy advocated here is by no means an attempt to return to models associated with the Frankfurt School, where teaching popular culture is understood as confronting students with an ideologically correct reading. Theodor W. Adorno's idea of teaching the pernicious effects of "mass culture" as he called it, was to take students to a movie, and afterwards spoil their fun by whacking them over the head with a water-proof ideological analysis.[30] Not only is the thought of Adorno going to a movie theatre (to actually witness first hand the object of his disgust) somewhat preposterous; anyone who has ever had the slightest classroom experience will know that such authoritarian methods almost automatically engender opposition. And rightly so, because they completely silence students, deny the pleasure of watching a movie, push aside the identifications produced by the movie, delegitimate the knowledge and even expertise which students undoubtedly have in the realm of popular culture, ridicule their meanings, and, in spite of all protestations to the contrary, treat them as objects, not subjects of pedagogy.[31] At least as far as method is concerned, Adorno's pedagogy is no less authoritarian than conservative models advocated by the likes of Bob Dole and the moral majority, because it merely imposes an omnipotent 'truth' on passive students.

Therefore, any pedagogy aiming at media literacy has to begin exactly with the identifications of teenage viewers and the pleasure produced by the participation in popular or 'mass culture'. Music, clothing, dancing, consuming are pleasurable, no matter for what age cohort, and to deny the pleasure and identifications of students is to lose them before the discussion has even begun. To make a movie like *Trainspotting* the subject of education, either formally in schools, or informally in youth clubs or at home, is already a step towards an education relevant to students' needs. But the movie has to be taken up in ways that takes students and their knowledge and concerns seriously.

Models for such an approach can be found in the work of the Brazilian educator Paolo Freire, who aims at a form of critical literacy which treats students once again as subjects, not objects of pedagogy. Freire conceives of pedagogy as a dialogue and therefore begins with the needs and desires of the learners, not with that of the educator who has a certain canon or world view to get across. The literacy programmes Freire practised in Brazil and elsewhere were not concerned with transmitting fixed canonical knowledge, traditional or revolutionary. Instead, Freire aimed at enabling students to produce and legitimate their own knowledges in critical dialogue with each other and the educator, to name the world they inhabit, and to gain the power to eventually transform it.[32]

American educational theorists like Henry Giroux, Peter McLaren or Roger Simon have adopted Freire's concept of liberation pedagogy and combined it with recent theories of Cultural Studies to suggest ways of becoming critical agents in the postmodern media world. They use the term "critical media literacy" to describe the ability to become agents in a society in which media representations play an increasingly important role for our self-perception, sense of possibility, and agency. Henry Giroux's "pedagogy of representation", which I will single out as an exemplary project, wants to enable students to understand how their own desires and identities are produced socially, for instance through the representations of popular culture, and to give them the means to question and transform these representations:

> I am referring to the various ways in which representations are constructed as a means of comprehending the past through the present in order to legitimate and secure a particular view of the future. How students can come to interrogate the historical, semiotic and relational dynamics involved in the production of various regimes of representations and their respective politics. In other words, a pedagogy of representation focuses on demystifying the act and process of representation by revealing how meanings are produced within relations of power that narrate identities through history, social forms, and modes of ethical address that appear objective, universally valid and consensual.[33]

In other words, students have to know about the media industry and the way in which images are produced, circulated and consumed. They have to be able to denaturalize representations and understand that representations are never objective, that there are always various 'interests' at work, whether they be commercial or political. It might be useful to contrast *Trainspotting* with other representations of working-class life, for instance in movies like *Small Faces* – not because these representations are more objective, but because the difference between the two might reveal different attitudes toward youth and help denaturalize the images of both. Students also bring different identities to the movie and come away with different impressions: girls will probably respond very differently, and so will students from different ethnic and social backgrounds. The classroom can become a site where different meanings of the movie are negotiated, again to denaturalize images and easy identifications.

Though Giroux's pedagogy is far removed from Adorno's, it is by no means to be confused with romantic or narcissistic anti-authoritarian pedagogies which merely affirm whatever identities students may bring to the classroom. Such approaches, popular since the seventies, do nothing to foster literacy or critical agency, but infantilize students and leave them at the mercy of media images of themselves. In critical media literacy, Adorno's term "critical" retains its central importance, and it is essential to challenge the identifications with which students come away from the movie. Therefore, the use of critical material in the form of newspaper articles or theoretical essays, depending on the age group, is of utmost importance. However, the values which inform this challenge and critique are not *a priori* established by the teacher, but have to be negotiated dialogically, in a conversation between cultural text, students and educators. What Giroux calls "pedagogy of representation" begins with the momentary desires, pleasures and identifications of the students, but does not stop there: it strives to make them critical by exposing them to a dialogue with other identifications and by putting them into larger social contexts beyond individual experience. The rationale is that only when they understand and question their own variously produced identifications can students become critical and transformative agents. Giroux's dialogic pedagogy does not for a moment abandon a radical notion of social justice, solidarity and democracy as reference points, though, unlike Adorno, he no longer pretends that he can define their exact contents.[34]

But Giroux does not confine himself to critique. Any pedagogical approach to popular representations remains incomplete as long as students remain consumers, albeit critical ones, of images of themselves.

> [E]ducators, artists, and other cultural workers must [...] develop educational approaches that teach kids how to use media as a mode of self-expression and social activism. We need to find ways to translate pedagogy into an activist strategy that will expand the opportunities for young people to acquire the knowledge and skills that will help them extend their participation into, and control over, those cultural, economic, and social spheres that shape their daily life (mass media, schools, media, workplace, policy making institutions, the arts).[35]

Giroux's goal is therefore what he calls a "representational pedagogy" that enables students not only to demystify popular culture, but to produce their own representations of themselves and their notion of solidarity and community in their own films, magazines, radio shows, internet homepages or music, and thus to sound their own voices and produce their own versions of the future. Students can learn to challenge that which reduces them for instance to mere consumers, and creatively appropriate and radicalize the elements of critique buried in movies like *Trainspotting*. They need access to the means of representation, which is equal to access to power: because the power to speak, to represent oneself, and to invent new forms of solidarity and community is equal to the power to shape one's destiny.

Of course, such a "representational pedagogy" requires political struggle outside the classroom as well: policy makers and educators have yet to be convinced that critical cultural literacy is an indispensable part of citizenship education, and that spending money on video equipment or dark rooms in schools and youth clubs is as important as funding the 'hard' sciences. Cultural workers have to understand that popular culture is not mere entertainment, but the terrain on which versions of the future are negotiated. Public life is about more than consumerism: cultural workers in all areas have to understand that a substantive notion of democracy cannot do without citizens who can read, contest, and re-write popular representations in order to transform public life.

Notes

1 All passages quoted from the screen adaptation are from Hodge (1996). For the opening sequence of the movie see *ibid.*, 3-5.
2 To name a single example, the German movie *Lola rennt* (1998) could be seen as an extended version of the opening sequence of *Trainspotting*, or a 90-minute MTV video-clip for that matter.
3 For a useful analysis of public life, identity and postmodern media cultures see Morley & Robins (1995). A note on footnotes: the need to maintain a minimum of readability requires that I simplify the theoretical debates on representation, literacy, subcultures, resistance, etc. In this essay, I draw mainly on the debates within British and American Cultural Studies. To give readers an impression of the implications of some of the questions, and the possibility to form their own opinions, I use these notes to supply additional bibliographical information.
4 Giroux (1997a: 59-60).
5 *Ibid.*, 60.
6 For the circuit of culture see Hall (1997: 3).
7 A casual keyword search for 'Trainspotting' with Alta Vista, performed some 18 months after the release of the movie, produced no less than 50,000 hits with reviews, sample chapters from the novel, photos, clips and soundbites from the movie and chat rooms, some on commercial, but most on personal sites.
8 See Giroux (1997a: 58).
9 For a very useful description of the American and British war on drugs, its impact on public life, and the creation of a 'moral panic' around youth see Reeves & Campbell (1994).
10 Young (1994: 14; my emphasis).
11 Welsh's American editor John Howard of Norton gives an example of a marketing strategy that successfully taps into the desire for the exotic. See Howard, "Hanging with the Scottish Homeboys".

12 The notion of rituals of resistance was developed by various cultural theorists at the Birmingham Centre for Contemporary Cultural Studies. See Hall & Jefferson (1993).
13 Welsh (1996: 15).
14 *Ibid.*
15 Willis (1993: 107). For a semiotic analysis of drug use and subcultural styles see also Hebdige (1979).
16 *Trainspotting* is problematic in more aspects than one. In a pedagogical situation it can and should be criticized as massively sexist to the point of degrading women. The representations of violence are also highly problematic. For strategic reasons, I have selected consumerism as one possible point of departure for a pedagogical intervention. I discuss issues like sexism and violence at greater length in Neubauer (1999).
17 Hodge (1996: 15).
18 Thompson (1996: 2).
19 The role of subcultural resistance has been the subject of extended arguments among cultural theorists. While Paul Willis, Dick Hebdige and especially Jonathan Fiske are known for their unproblematic and romantic approaches to subcultural resistance, critics like Stuart Hall, Angela McRobbie and others criticize them for their potential complicity with consumerism, their sexism or racism. See Hall (1981).
20 For an extended discussion of heroin chic see Giroux (forthcoming).
21 For a comparison between novel and movie see e.g. Sinfield (1994), Stedman (1997) and Neubauer (1999).
22 Hodge (1996: 51).
23 *Ibid.*, 106.
24 Sinfield (1997: xxvii).
25 Here, the novel is a lot more explicit than the movie can be. The junkies in *Trainspotting* burlesque Margaret Thatcher's call for a market unfettered by government control, and the competitive individualism that informed her infamous dictum, made in *Women's Own* in 1987, that "there is no such thing as society". In the words of Mark Renton: "Ah'm tempted tae quote Johnny n say that we wir aw acquaintances now. It sounds good in ma heid: 'We are all acquaintances now.' It seems tae go beyond our personal junk circumstances; a brilliant metaphor for our times." (Hodge, 1996: 11) Welsh's drug culture is not, as Reagan and Thatcher propagated, a moral aberration, but a carnivalesque replica of deregulated consumer capitalism, in which 'the need' has long obliterated any sense of solidarity: "Ah love nothing (except junk), ah hate nothing (except forces that prevent me getting any) and ah fear nothing (except scoring)" (21). In the moment of need (i.e. at every moment except the orgasmic high itself), the narcissistic ego tramples all social relations and altruist sentiments underfoot. Sick Boy neatly summarizes the neoliberal creed of limitless individualism and ego-inflation that feeds both drug culture and global laissez-faire liberalism: "[T]he socialists go on about your comrades, your class, your union, and society. Fuck all that shite. The Tories go on about your employer, your country, your family. Fuck that even mair. It's me, me, fucking ME, Simon David Williamson, NUMERO FUCKING UNO, versus the world." (30) Yet, like the movie, the novel does not question this cynicism, nor does it offer alternatives.

26 In marked contrast to the novel, the movie softens the ending. The last scene has Spud peering into a locker and taking out a wad of money, obviously put there by his good pal Mark. This ending is utterly hypocritical, because it does not offer a substantive view of solidarity and friendship. It is a merely a concession to an audience that might not relish the ugliness of greed and egotism.

27 Berman (1996: 57).

28 *Ibid.*, 60.

29 Stuart Hall's series "Culture, Media and Identities" is one of the first attempts to create useful classroom material for a critical pedagogical approach to popular culture. It offers useful hints, but should not be used as a definitive 'handbook' since this would exactly defeat the purpose.

30 Appropriately, in one of his conversations with Hellmut Becker he called his projected method "Pädagogik des Madigmachens". See Adorno (1971).

31 For a poignant critique of critical pedagogy of the Frankfurt School see Giroux (1997b).

32 The most comprehensive account of Paolo Freire's basic notion of pedagogy can be found in *Pedagogy of the Oppressed* (1997). The collection of essays entitled *Literacy* (1987), co-authored with his American translator Donald Macedo, is a highly readable attempt to provide a bridge from Freire's concern with peasant societies to postmodern media literacy.

33 Giroux (1993: 115).

34 For a useful discussion of "pedagogy of representation" see Giroux (1993).

35 Giroux (1997a: 62).

Bibliography

Adorno, Theodor W.: *Erziehung zur Mündigkeit. Vorträge und Gespräche mit Hellmut Becker 1959-1969*. Ed. Gerd Kadelbach, Frankfurt/M., 1971.

Berman, Jenifer: "Irvine Welsh", *Bomb* 56, 1996, 56-61.

Freire, Paolo & Donald Macedo: *Literacy. Reading the Word and the World*, Westport, 1987.

---: *Pedagogy of the Oppressed*. Tr. Myra Bergman Ramos, New York, 1997.

Giroux, Henry A.: *Living Dangerously. Multiculturalism and the Politics of Difference*, New York, 1993.

---: *Channel Surfing. Race Talk and the Destruction of Today's Youth*, New York, 1997a.

---: *Pedagogy and the Politics of Hope. Theory, Culture and Schooling. A Critical Reader*, Boulder, 1997b.

---: *Stealing Innocence. Youth, Corporate Power, and the Politics of Culture*, New York (forthcoming).

Hall, Stuart: "Notes on Deconstructing 'The Popular'". – In Raphael Samuel (Ed.): *People's History and Socialist Theory*, New York, 1981, pp. 227-240.

--- & Tony Jefferson (Eds.): *Resistance through Rituals. Youth Subcultures in Post-War Britain*, London, 1993 [first published as *Working Papers in Cultural Studies*, 1975].

--- (Ed.): *Representation. Cultural Representations and Signifying Practices*, London, 1997.

Hebdige, Dick: *Subculture. The Meaning of Style*, London, 1979.

Hodge, John: *Trainspotting. A Screenplay*, New York, 1996.

Howard, Gerald: "Hanging with the Scottish Homeboys. Adventures in Literature with James Kelman, Duncan McLean, and Irvine Welsh", http://www.wwnorton.com/scots.htm.

McLaren, Peter: *Critical Pedagogy and Predatory Culture. Oppositional Politics in a Postmodern Era*, New York, 1995.

Morley, David & Kevin Robins: *Spaces of Identity. Global Media, Electronic Landscapes and Cultural Boundaries*, New York, 1995.

Neubauer, Jürgen: *Literature as Intervention. Struggles over Cultural Identity in Contemporary Scottish Fiction*, Marburg, 1999.

Reeves, Jimmy & Richard Campbell: *Cracked Coverage. Television News, the Anti-Cocaine Crusade and the Reagan Legacy*, Durham, 1994.

Simon, Roger: *Teaching Against the Grain. Texts for a Pedagogy of Possibility*, New York, 1992.

Sinfield, Alan: *Literature, Politics and Culture in Postwar Britain*, London, 1997.

Stedman, Gesa: "'Scotland, the brave, ma arse'. *Trainspotting* – The Novel, Film and Soundtrack", *Hard Times* 59/60, 1997, 81-85.

Thompson, Ben: "The Interview. Irvine Welsh Talks to Ben Thompson", *The Independent on Sunday*, 2 June 1996, 2.

Welsh, Irvine: *Trainspotting*, London, 1994.

---: "City Tripper". – In *Trainspotting. The Play*, programme of the Whitehall Theatre, London, 1996, pp. 12-15.

Willis, Paul: "The Cultural Meaning of Drug Use". – In Stuart Hall & Tony Jefferson (Eds.): *Resistance through Rituals. Youth Subcultures in Post-War Britain*, London, 1993, pp. 106-118.

Young, Elizabeth: "Grubby Faces", *The Guardian*, 8 March 1994, Sect. 2, 14-15.

Merle Tönnies / Claus-Ulrich Viol, Bochum

Young Britain in Perspective. The Views of Rebbecca Ray, shez 360, Chandrasonic, Kathy Lette, and Anne Fine

In order to supplement the preceding case studies with more personal points of view, we asked a number of British authors, artists and musicians (either in the form of a questionnaire or in an interview) to give us their perspective on youth in Britain. The most pertinent answers are reprinted below. In order to represent the full panorama of opinions, we have included both young(er) respondents and those looking at British youth from a different generational standpoint. Young writer Rebbecca Ray's widely acclaimed first novel *A Certain Age* was published in 1998. The artist shez 360 brings commercial aesthetics and a postcolonial (Asian) perspective to the visual arts. Chandrasonic is the guitar player of Asian Dub Foundation (ADF), a politically committed band that fuses Eastern and Western traditions into a new form of dance music. The feminist Kathy Lette has written a number of popular and humorous novels, the most recent of which is *Altar Ego* (1999). Anne Fine is a recognised author of fiction for children and adolescents.

Rebbecca Ray
born: Mid-Wales, 1979
occupation: writer

a&e: What would you say are the most pressing problems for young people in contemporary Britain? Which political measures would you advocate to cope with them?

Considering the plans of Tony Blair's New Labour to create more chances for young people, for instance through improved education, would you say that young people are taken more seriously by the current British government than in the (post-)Thatcherite system? Has the new approach had any concrete effects?

Rebbecca Ray: As I'm sure is true of any country, there are a great many problems facing young people in Britain. I wouldn't like to say which is most pressing, but here are a few that could at least be addressed: There's a lot of young crime in Britain, there's an extremely high teen-pregnancy rate and – although I don't consider drugs in themselves to be destructive – I think there is a drug problem too.

I'm not a very politically aware person and I really don't know very much about the governmental system, but I do believe that these problems stem from one single source. I think a lot of young people lack a sense of opportunity, and because of this, a sense of hope.

One of Blair's selling points during his election campaign was youth opportunity, I know. I haven't seen any improvements in funding and jobs are, if anything, even harder to find. (Outside the cities, that is, which have received a great deal of money. Other areas have been neglected.) Unemployment figures are going down, I know, but then who'd put their faith in statistics?

Also, New Labour seems to consider youth-opportunity in a solely educational context. Our education authorities are moving further and further away from encouraging creativity and individuality. I think success, in a lot of schools now, is judged purely on an academic basis. There doesn't seem to be much respect accorded to either vocational skills or to abstract creativity. This must affect a lot of the young people that don't see themselves as future lawyers or doctors. I'd very much like to see support – both in and out of schools – for self-expression. Britain doesn't have much to export, except for the British people's creativity. I think it used to be a country known for producing inventors, artists, skilled workers. If you want funding for a good idea these days, your best bet is to look to Japan or the States. If the educational and funding systems were geared around utilising the individual skills that each person has, rather than attempting to streamline them (and abandoning those that don't fit), it would surely be beneficial, both for young people's self-esteem and sense of opportunity, and for Britain as a whole.

... Or at least that's what I think.

a&e: From your personal experience with the culture industry, is there a sufficient number of platforms for young people in Britain as far as non-commercial, challenging or even subversive representations are concerned? What changes would you like to see introduced in this respect?

Rebbecca Ray: I have to say, I think the creative industries succeed in providing opportunities for both non-commercial and potentially subversive material. (But then, what sells better than subversion and controversy?) Anyway, I could hardly criticise the publishing industry as failing to provide a platform for young people, could I? I think they do well, on the whole. And commercial encouragement from industry is certainly more common than the government-funded kind.

a&e: In an age of MTV, the 'Americanisation' of popular culture and an internationalised community of consumers, would you say that national identities are still relevant for young people? Does your self-image include any characteristics like British/English/?... and how important are such loyalties? Has the meaning of these terms been affected by the transition towards a multicultural society in Britain?

Rebbecca Ray: I don't think of myself as British. Or English. Or Welsh – Wales was where I grew up. I don't know, but I would imagine that national identity is far more important for young people from minority backgrounds. I must admit, there doesn't seem to be very much that encourages pride over a British identity. Having said that, I don't exactly have the right to complain. Thank God I wasn't born in Afghanistan.

As far as the Americanisation of British youth culture is concerned, I think Britain is still near the forefront of new cultural waves, most recently dance music. Youth sub-cultures will always force their way to the surface – isn't being a teenager all about dissent?

a&e: The 1990s have often been called the decade of 'post-feminism'. From your own experience and that of the women you know, would you say that the equality of the sexes has finally been achieved and the new self-confident woman is free to choose her own way of life or does this development constitute a sign of resignation?

Rebbecca Ray: I think we're pretty close now, in most areas of British culture, to achieving equality for the sexes. I was brought down a peg or two recently, hearing a discussion about feminism on the radio. Someone said that a lot of young British women will not now describe themselves as feminists because it has unfashionable connotations. I've told people that I'm not a feminist on many occasions myself. But it's wrong to take for granted the opportunities that women have in our society now. Maybe women should still be proud to be feminists – in a culture of equality. Although I'm sure they wouldn't describe themselves in this way, there are still plenty of men out there who are masculinists.

The other question, as far as our views on feminism are concerned, is whether we include immigrated cultural minorities in the spectrum. There is a very large Asian population in the area where I live. I don't know how much feminism – or post-feminism – might have affected the women in their society.

On the whole, I think Britain does pretty well now on gender equality.

a&e: It sometimes seems that the pace of living has accelerated today, so that relationships are only negotiated for short periods, identities are in a flux and values only retain validity for a few years at most. Would you agree with this view, specifically, how would you define the status of marriage / the family / long-term relationships for young people in the 1990s? In *A Certain Age*, the central elements of relationships seem to be dominance and subordination, so that the heroine, though in part a 'victim', develops towards using her power over other people. Does this lack of positive alternatives reflect your own views on human relations?

Rebbecca Ray: We're trying hard now, I think, all over the world, to determine our value system. Blair has opted, as did the Conservatives, to advocate marriage and the family as a defining factor in our morality. Politically, it must be easier to promote a return to outmoded – and, frankly, hypocritical – values than to attempt to deal with the many problems created by a more diverse, fragmented culture. I have never believed in marriage, my parents didn't believe in it. Personally, I think that the blind and permanent commitment required by marriage can only lead to future relationship problems. Divorce rates haven't gone up because more people are falling out of love, they have gone up because it is now socially acceptable to admit that a relationship is over.

On the other hand, I do think that long-term relationships can be extremely positive, especially for young people. They can often breed self-confidence – if the two people are right for one another. I also think there should be a place for a degree of promiscuity in every young person's life – although not during the long-term relationship, hopefully. Gaining sexual experience with new people, if you're doing it for the right reasons, creates independence and a strong sense of self.

It's true that the relationships in the book are strongly negative in many respects but this represents the other side of the coin. Long-term relationships can be very destructive between the wrong people – and depression so often feeds itself. It's very hard for two self-destructive people not to influence each other. What do they say? Misery loves company?

The book doesn't really reflect my views on human relations – I suppose it's meant to be an extreme, a sense of what *can* happen. There's nothing I can add to the understanding of human relationships, I think to communicate experience is enough. Love has always been, and always will be, one of the most beautiful, painful, complex human experiences. And thank God, or I'd be out of a job.

a&e: If you consider your own work, would you say that it is specifically produced from a 'youth' point of view and targeted at young addressees? Are you trying to influence your young audience / the general public and perhaps also to mediate between different age groups?

Rebbecca Ray: No. I just want to make lots of money.

I don't know. Although – I hope – I've gained more experience in the few years since I wrote the book, I think I could only have written from the perspective of a young person then. At the time, one of my ambitions for it was that it might end up school curriculum text. Who knows – maybe one day. I've always thought there was a lack of fiction about adolescence that was actually for young people. I was sick of reading rites-of-passage novels written by adults, for adults. I disliked the rose-tinted-spectacles nostalgia of novels like *Cider With Rosie*, and I found the imposition of the adult themes and ideas that saturated books like *The Catcher in the Rye* made them impossible to relate to as a teenager. It may be the case that, because the book I wrote avoids these things, it lacks the depth that adults look for in fiction. Maybe it doesn't matter; the responses I've had from young people have been overwhelmingly positive and personal. It's probably not a book for grown-ups, even though I would have liked it to be. But then, my writing has changed a lot. I wouldn't try to write *A Certain Age* now, and if I did it would be a lie.

I wasn't trying to influence anyone. And, if I'm completely honest, I didn't really expect so many adults to be shocked by it. When the reviews came out, there were a lot of statements like 'taps into the fears of parents everywhere'. If this was really the case, I can only say that these parents must be horribly distant from their children's lives in order to remain so naïve. What do parents *think* their kids are doing? Learning how to crochet? If adults didn't back away from issues like sex and drugs entirely, they might be able to create a framework within which teenagers can experiment safely. I think that once parents come to terms with the idea that sex and drugs aren't *innately* destructive, they might be able to stem some of the destructive situations that result from uneducated use and abuse. How can you explain to a teenager that taking three Ecstasy pills is excessive when you're also maintaining that taking it at all is morally wrong?

In the end, a book can't mediate between generations. I think only personal communication can do that.

a&e: When reading *A Certain Age*, it is striking that the whole question of the age of consent does not seem to pose a problem for both parents and the younger generation although your heroine is barely fourteen. Is this picture a 'realistic' depiction of changing sexual attitudes in Britain?

Rebbecca Ray: No, the book probably isn't realistic in its depiction of the parents' views towards underage sex. But then, if they'd banned the girl from seeing her older boyfriend, there wouldn't have been much of a story to tell. I think the age of consent still plays a huge part in parents' attitudes towards their children's sexuality, not least because it's the law.

Again, it's a case of avoidance, though. The parents in the book don't agree with the idea of underage sex – they just don't know how to deal with it. I think this is the case with most parents, and they either avoid the issue by ignoring it, as they do in the book, or by laying down indisputable rules. I think this has got to be one of the contributing factors of the high teen-pregnancy rate I'm criticising, but this is a generalisation. I know there are many liberal parents who see the value in dialogue – two of them brought me up – I think the majority still have a great fear, though, of really addressing the issues of their kids.

As far as young people are concerned, the proportion that care about the age of consent is tiny. Maybe this is the result of such a lack of communication, I don't know. But I think the thoughtlessness with which many teenagers approach sex can often lead to emotional damage.

a&e: When looking at the response to your novel on the internet, we were struck by the overwhelming mass of positive reactions. Did you also get critical responses, maybe along the lines that the heroine and her world could be a bad example for young people (as after all your novel refuses to be overtly didactic about such issues as drugs, paedophilia, masochism and violence)?

Rebbecca Ray: I've had a lot of negative reactions to the book – unfortunately they were mostly based around its quality. Although, as I said, many people seemed to be shocked by it, I don't think anyone reacted to that shock by denouncing the book's morals. I was worried, before its publication, that people might see it as promoting the behaviour it describes. In the end, though, the central character is forced to face the reality of the pain that her actions have caused. She is irresponsible – and thoughtless – and I didn't want to condemn her for that. But the situation in which she places herself, and which she then encourages, only brings her a great deal of pain – and it destroys her parents. I think these eventualities would be enough to put anyone off mimicking her behaviour.

Also, I tried to be careful not to depict her actions as 'cool'. She is never attractive in these situations, she feels ugly, and that isn't something any teenager wants to emulate.

As far as paedophilia is concerned, I think the book condemns it in the sense that, although Oliver isn't punished for his actions, he is revealed as a deeply unhappy person, a broken person. I wanted very much to describe the kind of painful, desperate need that leads an older man to begin a relationship with a teenage girl.

The violence is slightly different. I didn't want to denounce the character of Oliver for his violent behaviour because, as the end of the book, it's important for the girl to see that the responsibility lies with her as well. I wanted her to begin to understand that she is responsible for her own happiness, that creating a role for herself as a victim doesn't absolve her of blame. That's her coming-of-age. Maybe it wasn't expressed as well as it could have been – but then I wanted it to be a dramatic ending too. I probably fall short of making my points too often, just for the sake of a great big bang.

a&e: Is their any message / personal motto you would like to impart to other young people if that were possible – and if all of us were not too 'postmodern' to believe in mottos anyway?

Rebbecca Ray: I wouldn't want to try and impart any message – I'm still having trouble living by my own rules. And the whole point of being a teenager is that you don't take anyone's advice. Right?

shez 360
born: London, 1974
occupation: artist

a&e: What are the most pressing problems for young people in contemporary Britain? Which political measures would you advocate to cope with them?

shez 360: Awareness, above all. More and more newspapers and media take a non-commital centre-right position. This it seems is a sign of an overall transition to a less motivated, thoughtless society. The emerging value system (or lack thereof) seems born of a certain cynical apathy, characteristic of English attitudes. It is reinforced by the actions of culture – even as culture seems to diversify and embrace various different cultures it removes any true context, and everything becomes representation. As a result, it is harder than ever for young people to navigate their way around culture – 'culture' as being the locus for contemporary existence – and make a worthwhile contribution.

Whether government instigates culture, or is to some degree subordinate to it, there is some degree of symbiosis. Therefore political measures within national government could not counter this process without becoming self-damning.

a&e: In 1997, one of the main projects of New Labour was creating more chances for young people, for instance through improved education, and Tony Blair was being represented as the epitome of youthfulness. Would you say that young people are taken more seriously by the current British government than in the (post-)Thatcherite system? Has the new approach had any concrete effects?

shez 360: Young people are only taken 'seriously' at a superficial level – i.e. in terms of promoting New Labour through association with pop stars and designers to obtain 'the youth vote'. In real terms funding for education is worse now than it has ever been in this country, and opportunities for further education have decreased dramatically especially among poorer students. Education is therefore now as elitist as it was 100 years ago, and more students from universities are forced to take city-based employment to pay off their educational debt, rather than actually utilising their education for any progressive means.

a&e: From your personal experience with the culture industry, is there a sufficient number of platforms for young people in Britain as far as non-commercial, challenging or even subversive representations are concerned? What changes would you like to see introduced in this respect?

shez 360: There are less alternative platforms, but to my mind this is not a bad thing. The seventies and eighties saw some of the most self-indulgent and didactic forms of artistic expression, and to my mind it is these artists that have created the current marginalisation and distrust of a lot of art forms. I find it far more challenging and realistic to deconstruct the system from within. Yes, there is the speed at which things are assimilated by the mainstream, but to work counter to this and slow things right down in one's own mind gives one the ability to work between the lines of culture.

a&e: In an age of MTV, the 'Americanisation' of popular culture and an internationalised community of consumers, would you say that national identities are still relevant for young people? Does your self-image include any characteristics like British/English/?... and how important are such loyalties? Has the meaning of these terms been affected by the transition towards a multicultural society in Britain?

shez 360: National identities are still important to people, but this is rather retrogressive and is usually based around projected difference (ignorance) and sporting competitions (male aggressive syndrome). My self-image is both a rejection of all things British – as representing pompous imperialism – and a staunch defence of being British as an opposition to Americanisation and to inferior international advertising.

a&e: Surveying tendencies in fashion, leisure pursuits and the media, some critics (at least from among the old '68 generation in Germany) have alleged that young people today are living only for hedonism, are characterised by self-absorption, passivity and a lack of political awareness and could even be called 'conservative' again. Would you agree with regard to current trends in Britain?

shez 360: I believe this is changing. Perhaps rather optimistically I genuinely believe in a growing youth political awareness. But political truths become harder to ascertain in a culture where Anglo-American manipulation of media and representation are doctrinal. And it is an older generation that have failed to alter this chain of events as it came to pass. To truly alter culture one must be constantly striving to be ahead of it, rather than operating counter to it. This is the specific failure of the older generation, who should stop whinging and appreciate what is being done now. Otherwise they are just fulfilling their assigned roles in criticising and slowing down contemporary action, when in fact they share the same aspirations.

a&e: If you consider your own work, would you say that it is specifically produced from a 'youth' point of view and targeted at young addressees? In how far is it meant to be representative and in how far does it rather reflect individual experiences? Are you trying to influence your young audience / the general public and perhaps also to mediate between different age groups?

shez 360: This would depend on how far one felt fashion and advertising were a youth domain, or even culture at large. My work plays between established discourses within culture, attempting to remove boundaries between each. As such although one cannot fully divest oneself of an individual perspective, I am to pare my images down as much as possible to open them up to the widest spectrum of interpretation and accessibility. Humour as well is a major factor, rather than telling people what to think, I prefer to satirise existing prejudices/stereotypes to the point where they (hopefully) become ridiculous to maintain.

a&e: From your own experience, would you say young people from Asian backgrounds experience growing up in Britain differently than the majority? In how far are these differences due to Asian community traditions?

shez 360: Yes they do. There is an awareness of difference that is at first difficult and creates a tension between 'white' culture and tradition. In as much as everything one is taught at a young age gears one toward passive assimilation and a possible rejection of one's own origins. I don't know how much this has changed since I was at school.

However, this sort of 'limbo' has in the end forced me to go back to my own culture and become the best of both worlds, with the freedom of movement and association this brings. This is in fact something I see more and more, as artists from multicultural backgrounds begin to take on the possibilities this engenders, their work stands out much more than the already fading one-liners of tired 'Young British Art'. For example the works of Chris Ofili, Yinka Shonibare, Vhong Phaopanit, Runa Islam. But there is still more to come, in spite of English art schools still having a resistance to more diverse students.

a&e: Your work has often been seen as commenting on / making use of the stereotypes of advertising aesthetics. Do you think that the multicultural tokenism of advertising and the use of ethnicity for purposes of 'exoticism' are making it more difficult for young people today to develop a genuine multicultural awareness? Would you want your art to fulfil a function in this respect?

shez 360: Absolutely. You have pretty much echoed my mission statement. My work is about introducing a critical function, while aping the forms and means of advertising at its most effective. It is also about looking at the reality behind 'exotic advertising', which often leaves out any acknowledgement of a non-Western target audience or of the historical legacy behind such representations of difference.

a&e: Simply in terms of numbers, the reading public is far bigger than the section of society which is interested in art exhibitions and galleries. Would you say it is more difficult to 'reach' especially young people in your chosen medium than through literature and also music (from which one cannot get away today anyway)?

shez 360: Forget literature – there is almost no such thing as contemporary literature (of any intellectual or aesthetic merit). With the arrival of MTV, as you mentioned before, there has been a shift in favour of the visual and concise. This is only a bad thing if viewed in the light of developments to date – i.e. few people have taken it on board except advertisers, corporations and Hollywood. However, it does open up possibilities for a new artistry that might combine and shatter media at will. Agreed, art galleries are very limited. That is why at this moment I am already engaged on projects to insert my fake advertisements back into fashion and lifestyle magazines – thereby confusing and highlighting context. I am also trying to raise funding for an actual billboard site in the strongly Asian borough of Tower Hamlets in London. And music, well yes it does seem as if life now runs to a constant soundtrack, and I do have plans in this department but you'll have to wait and see.

a&e: Is their any message / personal motto you would like to impart to other young people if that were possible – and if all of us were not too 'postmodern' to believe in mottos anyway?

shez 360: Wake Up.

Chandrasonic (Asian Dub Foundation)
born: Acton/London, 1968
occupation: musician and teacher

a&e: What are the most pressing problems for young people in Britain today?

Chandrasonic: Unemployment, poor employment, actually. Unemployment is going down a lot in this country, but jobs are being replaced by deskilled, very low-paid jobs. Look at things like the media industry, MTV, TV companies – they get young people to work for nothing. It's the McDonaldisation of employment, especially for young people. Also, alongside that, the chances to go in further and higher education are rapidly diminishing as well.

a&e: From Germany it seemed that Tony Blair tried to change this or at least pretended to change something …

Chandrasonic: No, he's trying to make it worse.

a&e: So what happened to Blair's slogan "Education, education, education"? Has there been any improvement for young people since the election in 1997?

Chandrasonic: I don't think you need to ask *me* that one really. It's just the usual stuff. Basically higher education is being denied to a lot of people, it's closing up. The processes started with the Conservatives are being carried on with a vengeancc by Labour. No, there have not really been any improvements. I think this quite a continuation, really: the new deal to make it more difficult for young people to get dole and housing. None of this stuff has changed; in many ways it's just continuing the spiral downwards. We have heard about a tax on single mothers, we have heard about all kinds of stuff. It's business as usual, really.

a&e: What political measures would you advocate to cope with the situation?

Chandrasonic: Well, I don't know whether you know, but we run a lot of youth projects. I would say, stick some cash into projects like our ADFED [educational branch of ADF, helping young (Asian) musicians to develop their skills and providing opportunities for creative self-expression], which is all about increasing skills for people and self-empowerment and expression.

a&e: You have already referred to MTV and its exploitation of young people. Generally in Britain, are there enough platforms for young people's concerns?

Chandrasonic: I don't think there're any at all now and I think the issue is that we have a very self-centring society and a society which encourages people not to question, not to speak out, not to criticise.

a&e: What about the mainstream media like the BBC and Channel Four. Have you got any engagements with them? Is that a platform for you?

Chandrasonic: Yes, it is for *us*, you see you've got to be prepared to talk about something. We are one of the few music groups and musicians that actually talk about issues and socially conscious themes and, you know, a lot of people have a problem with that. We have a self-centring entertainment culture. Everything has got to be a laugh and everything has got to be connected with sex or consumerism, and you're not meant to criticise what is going on. There is a whole culture of self-censorship.

a&e: We have that phenomenon in Germany that people from the '68 generation criticise young people for lacking awareness and activity.

Chandrasonic: They should turn their criticism upon themselves because what they set up, what happened in the sixties and seventies got us where we are now. I really can't stand it when I hear the old generation say young people today aren't radical like they were.

a&e: But you also say that there is a bit of hedonism going on?

Chandrasonic: I don't think it's as simple as people deciding I'm not going to be interested in anything, I'm going to be hedonistic. I don't think it's as simple as that. That assumes that there is a kind of choice. You know, there are new forms of protest, there are new forms of things that are growing. You have to look at the Seattle thing [the disruption of the World Trade Organisation talks in November 1999 by international protesters], we have had things in London as well and there is also the internet and things like that. There are new avenues and new means and methods that are growing now. People from the '68 generation are just looking to see a repeat of their youth as evidence of radicalism. What they should be doing is getting out there, seeing new avenues, new areas where they can actually help to inspire a new kind of radicalism that's relevant for now. We don't want 1968 radicalism – it was in 1968, the economic and social conditions of the world are completely different now. So we have to look for new areas of protest, new areas of organisation. I think it is important that they are going to be on a global scale, internationalist, and they are going to be very much tied up with new technology.

a&e: So it is the older generation who have turned conservative?

Chandrasonic: It's just another version of that old thing: 'Oh, things aren't as good as they were in my day.' Only it's coming from a left-wing perspective, not a right-wing one. Anyone who talks like that without any alternative or way to raise consciousness should just shut up. If you've got a problem with it, let's have a solution, shall we? It's too easy. You see, they benefit from the status quo, in middle-class newspapers, academic institutions and things like that. They benefit from the way things are now. They are part of the problem.

a&e: What is the solution to activate young people from your point of view? Is it to get into the media or to do alternative projects?

Chandrasonic: I think both – the two aren't mutually exclusive at all. They are part and parcel of the same thing. There is a concept Hilary Wainwright came up with called 'revolutionary gradualism'. [H.W. is a prominent figure of the pro-Labour socialist movement and currently editor of *Red Pepper*, an independent magazine of the green and radical left.] I wouldn't necessarily say that she is a guru or anything, but it's the concept that I like: you build up strong organisations at the grass roots and you make links horizontally.

a&e: We would like to ask a question from a different realm, maybe not totally different. Does your own self-image include labels like British, English etc.? Is that important at all?

Chandrasonic: I don't know. I don't think I can categorise it really. We have debated this for many years and in the end, I'd rather just kind of say 'forget it'. I have very strong roots in India but I was brought up here. There is a whole load of subjects, even objective factors that relate together to create me as a person, which is the same for anybody to the point where it's very difficult to talk about a national identity. I think you can just talk about a personal identity, your relation to your self-perception and how others see you. I think that's the nature of identity, it's a relationship between how others see you, how you think others see you and how you see yourself.

a&e: Isn't that partly determined by – let's call it the Asian background, this upbringing? Is growing up in Britain different coming from an Asian background?

Chandrasonic: Of course it is. Very different, because there is a whole load of weight of preconceptions and prejudices that come with that.

a&e: Is there any improvement in the direction of a multicultural society?

Chandrasonic: There is a massive improvement in some areas, in other areas there is a complete stasis, especially in the criminal justice system etc.

a&e: What about Satpal Ram? What's the latest news? [The young Asian S.R. was sentenced for life in 1986 after lethally wounding one of a group of racist attackers in clear self-defence. The fact that he did not receive a fair trial has made a number of campaigns – including ADF – fight for his cause.]

Chandrasonic: The latest news is that they've got new people on the case and there is a motion put forward in Parliament to debate the case. It keeps moving step by step.

a&e: Your lyrics – and dub in general – are about creating a new culture that transcends national identity and things like that. Do you have the feeling that music can make that difference?

Chandrasonic: No, not on its own, it's just one part of a large whole. You could turn anything into a positive, empowering thing, the way you work in a factory, the way you talk to people, the way you make music, the way you make films. It's just part of a whole process.

a&e: You tour Europe a lot – France, Germany. Is there this community feeling in your performances that you can say you've left behind national identity?

Chandrasonic: Yes, yes. I think our vibe is very welcoming and includes everybody in the room.

a&e: Are there nevertheless differences among the national crowds? For instance that the German crowd is not that easy-going?

Chandrasonic: No, that's not true. We've had some of our best gigs ever in Germany – Berlin, Hamburg – incredible. Some places in Germany have been quite dead but I don't want to name names. There are a series of factors involved in this. Berlin and Hamburg have been tremendous places to play. Cologne is awesome – every gig we've played in Cologne has been fantastic.

a&e: What about the relationship between tradition and future; a lot of your programme is about leaving behind musical traditions …

Chandrasonic: No, it's not leaving behind, it's regenerating and seeing tradition as a moving, progressing thing rather than something that's stuck. I think tradition, in order to survive, has to be enriched.

a&e: Does that include the thematic orientation towards the past? In your songs like "Naxalite" or "Assassin" you're dealing with historical events. From your point of view, is it more important for young people to orient themselves towards the future, or is it more tradition and history, or is it a mix, what would you say?

Chandrasonic: Those two songs are actually a redress of historical perception; they're attempts to maybe look at aspects of Indian history that aren't normally associated with India. As to tradition and the future, I don't think you can have one without the other. The future is not a vacuum, is it? The future is built on what's happening now. As your own Karl Marx says, we make our own history but we do not do so on the conditions of our choosing.

a&e: There will be a new single called the "Real Great Britain". What is the song about?

Chandrasonic: It has to do with a lot of stuff to try and re-brand Britain. There was this notion of re-branding Britain that came from New Labour.

a&e: Have you got any message or motto that you'd like to impart to young people?

Chandrasonic: Don't just consume, make you're own tune!

Kathy Lette
born: Sydney/Australia, 1958
occupation: writer

a&e: What would you say are the most pressing problems for young people in contemporary Britain? Which political measures would you advocate to cope with them?

Kathy Lette: For British women the issue is equal pay. We're still only getting 75 pence in the pound, and yet we're supposed to be Post Feminists. Any woman who calls herself a Post Feminist has kept her wonder bra and burnt her brains.

a&e: In 1997, one of the main projects of New Labour was creating more chances for young people, for instance through improved education, and Tony Blair was being represented as the epitome of youthfulness. Would you say that young people are taken more seriously by the current British government than in the (post-)Thatcherite system? Has the new approach had any concrete effects?

Kathy Lette: Tony Blair is highly unusual – a politician who is passionate about his beliefs; a politician who cares about more than the size of his *election.*

a&e: From your personal experience with the culture industry, is there a sufficient number of platforms for young people in Britain as far as non-commercial, challenging or even subversive representations are concerned? What changes would you like to see introduced in this respect?

Kathy Lette: That question is too deep for me – I got exhausted treading intellectual water just reading it. "Cultural platforms?" – aren't they the shoes Ginger Spice wears?

a&e: In an age of MTV, the 'Americanisation' of popular culture and an internationalised community of consumers, would you say that national identities are still relevant for young people? Does your self-image include any characteristics like British/English/?… and how important are such loyalties? Has the meaning of these terms been affected by the transition towards a multicultural society in Britain?

Kathy Lette: The Americanisation of the world's culture is nauseating. Mainly because of its misogyny. Especially in the movie industry, in which I've worked in Hollywood.

I mean, imagine it. *Joan* Wayne leads a wagon train of helpless men to safety. Imagine it. *All the President's Women, Roberta* Redford and *Dusty* Hoffman, risk their lives to uncover the Watergate scandal. And then there's *The Godmother,* starring *Marilyn* Brando. *Melanie* Gibson shooting straight from the lip in *Lethal Weapon. A Fistful of Dollars*, starring *Clit* Eastwood …

But of course, this sort of focus-pocus will never happen. Because Hollywood hates women. I mean Real Women. Women like us. Women with the odd bit of armpit stubble. Women with cheek and chutzpah. Women who do *not* have love bites on our mirrors. No. Hollywood only likes one sort of female. The sort who has kept her bra … and burnt her brain.

Having lived in L.A. … sorry – living in L.A. is a contradiction in terms – having existed there for over a year, let me tell you that the term 'bimbo' is not gender specific. California is crawling with indistinguishable men called Andy/Sandy/Chuck or Hank. They all have blow-waved brain cells and I.Q.'s smaller than their jock straps. So, why don't they proliferate our screens, playing the token human handbags of high-powered female protagonists? Because Hollywood's D.I.Y. Guide to Becoming a Bimbo is for females only.

Apart from the odd 'Pretty Woman' prostitute or 'Fatally Attracted' psychopath, what role models do we girls have? I'll tell you. Sharon Stone and Kim Basinger, playing the sort of innocuous character whose sole concern is what side her bed is buttered.

It wasn't always like this. Once we had Mae West, Lauren Bacall, Barbara Stanwyck, Katharine Hepburn, Bette Davis … Women with black belts in the art of *tongue-fu*. So, what happened? The 1950s, that's what. The war was over, women were no longer required in the workplace … and suddenly, surprise, surprise our heroines were dipped in household disinfectant. We were in for an entire decade of film scripts sanitised by the likes of Jane Wyman, Donna Reed, Nancy Reagan; sinking into his arms … before sinking her arms in his sink.

But surely these attitudes go in one era and out the other. This is the Politically Correct 1990s. The days of 'designer' wombs and date rape. Surely things have changed? … Despite the advent of the Women's Movement, going to contemporary movies is *still* vocational guidance in bimbofication. Think about it.

Judging by the monosyllabically dull dialogue of the female characters in most modern movies, higher education for women is obviously out. Our only reading material consists of palms, menus and bank balances.

It appears to be a Hollywood rule that any female character with a witty line must die by the end of the film. The colour of her hair will be brunette. (In case you hadn't noticed, peroxide is the major contribution science has made to the Californian way of life. As Norma Jean knew only too well, there is a reason why blondes have more fun. It's because brunettes are kept busy bleaching, waxing, shaving and Nair-Hair removing.)

Then there's the skin of our current Hollywood heroines. There seems to be no law of gravity in L.A. Skin sags *upwards*. The bodies of our cinematic role-models are all of Barbie Doll uniformity. Bimbo etiquette requires you to have either a breast reduction (and you thought two were the normal number, right?) or silicone implants. But what about the environmental ramifications of the latter procedure? It's a shock, I know, but the immortal Barbie does have a shelf-life. Having passed her amuse-by date, the dilemma is what to do with the carcass? You see, the silicone won't melt in the crematorium, nor will it biodegrade in the ground. Hollywood hasn't as yet offered a solution. Should we simply make a kind of breast mountain, like the butter and grain mountains in Europe? Or perhaps mothers could bequeath their silicone implants onto their daughters. A kind of breast behest?

Okay, you're thinking, if all this is true, surely we're shooting too much footage and not enough producers? But the truth is, *things could be worse*. Movies may constantly portray women as brain-dead drongos, but at least we're *portrayed*. A disturbing new trend is emerging in Hollywood. Women, even the traditional bimbo, are about to become obsolete. It's well known that Californian men love their cars. Hollywood produces a series called *Knightrider* featuring a car which talks. Then there's the sit com, *My Mother the Car* – a kind of womb on wheels. A one-night stand is now referred to as a 'speed bump.' If American movie moguls could get their cars to make love to them, they wouldn't need women at all ...

Well, strap a shock-absorber to your brain because ... *it's happened*. A shop on Santa Monica Boulevard is now selling a gadget subtlety named the 'Auto Suck'. Men plug it into the cigarette lighter, attach it to the appropriate part of the anatomy and it performs fellatio whilst driving.

As if driving in L.A. isn't difficult enough, what with freeway shootings and traffic jams – without having to swivel your head from side to side to see who's motoring a tad too happily. It seems that Michelle Pfeiffer and Julia Roberts will soon have to have a steering wheel and rear-demister surgically attached.

I know. It gives a whole new meaning to the term 'sex drive'.

The truth is, the representation of women in popular culture won't improve until we girls high-jack Hollywood. Then we can give the blokes a taste of what it feels like to have no movie role models. Oh, we'll give them the occasional male prostitute in 'Handsome Guy' or the token toy boy in 'Scent of a Man' ... but for the most part, we'll just have them hanging around to laugh at our jokes, flick their blow waves about and service us sexually.

* * *

As for self image – I am 100 % Aussie sheila – raucous, raunchy and hedonistic. (In Australia we give very good hedonism.) You must stay true to who you are – especially as a writer, otherwise you'll lose your voice.

As for the importance of cultural loyalties – it's diversity which makes the world interesting. We don't want to live in a big, bland, Americanised world – McWorld. Oh no. ... but in a human minestrone, with a little bit of everything. Now *that's* palatable.

a&e: The 1990s have often been called the decade of 'post-feminism'. From your own experience and that of the women you know, would you say that the equality of the sexes has finally been achieved and the new self-confident woman is free to choose her own way of life or does this development constitute a sign of resignation?

Kathy Lette: As I said in the first question, British women are still only getting 75 pence in the pound, still doing all the house work (British men have increased their contribution to housework on average, by three seconds A WEEK!) and still getting concussion hitting our heads on the glass ceiling (and we're probably expected to Windex it while we're up there) and yet we're supposed to be Post Feminists. Any woman who calls herself a Post Feminist has kept her wonder bra and burnt her brains. Wake up and Smell the Sexism.

a&e: It sometimes seems that the pace of living has accelerated today, so that relationships are only negotiated for short periods, identities are in a flux and values only retain validity for a few years at most. Would you agree with this view, specifically, how would you define the status of marriage / the family / long-term relationships for young people in the 1990s? How important are they compared with other means of providing reliability in life and defining one's identity?

Kathy Lette: Marriage, well, yes. (oops, my type face just changed. Even my computer is two-faced!)

Girls, has the UN declared your love life a disaster area? Are you a romance fatality? A chalked outline in the marital stakes? Are you approaching the age of being dumped for a younger wife and you're not even married yet? Hell, if your *skin*'s cleared up, you're too old to marry. Men are walking down the aisle with a foetus in a veil. If you're over 30, you may be young at heart, but apparently you're middle-aged in all the other places.

In your frantic search for a member of the Ring-Buying Sex have you been on more laps than a portable PC? Has desperation forced you to downgrade your marriage expectations from Mr. Right to Mr. Kinda OK? A marital limbo dancer, you just keep getting lower and lower. Who said anything about looking for the perfect man? Interestingly flawed will do. Vaguely bearable. Two corpses short of a serial killer, even. What shocks your friends is not how much you expect from man, but how little. In the end, you choose your groom chiefly on the ground that *he's a male.*

But is this pathetic scenario really the case? The number of marriage ceremonies currently performed in the West is lower than Pamela Anderson's bikini line. And, as we now know that marriage suits men (married men live longer than their single counterparts, with less heart disease and mental problems; whereas single women live longer than married women and are physically and mentally healthier), it seems to me that it's *women* who are showing signs of PMT (Pre-Monogamy Tension).

Since girlhood, it's been grilled into us that getting married is the natural thing to do (unless you've got a very good excuse, you know, that you're lesbian or are so visually challenged that you need to get your mirrors insured). Love should end in marriage. Well, believe me, in many cases *it does.*

But come on! You've lived together and bought a microwave and shared a genital infection. Marriage is surely the next logical step? ... But should love be logical?

Speaking of which ... All your life you've found it hard to avoid temptation, right? Well, once wed, you'll find it impossible to find any. Marriage means never again getting the urge to do the lambada naked in front of your pets. Never again performing strip karaoke. Never again seducing the tumble-drier man with the washboard tum and torn-jeans bum. No. Now your life will be consumed by much more Important Issues. Locating lost dry-cleaning tickets. Taking pets you loathe for dental-descaling. Obsessing about whether your washing machine has a double duty agitator, as you run your fingers through what will be left of your husband's hair and wonder how you ended up living with a man who can wear a tartan terry towelling dressing gown without irony.

But being married does have some good points. What a relief not to have to go naked in front of a stranger ever again. Not to have to bikini-wax every five seconds. Or lie on your side to make your breasts look bigger. A husband is the person who knows all about you ... and still likes you anyway.

Marriage is also an immunisation against loneliness. Who wants to become one of those women who pretend to be fulfilled by the new medieval history lecture series they've signed up for? To get bath salts every birthday and Christmas. A Sahara of bath salts. Forever doomed to tick the box marked 'Single'. Spending your childbearing years in board meetings, then trying to conceive with a turkey baster at 45. Forever doomed to wear full make up to the supermarket, *just in case you meet somebody.* Ugh. It's enough to make your nipples go numb.

Besides, Engagement, Marriage, The First Baby – aren't these the traditional greetings-card landmarks of life? Yes … *Till Divorce Us Do Part.* Perhaps America's collective cold feet is due to the fact half of all marriages today end in divorce. (And let's face it, *more ought to.*) It's tempting just to save time and money and marry your divorce lawyer. So quick; so easy. A drive-through McMarriage … Hell, if matrimony were a horse, no self-respecting gambler would take a punt on it.

If the institution of marriage is not to be jilted at the altar, we need to love more realistically, with the inoculation of experience.

a&e: If you consider your own work, would you say that it is specifically produced from a 'youth' point of view and targeted at young addressees? Are you trying to influence your young audience / the general public and perhaps also to mediate between different age groups?

Kathy Lette: I just always write the book I wish I'd had at the time. *Puberty Blues* was about what it's like as a young girl growing up in Australia with Neanderthal men – those men who'd look more at home if they just squatted on their haunches and groomed each other.

Girls Night Out was a book about what it's like trying to find a man who isn't married or gay. Or married AND gay. *The Llama Parlour* was a satire on the Americanisation of our culture. *Foetal Attraction* was about the horrors of natural childbirth (a case of stiff upper labia) and the weirdness of the English (they have a condescension chromosome – most of them have graduated from Oxford in Advanced Smugness); *Mad Cows* was about how motherhood leaves you a few nappies short of a full pack of Pampers and, my favourite, *Altar Ego* is an antidote to the Bridget Jones books of this world – the books which imply that you are nothing without a man.

I just write my books because it's cheaper than therapy. Otherwise I'd be a resident of Couch Canyon.

a&e: Is there any message / personal motto you would like to impart to other young people if that were possible – and if all of us were not too 'postmodern' to believe in mottos anyway?

Kathy Lette: Do be a Feminist, but don't be Politically Correct (surely, a contradiction in terms). Be yourself. Always remember that life's too short to be subtle and, most important of all, give good hedonism!

Anne Fine
born: 1947
occupation: writer of fiction for young people

a&e: What would you say are the most pressing problems for young people in contemporary Britain? Which political measures would you advocate to cope with them?

Anne Fine: I think the most pressing problem for the great majority of young British people is their thin – not to say poor – education. The ones at the top of the heap probably have as good and enriching an education as they always did. But expectations were allowed to slip so low for the great bulk of our young people during the years of ideological concerns about 'anti-elitism', etc.

a&e: In 1997, one of the main projects of New Labour was creating more chances for young people, for instance through improved education, and Tony Blair was being represented as the epitome of youthfulness. Would you say that young people are taken more seriously by the current British government than in the (post-)Thatcherite system? Has the new approach had any concrete effects?

Anne Fine: I'd say Tony Blair is trying to grasp this nettle. He has remained loyal through difficult times to Chris Woodhead, who fights this battle for raised standards openly, in the teeth of strong opposition from various sectors of the 'educational establishment'. If I can judge by the fan letters I get, just at the most basic levels, standards – and expectations – are rising again quite steadily. I feel almost hopeful. (Almost.)

a&e: From your personal experience with the culture industry, is there a sufficient number of platforms for young people in Britain as far as non-commercial, challenging or even subversive representations are concerned?

Anne Fine: I hate to link everything to education, but I think that there have never been problems in Britain offering young people platforms so much as in getting them interested in wanting to use those that are available.

a&e: In an age of MTV, the 'Americanisation' of popular culture and an internationalised community of consumers, would you say that national identities are still relevant for young people? Characteristics like British/ English/? ...: how important are such loyalties? Has the meaning of these terms been affected by the transition towards a multicultural society in Britain?

Anne Fine: I suspect national loyalties are still relevant to the young people I know. On the minus side, we suffer a rather dismal xenophobia. On the plus side, I think, within our own national boundaries, we have a vastly wider sense of what a range of groups make up the new Britain. And the great majority of us, especially our young people, seem perfectly comfortable with this. In fact I'd say that multiculturalism has taken on pretty well, here.

a&e: The 1990s have often been called the decade of 'post-feminism'. From your own experience and that of the women you know, would you say that the equality of the sexes has finally been achieved and the new self-confident woman is free to choose her own way of life or does this development constitute a sign of resignation?

Anne Fine: I look at educated young women I know, and they assume their own careers and lives are as important and valuable as those of their male friends. So here's a revolution won. But, if I know life, it'll take eternal vigilance to keep things that way. And I suspect quite a percentage of our less well-educated young women only pay lip service to the principles during school years, and fight the good fight for almost no time at all after leaving school.

a&e: It sometimes seems that the pace of living has accelerated today, so that relationships are only negotiated for short periods, identities are in a flux and values only retain validity for a few years at most. Would you agree with this view, specifically, how would you define the status of marriage / the family / long-term relationships for young people in the 1990s? How important are they compared with other means of providing reliability in life and defining one's identity?

Anne Fine: I get the feeling that many young people – especially those from divorced families – value, and depend on, their intimate circle of friends almost more than their relations. This could be, as Professor Allan Bloom put it in *The Closing of the American Mind*, that they have 'been raised in a world of conditional relationships' and so view things accordingly. I think they idly talk and feel romantic. But they wouldn't stay frustrated, miserable and thwarted for years and years to try and stay true to some romantic ideal out there on the planet, as their grandparents did, and their parents tried – and failed – to do. And, for well-educated girls now, a successful career appears to be as appealing as the idea of a wedding used to be.

a&e: Is there any message / personal motto you would like to impart to young people if that were possible?

Anne Fine: What I remember was so awful about being young was the absence of any real sense of proportion. This is the strength of being young, and the weakness. My advice would be, if you ever feel (1) things are so bad you don't want to stay on the planet, or (2) so pointless you can't be bothered to do anything useful with your time here, don't *ever* do anything really stupid. Just take it on trust from the oldies for once: (1) things aren't, and (2) you can.

Publications Received

Bernhart, Walter, Steven Paul Scher & Werner Wolf (Eds.): *Word and Music Studies. Defining the Field. Proceedings of the First International Conference on Word and Music Studies at Graz, 1997*, Word and Music Studies 1. Amsterdam / Atlanta, GA: Rodopi, 1999. 352 pp., bound: Hfl. 160,– / US-$ 89,– (ISBN 90-420-0587-4), paper: Hfl. 55,– / US-$ 31,– (ISBN 90-420-0577-7)

The nineteen interdisciplinary essays assembled in "Word and Music Studies 1" were first presented in 1997 at the founding conference of the International Association for Word and Music Studies (WMA) in Graz, Austria. Diverse in subject matter, theoretical orientation, critical approach, and interpretive strategy, they share a keen scholarly interest in contemporary word-music reflection. Registering the impact of cultural studies on word-music relations, as manifested in the 'new musicology' and other 'historicist' approaches, the volume aims to assess the entire field of word and music studies, to define its subject, objectives, and methodology and to describe the field's state of the art.
Within the broader context of generic, structural, performative, and ideological considerations concerning the manifold interrelations between literature and music, contributors explore wide-ranging topics, such as the vexing question of terminology (e.g. 'word and music', 'melopoetics', 'interart', 'intermedial', 'transmedial'); inquiry into the meaning, narrative potential, and verbalization of music; analysis of texted music (the Lied and opera) and instrumental music; and discussion of individual issues (e.g. 'ekphrasis', 'musicalization of fiction', 'word music', and 'verbal music') and interart loanwords (e.g. 'narrativity', 'counterpoint', and 'leitmotif').

Doyé, Peter: *The Intercultural Dimension. Foreign Language Education in the Primary School.* Berlin: Cornelsen, 1999. 124 pp., DM 19,80 (ISBN 3-464-02315-X)

Der Fremdsprachenunterricht in europäischen Grundschulen kann sich heute nicht mehr auf die Förderung sprachlicher Fertigkeiten beschränken. Er muß versuchen, einen Beitrag zur Befähigung der Kinder zu interkultureller Kommunikation zu leisten.
Das ist die zentrale These dieses Buches. Der Autor Peter Doyé schafft die theoretische Grundlage für seine These durch die Zusammenstellung zwingender Argumente aus Pädagogik, Psychologie und Soziologie, und er präsentiert 25 Beispiele für die praktische Umsetzung seiner Ideen. Die Beispiele stammen aus sieben europäischen Sprachen und reflektieren die Erfahrungen des Autors aus seiner Arbeit im *Modern Languages Project* des Europarats.
Das Buch richtet sich an Lehrerinnen und Lehrer an Schulen und Hochschulen sowie Lehrplanentwickler und politische Entscheidungsträger.

Dretzke, Burkhard: *Modern British and American English Pronunciation. A Basic Textbook*, Uni-Taschenbücher UTB 2053. Paderborn *et al.*: Schöningh, 1998. 247 pp., DM 36,80 (ISBN 3-8252-2053-2)

Als praktische Einführung für Studenten des Englischen behandelt das vorliegende Lehr- und Lernbuch die Aussprache der beiden nationalen Varietäten *British English* und *General American English*. Dabei werden sozioregionale Varianten – wie etwa die Aussprache in London – mit berücksichtigt. Neben artikulatorischer, auditiver und akustischer Phonetik und Phonologie wird die Diskrepanz zwischen Schreibweise und Aussprache thematisiert. Besonderer Wert wurde auf typisch deutsche Falschaussprachen und auf Transkriptions- und Ausspracheübungen gelegt. Eine selektive Bibliographie bietet weiterführende Informationen.

Gehring, Wolfgang: *Englische Fachdidaktik. Eine Einführung*, Grundlagen der Anglistik und Amerikanistik 20. Berlin: Erich Schmidt Verlag, 1999. 222 pp., DM 39,80 (ISBN 3-503-04931-2)

Das Buch bietet eine umfassende Einführung in die zentralen Bereiche der englischen Fachdidaktik. Aus theoretischer wie aus unterrichtspraktischer Perspektive werden Fragen der Sprachaneignung, unterschiedliche Lehrverfahren, der Umgang mit literarischen Texten sowie Modelle der Unterrichtsplanung und der Textkonzeption eingehend behandelt. Dabei geht es unter anderem auch um die verschiedenen Formen des Spracherwerbs oder um die Möglichkeiten einer handlungsorientierten Englischmethodik.
Die Einführung ermöglicht nicht nur Studierenden oder Lehramtskandidaten einen schnellen Zugriff auf aktuelle Informationen über die wichtigsten Aspekte der Fremdsprachenvermittlung. Auch erfahrenen Lehrkräften liefert der Band neue Impulse für eine reflektierte Unterrichtsgestaltung im Fach Englisch.

Gelfert, Hans-Dieter: *Kleine Kulturgeschichte Großbritanniens. Von Stonehenge bis zum Millennium Dome*. München: Beck, 1999. 364 pp., DM 28,– (ISBN 3-406-42121-0)

Diese Kulturgeschichte Großbritanniens umfaßt den gesamten Zeitraum von der ersten Besiedlung bis zur Gegenwart. Jede Epoche – ab 1500 jedes Jahrhundert – beginnt mit einer Zeittafel und einer kurzen Darstellung des gesamten Jahrhunderts. Dann folgen Kapitel zur Stilgeschichte, zur wirtschafts- und sozialgeschichtlichen Einbettung und zu den einzelnen Kulturphänomenen: Religion, Erziehung, bildende Kunst, Musik, Literatur und Philosophie. Vergleichende Ausblicke auf die deutsche und europäische Kultur verdeutlichen die Eigenart der britischen Kultur.

Gibson, Andrew & Robert Hampson (Eds.): *Conrad and Theory.* Amsterdam / Atlanta, GA: Rodopi, 1998. 204 pp., Hfl. 65,– / US-$ 36,– (ISBN 90-420-0369-3)

"This volume was designed to stage an encounter between Conrad and theory – or rather, to see what kinds of encounter between Conrad and theory were taking place in the late nineties. It was not conceived of as subjecting Conradian texts to various theoretical approaches, but rather as an exploration of the relevance to Conrad studies of some of the kinds of theoretical work that is currently taking place, where one of the issues might be the direction in which theory itself might be moving. [...]
The essays in this volume, then, are intended to demonstrate the usefulness of recent and current developments in philosophy and literary and critical theory in shedding new light on a range of Conrad's works. They recognize and address contemporary debates about Conrad's ethics, politics and aesthetics, and, in particular, the relationship between all three. But they also set out to shift some of the terms in which such debates have previously been couched. In other words, they raise questions for Conrad criticism. Above all, perhaps, they raise some of the questions that theory precisely exists to raise: questions, not only of the limits of the power of established critical vocabularies, but of premises, values, even modes of constructing Conrad that such vocabularies cannot help but bring with them."

Grice, Helen & Tim Woods (Eds.): *'I'm telling you stories'. Jeanette Winterson and the Politics of Reading*, Postmodern Studies 25. Amsterdam / Atlanta, GA: Rodopi, 1998. 136 pp., Hfl. 60,– / US-$ 33,– (ISBN 90-420-0340-5)

"Despite the equivocal reception accorded to her [Winterson's] work, we think that this substantial body of writing warrants serious and sustained attention, and that the current lack of any book-length study available to people interested in her work might be rectified by this collection. Given such a dearth of material on her writing, and the extensive teaching of her fiction as part of literature courses both at schools and at universities, we hope that such a book will provide an exciting opportunity to initiate a broader discussion about the merits, affiliations and preoccupations of Winterson's fiction. The intention of this book is to draw together a number of essays by acknowledged readers and prominent academics, which explore the cultural context of Winterson's writing to date. The essays are comparative in their attention to Winterson and other contemporary writers, theoretically and methodologically informed, and deal with topical cultural issues. The book contains both essays which are directly focused on individual novels, and some which are more general in their focus on Winterson's writing and the context of her feminist, lesbian, historical and philosophical concerns."

Hellwig, Karlheinz: *Anfänge englischen Literaturunterrichts. Entwicklung, Grundlagen, Praxis. Primarstufe – Jahrgang 11*. Frankfurt/M. *et al.*: Peter Lang, 2000. 343 pp., DM 89,– (ISBN 3-631-34556-9)

Literatur im Englischunterricht von Anfang an: Das Programm des Buches beinhaltet ein literaturdidaktisches Konzept, das Literatur einfacher und komplexer Art – im Zusammenspiel mit anderen Kunsttexten – als integralen Bestandteil des Unterrichts einbindet – von der Primarstufe bis zum Beginn der Studienstufe. In der Praxis geschieht literarisches Lernerfahren prozeßorientiert im handelnden Umgang mit Literatur, konkret in Form *elementaren Literarisierens.* Die Unterrichtspraxis wird dargestellt vor dem Hintergrund einer historischen Skizze sowie auf der Grundlage von bildungs- und zeitgeschichtlichen Entwicklungen einerseits und andererseits unter Berücksichtigung neuerer fachwissenschaftlicher und lernerbezogener Impulse.

Klein, Holger, Sabine Coelsch-Foisner & Wolfgang Görtschacher (Eds.): *Poetry Now. Contemporary British and Irish Poetry in the Making*, Studies in English and Comparative Literature 13. Tübingen: Stauffenburg Verlag, 1999. 406 pp., DM 120,– (ISBN 3-86057-313-6)

In October 1996 some 30 British and Irish poets as well as some North American ones, many among them also active as critics, lecturers and editors of poetry magazines, congregated in Salzburg with critics, translators, and some publishers from Germany and Austria to discuss the kinds of poetry and the situation of poetry in the British Isles today. All phases were of interest, from composition to publication. Poetry was treated both as an aesthetic object and as a social process. The present volume unites the majority of the papers given in revised form and some in an expanded version. There emerges, as in a mosaic, a unique impression of anglophone lyric and epic poetry in our time, joined to critical assessments and systematizations. The book offers a broadly-based stock-taking of what there is, encompassing many different currents and single works, some of them very much in the limelight today, others less noted, but all of them valuable. Because most contributions were written by creative personalities, the collection assumes a character which leaves mere stock-taking in the usual sense far behind.

Kramer, Jürgen: *British Cultural Studies.* München: Fink, 1997. 255 pp., DM 36,80 (ISBN 3-8252-8134-5)

Die Einführung in die *British Cultural Studies* macht Studierende der Anglistik mit einem Bereich bekannt, der lange Zeit als *Landeskunde* ein Schattendasein innerhalb der Literaturwissenschaft führte. In einer Zeit, da die kulturwissenschaftliche Dimension aus guten Gründen mehr und mehr ins Zentrum der Lehrerausbildung und der alten Philologien rückt, füllt Jürgen Kramers Lehrbuch eine schmerzliche Lücke in der bisherigen Fachliteratur aus. Es skizziert die fachgeschichtlichen Zusammenhänge, kennzeichnet den Ort der Cultural Studies innerhalb der deutschen Anglistik, beschreibt Lehr- und Lernziele sowie deren Form, stellt wichtige Theorieansätze und exemplarische Projekte vor und gibt Anregungen für die Zusammenstellung einer Studienbibliothek sowie Informationen zum Studium in Deutschland und Großbritannien.

Mosthaf, Franziska: *Metaphorische Intermedialität. Formen und Funktionen der Verarbeitung von Malerei im Roman. Theorie und Praxis in der englischsprachigen Erzählkunst des 19. und 20. Jahrhunderts*, Horizonte 25. Trier: WVT Wissenschaftlicher Verlag Trier, 2000. 218 pp., DM 48,00 (ISBN 3-88476-389-X)

'Intermedialität' im Sinne von Wechselbeziehungen zwischen konventionellerweise distinkten Medien ist in einem Zeitalter zunehmender Medienkonvergenz auch verstärkt in das Interesse der Literaturwissenschaft gerückt. Jedoch fehlt bisher ein methodisches Instrumentarium zur Analyse 'literarischer Intermedialität'. In diesem Sinne stellt die vorliegende Studie einen Versuch dar, die Verarbeitung von Malerei in der englischsprachigen Erzählkunst systematisch aufzuarbeiten.
Im ersten Teil wird ein theoretische Instrumentarium zur Analyse verschiedener Formen und Funktionen der Verarbeitung von Malerei in Romanen entwickelt. Dabei wird ein narratologischer Ansatz gewählt, der es erlaubt zu untersuchen, wie die typischen Bauformen von Erzähltexten, z.B. die Erzählsituation, die Perspektivenstruktur, der Stil, die Raum- und die Zeitdarstellung zur Verarbeitung von Merkmalen der Malerei eingesetzt werden können. Mithilfe eines Modells werden Schnittstellen zwischen den beiden Medien dargestellt und anhand einer Vielzahl von Beispielen aus Literatur und bildender Kunst illustriert.
Im zweiten Teil wird das entwickelte Analyseinstrumentarium exemplarisch auf Werke aus der englischsprachigen Literatur angewendet, um die interpretatorische Relevanz der Theorie zu veranschaulichen und um einen Einblick in die historische Entwicklung der Verarbeitung von Malerei in der englischsprachigen Erzählkunst seit Mitte des 19. Jahrhunderts zu vermitteln. Die vier Kapitel behandeln (1) Herman Melvilles *Moby Dick* unter dem Gesichtspunkt der Verarbeitung der Malerei William Turners, (2) George Eliots Bezüge zur niederländischen Genremalerei des 17. Jahrhunderts in ihrem Roman *Adam Bede*, (3) Virginia Woolfs Roman *To the Lighthouse*, in dem die Autorin auf die Ästhetik des Postimpressionismus von Cézanne und Roger Fry zurückgreift, und (4) zwei postmoderne Erzähltexte von Julian Barnes (aus seinem Roman *A History of the World in 10 ½ Chapters*) und John Fowles ("The Ebony Tower"), in denen Aspekte der Malerei dazu funktionalisiert werden, den Werken metafiktionalen Status zu verleihen.

Pfister, Manfred & Barbara Schaff (Eds.): *Venetian Views, Venetian Blinds. English Fantasies of Venice*, Internationale Forschungen zur Allgemeinen und Vergleichenden Literaturwissenschaft 37. Amsterdam / Atlanta, GA: Rodopi, 1999. 255 pp., bound: Hfl. 130,– / US-$ 72,– (ISBN 90-420-0757-5), paper: Hfl. 40,– / US-$ 22,– (ISBN 90-420-0747-8)

Half a millennium of English and American fantasies of Venice: this collection of essays by leading critics in the field explores the continued and continuing fascination of travellers, writers, artists, theatre workers and film makers with the amphibious and ambiguous city in the lagoon. There is hardly another place in Europe that has become so much of a palimpsest, inscribed with the fantasies, the dreams and nightmares of generations of foreigners, and this turns *Venetian Views, Venetian Blinds* into a particularly pertinent case study of the ways cultural difference within Europe is experienced, enacted and constructed. The essays range across five centuries – from the Renaissance to our postmodern present, from Shakespeare and his contemporary Coryate to recent novels, detective fiction and films – and, in contrast to previous studies focussing on the Grand Tour, they emphasise more recent developments and how they continue or disrupt traditional ways of perceiving – or being blind to! – Venice.

Schiffer, Reinhold: *Oriental Panorama. British Travellers in 19th Century Turkey*, Internationale Forschungen zur Allgemeinen und Vergleichenden Literaturwissenschaft 33. Amsterdam / Atlanta, GA: Rodopi, 1999. 445 pp., bound: Hfl. 200,– / US-$ 110,– (ISBN 90-420-0407-X), paper: Hfl. 65,– / US-$ 36,– (ISBN 90-420-0796-6)

This survey of the long 19th century reconstructs the impact of Ottoman Turkey and its societies on Romantic and Victorian travellers. Whereas European discourse regarding the Orient has been criticised lately as unremittingly hegemonial and monolithic, here, in contrast, new evidence is presented of historically changing and ideologically fractured British representations of Ottoman Turkey in texts and, partly, the visual arts. The study traces the political, anthropological, religious and aesthetic assumptions and reactions in Turcophiles and Turcophobes alike; moreover, it analyses the critique which the great reviews brought to bear on travellers and offers sketches of their lives and reputations. There are lavish quotes as many texts are not easily accessible.
Travellers encountered dangers to health and lives from plague and bandits – natural and architectural beauties – classical ruins – everyday life in the cities and in the country – ethnic diversity and Oriental sameness – Muslim piety and hospitality – the court of the Sultans – the mysteries of the harem.
The new findings, by an authority on travel literature and frequent traveller to Turkey, are based on some 160 travel accounts. No comparable study examines sources only remotely approaching this number.

Siebers, Winfried & Uwe Zagratzki (Eds.): *Deutsche Schottlandbilder. Beiträge zur Kulturgeschichte.* Osnabrück: Universitätsverlag Rasch, 1998. 222 pp., DM 38,– (ISBN 3-932147-58-8)

Die schottische Kultur ist von den Kontinentaleuropäern lange Zeit nur als Teil der britischen wahrgenommen worden. Erst mit dem europaweiten Erfolg der schottischen Moralphilosophie im 18. Jahrhundert wurde die sprachliche sowie die rechts-, konfessions- und kulturgeschichtliche Eigenständigkeit und Eigenart der Schotten sichtbar. Die historischen Romane Sir Walter Scotts prägten dann zu Beginn des 19. Jahrhunderts die bis heute andauernde, touristische und oft von Stereotypen durchsetzte Auffassung Schottlands.
Historische und kulturelle Ursachen für diese Schottlandbilder der Deutschen und für das besondere Interesse and Schottland in der deutschen Öffentlichkeit werden hier erstmals von Experten aufgedeckt und erklärt. In den Essays geht es um Schottland in Literatur, Film, Musik, Alltagskultur und Sport.
Die Beiträge sind spannende, unterhaltsame und aufschlußreiche Lektüre für Schottlandfreunde, Schottlandreisende, für kulturinteressierte Laien und Fachleute.

Teske, Doris: *Die Vertextung der Megalopolis. London im Spiel postmoderner Texte*, Horizonte 26. Trier: WVT Wissenschaftlicher Verlag Trier, 1999. 297 pp., DM 54,50 (ISBN 3-88476-363-6)

An der Schwelle zum neuen Jahrtausend erscheint eine lang dominante historisch orientierte Weltsicht durch verstärktes Interesse an räumlichen Phänomenen angefochten. Auch das Thema Stadt hat in jüngster Zeit neue Popularität gewonnen, wie sich in verschiedensten Textgattungen, aber auch in einer "städtischen Renaissance" neuer Architektur und Stadtentwicklung zeigt. Die vorliegende kultur- und literaturwissenschaftliche Studie beleuchtet diese Entwicklung für London, das mit seiner globalen Bedeutung und seinen Tendenzen hin zur "virtuellen Stadt" als prägnantes Beispiel für die postmoderne Megalopole gesehen wird.
Im Mittelpunkt der Untersuchung steht die verschiedenartige Konzeptualisierung und Vertextung der heutigen Stadt in zentralen Schriften urbanistischer Wissenschaften, in populären Essaysammlungen und in ausgewählten Stadtromanen. Es wird gezeigt, wie diese traditionell voneinander abgegrenzten Gattungen ineinandergreifen und miteinander in Austausch treten und wie in der gemeinsamen Ablehnung von Wissenschaftskonventionen und Weltverständnis der Moderne die Grenzen zwischen den verschiedenen Textarten verschwimmen. Hierbei greifen die Stadtvertextungen auch Beschreibungsraster des 18. und 19. Jahrhunderts auf, wie bei einer näheren Betrachtung des Einflusses populärer Gattungskonventionen aus Kriminalroman, *gothic fiction* und Bildungsroman auf die heutig Darstellung von London gezeigt wird. In Auseinandersetzung mit den Grundlagen ihrer jeweiligen Textgattung streben die disparaten Texte durch gemeinsame Bilder und Konzepte sowie durch vergleichbares Vorgehen bei der Vertextung der Stadt auf einen geeinten postmodernen "Stadtdiskurs" zu.

Tönnies, Merle: *Samuel Beckett's Dramatic Strategy. Audience Laughter and the Postmodernist Debate*, Horizonte 23. Trier: WVT Wissenschaftlicher Verlag Trier, 1997. 239 pp., DM 48,50 (ISBN 3-88476-224-9)

Critical literature on Samuel Beckett contains innumerable conflicting attempts to cope with his dramatic works by tying them down to a definite "meaning" or assigning them a fixed place in literary modernism or postmodernism. This increasingly airy discussion can best be brought down to earth again by proceeding from a tangible "reality": the perception of the plays by the theatre audience. From this perspective, one becomes aware of the striking parallel between Beckett's refusal to provide "interpretations" of his drama and the tendency of postmodernism to concentrate on the act of presentation instead of the representation of an underlying "message". This study therefore sets out to establish whether the specific ways in which Beckett's plays manipulate the spectators' reactions confirm or refute the general affinity with postmodernism.
In this process, the focus is on the interaction between audience laughter that expresses detachment from the characters and laughter which shows the spectators' emotional involvement. The development of these techniques and their relationship with postmodernism is traced throughout Beckett's dramatic *oeuvre*, distinguishing between three basic groups of plays: the early drama (contrasting the first full-length play, the recently published *Eleutheria*, with the works from *Waiting for Godot* onwards), the later *Happy Days* and *Play*, where laughter is gradually stifled, and the short late plays, which concentrate on the structural side of the devices.

Viol, Claus-Ulrich: *Eighteenth-Century (Sub)Versions of Stage Irishness. Prevalent Anti-Irish Stereotypes and their Dramatic Functionalisation*, Horizonte 24. Trier: WVT Wissenschaftlicher Verlag Trier, 1998. 133 pp., DM 34,50 (ISBN 3-88476-299-0)

This book offers a concise and systematic account of the stage Irishman's eventful career in the 18th century. Foregrounding dramatic potential and functions rather than questions of linguistic or cultural '(non-)authenticity', this study explores both the social and the textual strategies that are at the bottom of this most durable and controversial ethnic stock-type in British culture. It also contextualises these different functional variants within the wider social and intellectual background of the 18th century.
Based on an application of the conceptual tools of textual stereotype research, the close analysis of a number of exemplary plays – including Colman's *Jealous Wife*, Garrick's *Irish Widow*, and Cumberland's *West Indian* – thus results in a typology of 18th-century stage Irishmen that accounts for the different ways of employing the stereotypes of the time. These range from 'mechanical' adoptions and gradual modifications to 'subversive' treatments that seem to anticipate rather modern developments.

Wolf, Werner: *The Musicalization of Fiction. A Study in the Theory and History of Intermediality.* Amsterdam / Atlanta, GA: Rodopi, 1999. 272 pp., Hfl. 90,– / US-$ 50,– (ISBN 90-420-0457-6)

This volume is a pioneering study in the theory and history of the imitation of music in fiction and constitutes an important contribution to current intermediality research. Starting with a comparison of basic similarities and differences between literature and music, the study goes on to provide outlines of a general theory of intermediality and its fundamental forms, in which a more specialized theory of the musicalization of (narrative) literature based on contemporary narratology and a typology of the forms of music-literary intermediality are embedded. It also addresses the question of how to recognize a musicalized fiction when reading one and why Sterne's *Tristram Shandy*, contrary to what has been previously said, is not to be regarded as a musicalized ficition.
In its historical part, the study explores forms and functions of experiments with the musicalization of fiction in English literature. After a survey of the major preconditions for musicalization – the increasing appreciation of music in 18th and 19th-century aesthetics and its main causes – exemplary fictional texts from romanticism to postmodernism are analyzed. Authors interpreted are De Quincey, Joyce, Woolf, A. Huxley, Beckett, Burgess and Josipovici. Whilst the limitations of a transposition of music into fiction remain apparent, experiments in this field yield valuable insights into mainly a-mimetic and formalist aesthetic tendencies in the development of more recent fiction as a whole and also show to what extent traditional conceptions of music continue to influence the use of this medium in literature.
The volume is of relevance for students and scholars of English, comparative and general literature as well as for readers who take an interest in intermediality or interart research.

Wolff, Leslie Bobb (Ed.): *Learner Autonomy as a Central Concept of Foreign Language Learning.* La Laguna, Tenerife: Universidad de La Laguna, 1999. 275 pp., 1.500 ptas. (ISSN 0211-5913 / = *Revista Canaria de Estudios Ingleses* 38)

"Learner autonomy has developed into a central concept in foreign language learning in recent decades. This has come about in part due to language educators' concerns for improving their students' learning process and has certainly been forwarded by at least two sources. On the one hand, work generated from what is generally considered the foundation document prepared by Henri Holec for the Council of Europe titled *Autonomy in Foreign Language Learning*. At the same time, at least two of the humanistic approaches, Community Language Learning and Silent Way, considered learner autonomy (although without using the term itself) central to their aims for learners. While few, if any, professionals today in the field of foreign or second language learning would argue against the need for learners becoming autonomous in their learning process of the language, there is still a good deal of work to be done to put this desire into practice. The contributions to this monograph issue hope to offer one more step in this direction. […]

In part the complexity of applying/using learner autonomy in a classroom can be seen as due to this need to help students become less passive learners. At the same time, since learner autonomy affects every aspect of the curriculum, each needs to be re-examined. In this monograph several of these have been covered. Among them are the role of the teacher, the teacher's own development, the use of learning strategies, the treatment of grammar, the social-interactive aspect of the class, the use of tutorials and the role of self-assessment."

Zacharasiewicz, Waldemar: *Das Deutschlandbild in der amerikanischen Literatur.* Darmstadt: Wissenschaftliche Buchgesellschaft, 1998. 419 pp., DM 85,– (ISBN 3-534-12467-7)

Die komparatistische Imagologie hat in den letzten Jahrzehnten im Bild fremder Länder und Völker ein besonders ergiebiges und instruktives Forschungsfeld entdeckt. Der hier vorliegende Band bietet zum ersten Mal eine Gesamtdarstellung der Entwicklung des Deutschlandbildes in der amerikanischen Literatur des 19. und 20. Jahrhunderts. Beleuchtet werden die vielfältigen Varianten des Bildes der Deutschen bzw. Deutschlands, wie sie uns in der Erzählliteratur, aber auch in Briefen, Reisebüchern, Autobiographien usw. begegnen. Die Wiederkehr bestimmter Figurentypen wird in den (kultur-)historischen Zusammenhang gestellt, und es werden mehrere Phasen in der Verbreitung und Nutzung beliebter Formen des Heterostereotyps der Deutschen aufgezeigt. Die Darstellung stützt sich auf eine größere Anzahl vorliegender Einzelanalysen und bietet auch dem Nichtfachwissenschaftler, für den sämtliche Originalzitate ins Deutsche übersetzt wurden, die Möglichkeit, sich näher mit diesem spannenden interdisziplinären Forschungsfeld zu beschäftigen.

Contributors' Addresses

Dr. Peter Bennett, Englisches Seminar, Universität Hannover, Königsworther Platz 1, 30167 Hannover (Germany).

Martin Brüggemeier, Dipl.-Übersetzer, An der Hochschule 3, 76726 Germersheim (Germany).

Professor Dr. Horst W. Drescher, Scottish Studies Centre, Institut für Anglistik und Amerikanistik, Johannes Gutenberg-Universität Mainz, An der Hochschule 2, 76711 Germersheim (Germany).

Professor Dr. Janet Holland, Social Science Research Centre, Faculty of Humanities and Social Science, South Bank University, 103 Borough Road, London SE1 0AA (United Kingdom).

Dr. Jürgen Neubauer, Waidmannstr. 35, 60596 Frankfurt/Main (Germany).

Dr. Bill Osgerby, School of Social Sciences, University of North London, Ladbroke House, 62-66 Highbury Grove, London N5 2AD (United Kingdom).

Mike Storry, John Moores University, Rodney Street, Liverpool L3 5UX (United Kingdom).

Professor Dr. Gerd Stratmann, Englisches Seminar, Ruhr-Universität Bochum, 44780 Bochum (Germany).

Dr. Rachel Thomson, Social Science Research Centre, Faculty of Humanities and Social Science, South Bank University, 103 Borough Road, London SE1 0AA (United Kingdom).

Dr. Merle Tönnies, Englisches Seminar, Ruhr-Universität Bochum, 44780 Bochum (Germany).

Claus-Ulrich Viol, M.A., Englisches Seminar, Ruhr-Universität Bochum, 44780 Bochum (Germany).